Open Catholicism

The Tradition at Its Best:
Essays in Honor of Gerard S. Sloyan

Mahmoud Ayoub
James E. Biechler
Regina A. Boisclair
Mary Collins, O.S.B.
Charles E. Curran
Monika K. Hellwig
Elizabeth A. Johnson, C.S.J.
Gabriel Moran
June O'Connor
Gerard S. Sloyan
Leonard Swidler
Paul M. van Buren

David Efroymson
John Raines
Editors

A Michael Glazier Book
 THE LITURGICAL PRESS
Collegeville, Minnesota

A Michael Glazier Book published by The Liturgical Press

Cover design by David Manahan, O.S.B. Illustration by Frank Kacmarcik, Obl.S.B.

1   2   · 3   4   5   6   7   8

Library of Congress Cataloging-in-Publication Data

Open Catholicism : the tradition at its best : essays in honor of Gerard S.
   Sloyan / [contributors] Mahmoud Ayoub . . . [et al.] ; David
   Efroymson, John Raines, editors.
        p.   cm.
        "A Michael Glazier book."
        Includes bibliographical references.
        ISBN 0-8146-5879-2
        1. Catholic Church—Doctrines. 2. Catholic Church—Education.
   3. Catholic Church—Liturgy. 4. Catholic church—Government.
   5. Christian ethics—Catholic authors. 6. Bible. N.T.—Criticism, interpretation, etc. 7. Sloyan, Gerard Stephen, 1919–   .
   I. Sloyan, Gerard Stephen, 1919–   . II. Ayoub, Mahmoud.
   III. Efroymson, David P. (David Patrick), 1931–   . IV. Raines, John C.
   BX1751.2.064   1997
   282—dc21   97-6710
                                                                    CIP

Contents

Introduction   v

1   I Was There When Some of It Happened   1
    Gerard S. Sloyan

2   Does God Play Dice? Providence and Chance   9
    Elizabeth A. Johnson, C.S.J.

3   The Gospel According to the Scriptures   26
    Paul M. van Buren

4   On Rescuing the Humanity of Jesus:
    Implications for Catholicism   40
    Monika K. Hellwig

5   A Call for a Catholic Constitutional Convention:
    The Beginning of the Third Millennium   49
    Leonard Swidler

6   The Conciliar Constitution of the Church:
    Nicholas of Cusa's "Catholic Concordance"   87
    James E. Biechler

7   On Becoming a Sacramental Church Again   111
    Mary Collins, O.S.B.

8   *Veritatis splendor* and Contemporary
    Catholic Moral Theology   129
    Charles E. Curran

9   Religious Education after Vatican II   151
    Gabriel Moran

10   On Being Bi-Religious:
     Colonialism, Catholicism, and Conversion   167
     June O'Connor

11   Pope John Paul II on Islam   190
     Mahmoud Ayoub

12   The Writings of Gerard S. Sloyan: 1950–1995   206
     Compiled by *Regina A. Boisclair*

Contributors   223

Introduction

The purpose of this collection of essays is to honor Gerard S. Sloyan. He was at The Catholic University of America for seventeen years (and now there again, as a post-retirement visiting professor), then at Temple University for twenty-three years; a Catholic priest since 1944; and, for a substantial lifetime, a "man of the Church" (Jean Danielou's final characterization of Origen). But a few more public items are worth noting.

He was born in 1919 and enjoys pointing out that he has been a Catholic longer than Pope John Paul II. He served on the editorial board of the Institute for Judeo-Christian Studies in the 1950s, and he serves today on the board of directors of the Association for the Rights of Catholics in the Church. An active member of the Catholic Biblical Association and the Society of Biblical Literature, he has been president of the Liturgical Conference (and chair of its board of directors), of the College Theology Society, and of the Catholic Theological Society of America, which voted him the recipient of its John Courtney Murray Award in 1981. Other honors include the Berakah Award from the North American Academy of Liturgy in 1986, the Pro Ecclesia et Pontifice Medal of 1970, and the Johannes Quasten Medal from The Catholic University in 1985.

This list is not complete. But it gives some sense of the range and duration of his service to the Church and academy, as well as the respect of his colleagues in diverse fields. A glance at Regina Boisclair's bibliography at the end of this collection points in the same direction. His substantial scholarship is sharpened, never impoverished, by his pastoral, ecumenical, and catechetical concerns. Conversely, it is his biblical, theological, liturgical, and historical competence which makes what he has written for the Church so trustworthy and wise. It would make no sense to comment on, or to attempt to assess, what he has written. Gerry himself singles out the six books on New Testament topics written while at Temple. One might add that, for a smaller sample of the combination of scholarly competence and pastoral sensibility, it would be instructive to examine his reflections on the recent *Catechism of the Catholic Church* in *Horizons*, 1994, and in his essays in Berard Marthaler's *Introducing the Catechism of the Catholic Church*. Any representative selection of his carefully crafted book reviews would also reveal the same self-definition of his life's journey and task.

In his brief essay Gerry speaks of an earlier time, when he and some of his colleagues at The Catholic University, and other Catholic faculties elsewhere, were "contributing to what became Vatican II rather than deriving from it." This is not only accurate but important. The temptation today, over thirty years after the end of that council, is to think of it and its spirit as something which happened "over there," in Rome, and about which there continues to be dispute. But without that earlier biblical, ecclesiological, liturgical, and catechetical ferment, to which Gerry Sloyan was a significant and persistent contributor, there would not have been the Vatican II we now know. Many today, in the Catholic Church and beyond, especially in the United States, stand on his shoulders.

When the Temple University Religion Department decided to sponsor a *Festschrift* it was clear that contributors would also have to be drawn from elsewhere. Counting the editors, there are eight with Temple connections (four colleagues and four whose Ph.D.s were earned during the Sloyan tenure), four from The Catholic University, and one from the Catholic Theological Society of America. Most have worked with Gerry in other associations (NAAL and Liturgical Conference, CBA, CTS, and ARCC). Several are well known, others less so. All are proud to be his friends and have their thoughts appear here as witness to that continuing gratitude.

His own narrative adds a personal dimension but also evokes a time and a spirit of a generation ago which are worth recording.

Elizabeth Johnson's lead essay is a fine example of the Catholic tradition at its best. To deal with the problem of *God* and the post-mechanistic world now described by contemporary science—a world of randomness, indeterminacy, and chance—she offers a healthy and viable re-consideration of primary causality in the Thomist system.

Paul van Buren argues that the "meaning" of *Jesus* in the "gospel" which Paul received had been arrived at by means of a thoroughly Jewish understanding and exegesis of Scripture. Thus the Jewishness of Jesus that should matter to the Church is not only that of his Galilean ministry but even more that of those Jewish Scriptures according to which his death and exaltation were understood from the first.

Monika Hellwig's essay underlines the importance of retrieving the authentic humanity of Jesus, as well as the stakes involved in that task for the Church and for Christian life and responsibility.

Leonard Swidler's plea for a Catholic Constitutional Convention is, at the same time, a rehearsal of the arguments for a more participatory *church* and a useful inventory of the many groups now actively working toward that goal. James Biechler then demonstrates the lasting value of the ecclesiological insights of the best of the conciliarist theologians, Nicholas of Cusa.

Mary Collins points to the not-always-perceived connections between control of the *liturgy* and the growth of Romanizing authoritarianism, on the one hand, and the material, experiential, more spontaneous resources within the liturgy, on the other.

Charles Curran's essay is a model of dialogue: appreciative of much Pope John Paul II says in *Veritatis splendor,* but raising serious questions about certain apparent assumptions and implications of that important recent encyclical on the Catholic *ethical* tradition.

Gabriel Moran's reflections on the two "faces" of religious education is a significant effort at clarification of certain ventures and issues which have become muddled since Vatican II, to the detriment of all concerned.

June O'Connor's contribution, like Johnson's and van Buren's, can be construed as experimental. It explicitly raises the question of conversion as an "addition" in some cases, rather than as substitution and abandonment. It raises the further crucial question of what kind of thing "Catholicism" is. Does it consist primarily as truth-claim(s) or as a way of being in the world? Can Catholicism be "shared" with another tradition within the mind and heart of one person without contradiction?

Mahmoud Ayoub's critical highlighting of what he sees as the "ambivalence" of John Paul II on Islam is a valuable view "from outside." Catholics can learn from the way he understands words such as "witness" and "dialogue." To see ourselves also from outside ourselves seems to mark the concrete steps and vocational decisions Gerry Sloyan chose to follow in his own life.

Clearly, there might have been other contributions, testifying even more fully to the range of Dr. Sloyan's scholarly and pastoral interests. The essays here are offered in gratitude and in affection. All were written expressly for this volume.* They are, even as the life they honor and celebrate, markings of a generous and open spirit.

The Editors

---

*With the permission of the editors, Johnson's essay will also have appeared in *Theological Studies* 57/1 (March, 1996), and Curran's in *Veritatis Splendor. American Responses.* Ed. by Michael E. Allsopp and John J. O'Keefe (Kansas City: Sheed and Ward, 1995).

ONE

I Was There
When Some of It Happened

Gerard S. Sloyan

George Orwell, born in Burma though he was, wrote a book called *England Made Me.* It was the Catholic Church that made me, through its incarnation in this country over the present century. The editors of this collection have asked me to set out how it all came to pass. I may be the least reliable witness in this matter but one has one's memory to turn to, unreliable though it may be.

I am a native of no mean city, the Fordham section of the Bronx. My family moved to central New Jersey near but not on the ocean when I was seven after a two-year stay in Westchester County, New York. All talk around our house was of the two populous boroughs, the other being my parent's birthplace, Manhattan. Ogden Nash's dismissive exchange of the former ran: "The Bronx. No thonx." But not in our house.

My mother had graduated from the New York Training School for Teachers where most of her close friends were Jewish. Her classroom teaching career was brief because in those days at marriage you resigned. It included one stint in Throggs Neck, thought by Manhattanites to be just south of Montréal, and another in the part-empty St. Anslem's Parish School (universal local pronunciation), which rented classrooms to a city system bulging with immigrant children. All this culminated for her in a smashing success with "dull normals" in that far-off, euphemism-free day. She emerged, the eldest of three of a mother widowed by Edward Kelley's early death, as a dedicated reader with a great love of learning.

1

My father was from the same neighborhood as she and very close in age, the son of immigrant parents born fifteen miles apart, in Knock and Ballinrobe, Ireland, but who first met at the Mayo Men's Ball in New York. He, like her, was a product of the public schools, P.S. 33 and the newly opened Stuyvesant High School, where he repaid his technical education with a lifetime fidelity to the alumni association into his eightieth year. It was a devotion greater than that to Cornell University's School of Agriculture, although he did join the Princeton, New Jersey, Cornell Club after he had been gone from Ithaca many decades. His studies in what was then called "scientific dairy farming" were motivated by his summers as an only child with eight roistering first cousins, six of them boys, in Suffolk County, Long Island. His aunt Matilda Sloyan had come over as a greenhorn and entered a largely arranged marriage with Yankee-stock Oliver Hubbard that lasted sixty years. My father's maternal aunt Mary Flannery, a U.T. ("unclaimed treasure"), always lived with my Grandmother Sloyan and her husband James, who was on the pó-lice. Margaret Flannery (always "Maggie"; it had not yet become stylish) did piece-work as a seamstress in her youth, and the family legend was that she could follow a conversation in Yiddish because she heard nothing else all day long.

My father tested cows in Florida, Illinois, and New Jersey before World War I, and in Iowa after it. In the Navy for the brief U.S. participation in that four-year war, he repaired fighter planes in Southampton and St. Nazaire and was back in New York within three weeks of the armistice. I was born a year later (my sister during his absence, a year after their marriage), and off the young foursome went to a dairy farm in Cedar Rapids. There they found neither fame nor fortune but two ice-cold winters in an ill-heated farm house "on the property." My mother feared for the life of her youthful pair so back they came to Gotham, my father taking what work he could find. It happened to be maintaining a fleet of cars for hire, from which he moved into a White Truck repair business of his own on West 23rd Street. We were a prosperous young family from 1922 to '32, but the depression brought an end to that. Those years were followed by the development of an oil burning unit on a jet principle; the same with an automatic coal furnace called Califac of New York; finally a salaried job in a gear-reduction plant for the amphibious L.S.T. during the last years of World War II. After the war, but slowly, there came a measure of success with the Automatic Motor Base Co. which he bought and developed. My mother, safe in her grave the last twenty-five years of his life, missed all that. What she knew well was living meagerly off savings during the depression and watching endless manila envelopes come in the mail from Hoguet and Neary, patent attorneys. One day when we were small she saw a popsicle stick with the imprint "Patent Pending" and said with a grin, "Why couldn't your father have invented that?" My youthful memories were of a mother falling asleep on the couch every night with a Rumer Godden or Mary Roberts Rinehart novel slipping to the floor as she dozed off, while my father was deep in the *Journal of the Society of Automotive Engineers* or the *Rural New Yorker.*

My older sister and I left our early schooling in New Rochelle behind and found ourselves in a newly built, combined grammar and high school staffed by young, hand-picked Sisters of Mercy. I have never brought myself to see *Nunsense* or *Do Black Patent Leather Shoes Really Reflect Up?* because the next nine years were such an intelligent, no-nonsense operation. I can see Sister Mary Wilfred or Sisters Edith or Robertus snorting in disgust to hear any anxiety about seeing little girls' underpants attributed to them. The high school regimen was four years each of religion study, gymnasium, English, Latin, and the sciences, three of mathematics and French, two of bookkeeping, and one of typing (there *was* the depression), and a semester each of economics and Problems of American Democracy. The town's public school had study periods, at which we marveled. The Sisters of Mercy were long on homework and parent-teacher conferences, with an operetta every spring.

This all work and one play routine prepared me for Seton Hall College where the curriculum was equally unimaginative. There, 350 young men pursued either a classical or a scientific course. For me that meant Latin and Greek, mathematics, religion, seminary-type theology junior grade, chemistry, history, French, and public speaking. Half of my professors were lay men, the other half diocesan priests. The latter came as an eye-opener; men like the genial, athletic priests of my parish devoting their lives to study and teaching. This bore looking into. The pace in Livy and Horace, the Rutherford-Bohr theory, and the Defenestration of Prague was fast. It left little time for more important matters, like managing varsity basketball or the college newspaper, but I found it.

In the first of those summers, I worked as a checker in the kitchen of the town's hotel and as a cashier behind the bar of a shore night club the second. They were different worlds from the theological seminary where I spent the next six years. The instruction in doctrinal, ascetical, and moral theology and in Church law was earnest but uninspired, as had been the two years of philosophy study that preceded them. The courses in Bible and Church history, on the other hand, were good to the point of exciting. Academic study of the liturgy and homiletics was non-existent in those years; we just did it, the worship tolerably well, the preaching, under supervision, again earnestly but indifferently.

Summers, paradoxically (we stayed on at the extensive rural property) were a better experience: seminars in patristics, a follow-up tutorial in biblical Hebrew, a course in the theologies of the Orthodox Churches of the East and one in *Fundamentaltheologie* by a thoroughly Innsbruckized Irish American who did not complete his material of the school year even then. It was an unimaginative, old-style theological education such as all of my generation received, whether preparing for the priesthood as seculars or regulars. It was, in a word, as good as the best in parts, in others as bad as the worst. I later learned, though, that Jaroslav Pelikan's five-volume *The Christian Tradition* had not much to tell me about the doctrinal debates and conclusions.

Over the course of three years I was one of several classmates who took externally administered examinations leading to the licentiate in sacred theology awarded by The Catholic University of America. A year of residence was required before ordination and I spent it in Washington, D.C., while World War II was in progress. Daily living and spiritual formation were in the Theological College of the university, a seminary conducted by diocesan priests of the Society of Saint Sulpice. In the university classroom I was introduced to *Dogmengeschichte*, the history of the development of the Church's doctrines, through a two-semester course on the sacraments. The presentation had been largely ahistorical up to that point. The seminary student body was from around the country, a gifted, "can-do" population. In the university lecture halls we joined men from a variety of religious congregations, but regrettably no Jesuits or Dominicans. They were sequestered in houses of study of their Society and Order respectively and paid a price for the isolation. I did, however, take a seminar for a quarter with a young priest candidate for the S.T.D. degree who showed promise, a Syracuse native named Hesburgh whose sister had been in college with my younger sister Elizabeth.

Many of the weekends that year were spent in the company of a half-dozen classmates in deacon's orders taking a census for the basement-church parish that later became the cathedral church of the Arlington Diocese. I was amazed to learn how many people would admit a twenty-four-year-old in white shirt and black tie into their homes to pour out the pain that the war was bringing them. There was also a measure of door-slamming in the face by good Christians who had been brought up right.

Three years before this I had been asked by the bishop of Trenton if I would like to earn a Ph.D. in education in order to be the diocesan superintendent of schools. There were a dozen parish and central high schools at the time and close to forty elementary in the eight central counties of New Jersey that made up the diocese. The man who was bishop at the time had a whim of iron, and it was so ordered. The three years after ordination were therefore spent in the graduate school of the university where I had already been enrolled for a year. Fellow graduate students in the priest-residence situation included many mustered-out military chaplains and men from Canada and Latin America. Most of these were being groomed in canon law, education, and social work, a few in theology, philosophy, and the liberal arts and sciences. For some these were steps to ecclesiastical preferment, as the Church of England discreetly terms it. On the whole, the clergy and laity headed for full-time academic careers were the more interesting lot.

As in all graduate education, especially where there is common residence, my peers were as effective agents of intellectual formation as the courses and professors. I dutifully studied the psychology of learning, statistics, the administration of school systems, and curriculum. This was enriched by a minor in cognitive and dynamic psychology, as the Wilhelm Wundt-trained professor called the intellectual and affective orders. In an attempt to retain sanity from the leaden prose of education textbooks, I audited courses in anthropology, literature, U.S. history, and Fulton J. Sheen. The last-named had by that time become a fairly shallow philosopher by virtue of his absorption with radio and occasion-preaching, but he was an excellent pedagogue. Public lectures proliferate on university campuses. I well remember having heard Sigrid Undset, John A. Ryan, Edward Kennard Rand, Etienne Gilson, Nazi-resisting Konrad Cardinal von Preysing, Lisa Meitner, and Jacques Maritain in those years and a bit later.

All this exposure to the world of ideas was to be shared with the youth of institutions like Sankt Franziskus von Assisium parish school in Trenton and the two St. Mary's High Schools of Perth and South Amboy. This I well understood. It never came to pass. With the death of the bishop who had plotted this career and then grown uneasy at the fruit it bore (a proposal for sex education in the schools at an annual parent-teacher meeting among them, not *doctrina communis* in 1948), his successor acceded to the request of my parent university that I join its religion department. I began at $2,625 per annum plus board, room, and laundry at the rank of instructor with a Ph.D. in hand. It was a different world. But in the classroom it was much the same as now. In the first year I taught undergraduate courses in the faith of the Church and Christian morality, but a year later and from then on, both testaments of the Bible only. The death of the department head in my third year catapulted me into a graduate course in the gospels. Four years later I inherited the headship and held it for ten years, making slow progress along with my colleagues from academic famine to feast in M.A. and Ph.D. programs. The last five of these years were spent contributing to what would be Vatican II rather than deriving from it. Such was the reality of the better Catholic faculties of 1945–1962 worldwide. Not every bishop appreciated the fact. Understandably, they thought it was they who had achieved the reforms.

Young faculty there as everywhere were subjected to numerous demands. Nowadays it is listed on annual reports to the dean as "community service." In my case, telephone calls to the university switchboard about a speaker for "our Protestant church (or synagogue) adult/youth group" were referred to the religion department. Being young and full of zeal I took on many of these fee-free engagements on both sides of the Potomac and also in the many, now defunct campus "Religious Emphasis Weeks." The hosts probably reckoned me lucky to be able to explain, if I could, why we worshiped Mary or sacked the Jewish neighborhoods of cities on our way to the crusades. This was ecumenical and interfaith dialogue in its infancy, although the National Conference of Christians and Jews already existed and the World Council of Churches was coming to birth. I remember particularly a luncheon date with a Belgian monk, the editor of *Irénikon,* who had come to Evanston as an observer of the W.C.C. meeting there and been told by the then archbishop of Chicago that he was not free to attend. This same son of Kentucky, I was later told by Robert Maynard Hutchins in a long visit at Santa Barbara, had responded when Hutchins asked him to propose the best Aquinas scholar he could name for appointment to the University of Chicago, that it was impossible because of the university's Baptist roots and continuing loose commitment to that tradition. It was a different world.

Coming to Temple University in 1967 at the invitation of its chairman with the acquiescence of Trenton's bishop who had released me seventeen years before, I encountered a situation not unlike the one I had left but with a few important differences. I had not previously known Jewish or Muslim students and colleagues. I had not realized the impact on Protestant scholarship of the leaps from Paul to Augustine to Luther and Calvin to Kant and Ritschl, the only waystations recorded being those in a popular, one-volume church history. Another not so welcome discovery was the unsophisticated condition of the doctoral program in the state-related university I was now a part of. We who had been recently hired attempted reforms. They succeeded. But the price was parricide. After three years the department's founding father was asked by the dean to step down, and I was elected in his place. The obvious tensions followed, and they lasted four years until his early death. That was a small step on the way to a large and vigorous department which shortly added Buddhist and Hindu studies to the examination of the three that had originated in the Middle East. The department never engaged in the popularly misnamed "comparative religion" because no faculty member ever knew any two in depth, not to say more than two, so as to compare them. But we learned a lot from each other by trading our mutual misconceptions. To these, most gave ear but some never.

In those Washington and Philadelphia years, I found the strongest intellectual influence to be private study in preparation for classroom teaching. The research that went into the six books on New Testament topics written while at Temple came second. As to the influence of learned papers heard and conversations engaged in, who can measure it? I took great comfort from reading a Karl Rahner essay that appeared late in his twenty-three volumes of *Theological Investigations* in which he said he would never speak ill of popularizers for he was one himself. He named only one paper done early in his career that he would label research scholarship, and he said it had no observable impact whatever. I can only hope that my *vulgarisation* approaches the *hauteur* of his.

What human contacts were the most formative, looking back from the vantage point of middle age (though how many people of 154 do you meet nowadays)? The first, surely, is the Liturgical Conference, Catholic in foundation but now fully ecumenical. All my convictions about the Church's public prayer were hammered out in the framework of its annual Liturgical Weeks and later periodical publications. The College Theology Society, now in its forty-third year, and its journal *Horizons* was another such influence; so too the *Catholic Biblical Quarterly,* which ranks in importance along with the association that produces it, and the Catholic Theological Society of America which I joined early and returned to hesitantly after its nonbiblical lapse into systematic and canonical-moral dullness of several decades. Service on four U.S. bilateral dialogues and as an observer over nine years of the commission on church order of the former Consultation on church Union, now the Church of Christ Uniting, was important, as was membership from the beginning on the board of the Philadelphia (now Interfaith) Council on the Holocaust; likewise on the editorial board of the *Journal of Ecumenical Studies* and as one of its outcomes assisting my colleague Leonard Swidler and the Anti-Defamation League of B'nai B'rith in achieving substantial changes in the text and staging of the 1990 Oberammergau *Passionsspiel.* Contacts with a variety of publishers and editors rank high. By and large they are a remarkable company that makes things happen.

The narrator of Damon Runyon's stories about the racetrack crowd of hangers-on at Mindy's always described himself as "just a guy who was around." That is who I have been in the worlds of Bible and worship, theology, religious education, and interfaith discourse. My sole distinction is that I have been "around" with some splendid men and women, discussing the most important things imaginable in our short life.

The parish pastor of my youth, I well recall, used to go through the rectory singing to a tuneless tune of his own, devising a chant of regret at the latest misplaced object in his house, "Ah, such is life/without a wife!" I have been blessed with the love of women over the years, and they have rewarded me with what Aquinas calls the highest of loves, friendship. Two other of my sisters have survived well after the first-mentioned who died at forty-one. In their devotion to the faith that made them and their lifetimes of intellectual concern attending it, they have seen me through many a rough passage, helping me find not lost objects but frequently myself.

TWO

Does God Play Dice?
Providence and Chance

Elizabeth A. Johnson, C.S.J.

Theology in every age interacts with the science contemporary to it, an indispensable task if theology is to fulfill its mission with respect to each generation. The dialogue may enkindle new theological insights, inspire more appealing metaphors, provide a context for new interpretation of religious tradition, or evoke a more profound sense of mystery. In any event, the interaction of theology with science is intended to make religious faith both credible and relevant within a particular view of the world and how it works. This means that in our day religious affirmations must speak about God's relation not to an ancient or medieval or Newtonian world, but to the dynamic, emerging world that the natural and biological sciences describe.[1]

This is not an easy world either to comprehend or to comprise within a religious perspective. Albert Einstein's famous remark denying that God plays dice with the universe is in fact an expression of his religiously-based refusal to accept the uncertainty principle encountered at the heart of quantum reality. However, thanks to the recent dialogue fortunately occurring between theology and science, the issue is being squarely faced by religious thinkers. The ancient religious view of a static, predictable, divinely governed universe is encountering the contemporary scientific view of an emergent, self-organizing universe that develops through the interplay of law and chance, to critical effect. Schooled in this dialogue, a contemporary religious mind finds aspects of the classical, monarchical idea of God along with God's attributes, relation to the world, and ways of working in the world inadequate, at least in part. Once again the theological search is on for language, models, and metaphors that will give expression to faith experience in ways coherent with the scientific sensibility of this era.[2]

In this essay, written in tribute to Gerard Sloyan, whose scholarly life bears witness to his own ever-present willingness to tackle new questions, I will engage the particular question of how God's providential activity can be affirmed in a world where chance plays a more essential role than ever before imagined. The conclusion, that divine providence is compatible with genuine randomness and that this compatibility in turn can shed light on the incomprehensible, gracious mystery of God, will be arrived at in a three step exploration: of the relevant scientific data, the Thomistic notion of dual agency, and the interface between the two. In no way does this discussion exhaust the topic. Rather, it simply traces and contributes to one line of discussion in this ever-expanding debate.

Science: The Interplay of Law and Chance

It is a truism by now that twentieth-century science has brought to an end the mechanistic view of the world associated with Newtonian physics and replaced it with a dynamic, open-ended view of the world in which some events are in principle unpredictable, although in retrospect they may make sense. This holds true for events at very small and very large magnitudes of space as, well as for events through the long reaches of time.

At the infinitesimal level of the atom and its sub-atomic particles, quantum mechanics uncovers a realm where time, space, and matter itself behave according to laws whose very functioning have uncertainty built into them. Statistical probability lends a measure of order to this realm, but precise sub-atomic events do not seem to occur according to any discernible regularity. For example, while it can be predicted that a certain mass of radioactive uranium will decompose within a given time, there is no way to predict which atom will decompose next, or why.[3] Furthermore, as the Heisenberg uncertainty principle asserts, a human observer cannot simultaneously plot both the position and velocity of a sub-atomic particle, for by charting one we disturb the other. Does this human inability to nail down and predict sub-atomic events point to the poor state of our equipment or rather to an ontological indeterminacy in reality itself? Many philosophers of science argue for the latter. Judging from the realm of the infinitesimally small, the fundamental building blocks of the world are neither mechanically pre-programmed nor utterly chaotic, but spontaneous within an orderly system.

At the macro level of non-linear, dynamical systems such as weather, chaos theory explores how very slight changes in initial conditions are ramified to produce massive effects.[4] A butterfly fluttering its wings in Beijing may set up an air current that amplifies upward through different levels of intensity to produce a major storm in New York a week later. While the ramifications of change through chaotic, non-linear systems are regular enough to be traced in mathematical equations, the number of initial conditions that affect each system is so immense and their confluence so unique that human observation will never get a total handle on them. We will never have an accurate weather forecast earlier than a week ahead, and this is due not to the limitation of our instruments but to the nature of the weather system itself. Being intrinsically unpredictable in an epistemological sense, dynamical systems thus represent a form of "structured randomness" in the world.[5] Does this indicate an ontological indeterminacy in the dynamical systems themselves? Many philosophers of science think so.

The immensely long evolution of the cosmos from the Big Bang to the present and still evolving clusters of galaxies, as well as the evolution of matter on earth from nonorganic to living states and from simple life to human consciousness, is another story fraught with the subtle interplay between chance and law.[6] To stay with the example of life on earth, mutations in genes caused by the sun's ultraviolet rays or exposure to chemicals issue in variations on life forms. Natural selection then rewards the ones who adapt best to their environment and reproduce. On and on goes this process of a hundred thousand variables, dead-ends, and breakthroughs. Roll back the clock to before the appearance of life on earth and then let it roll again: would humanity appear as we are now? Science is unanimous in saying no, so multiple and diverse are the factors that combined to produce our species. Intelligent life would probably develop, for the matter of the universe has the potential to evolve into complex structures (brains) from which consciousness emerges. But it would be a group with a different history, even a different physical appearance.

The emergence of human mind sheds light on a wondrous ability of matter, namely its capacity so to organize itself as to bring forth the truly new from within itself. Beginning with the featureless state right after the Big Bang, a rich diversity of physical systems and forms have emerged in a long, complex sequence of self-ordering processes even to the point where mind emerges from matter—and seeks to understand the process by which it came to be! This evolutionary interpretation of mind as emergent within the material process of self-organization leads to a holistic, non-dualistic idea of the human person. Not a composite of the isolable elements of material body and spiritual but somehow substantial mind, the human being is a single entity whose physical structure enables and supports the emergence of mind. As Paul Davies graphically puts it, mind is not some sort of extra ingredient glued onto brains at some stage of evolution; it did not require any factors external to the world itself.[7] Rather, consciousness is a power that emerges gradually in and through the increasing complexity of those intricately ramified and interlaced structures we call brains. We are the universe become conscious of itself. Material, physical reality is much richer in its possibilities than we are accustomed to think.

Taken together, scientific understandings of the indeterminism of physical systems at the quantum level, the unpredictability of chaotic systems at the macro level, and the emergence of new forms through the evolutionary process itself undermine the idea that there is a detailed blueprint or unfolding plan according to which the world was designed and now operates. Rather, the stuff of the world has an innate creativity in virtue of which the new continuously emerges through the interplay of chance and law: "there is no detailed blueprint, only a set of laws with an inbuilt facility for making interesting things happen."[8] The genuinely random intersects with deep-rooted regularities, issuing in a new situation which, when regularized itself, becomes the basis for a new play of chance. The world develops, then, according to neither anarchy nor teleology, but purposively if unpredictably. Physical phenomena are constrained in an orderly way, but themselves give rise to novelty due to the intrinsic indeterminism and openness of physical processes.

In this construal of nature's constitutive dynamic, it becomes clear that the classical idea of the laws of nature also requires revision. These are now understood to be descriptive rather than prescriptive, that is, abstract descriptions read off from regularities in the universe that approximate what we observe, rather than rules that pre-exist platonically apart from the universe and dictate or enforce behavior.[9] The laws of nature approximate the relationships in nature but do not comprehend them to their depths, which remain forever veiled. Nature itself is a mystery.

Furthermore, the laws of nature require the workings of chance if matter is to explore its full range of possibilities and emerge toward richness and complexity. Without chance, the potentialities of this universe would go unactualized. The movement of particles at the subatomic level, the initial conditions of non-linear dynamic systems, the mutation of genes in evolutionary history, all are necessary for the universe's becoming, though none can be predicted or controlled. It seems that the full gamut of the potentialities of matter can be explored only through the agency of rapid and frequent randomization. This role of chance is what one would expect if the universe were so constituted as to be able to explore all the potential forms of the organization of matter, both living and non-living, which it contains.

It can even be seen in retrospect that the emergence of human nature as we know it requires such an infrastructure. There is a deep compatibility between the autonomous ways physical, chemical, and biological systems operate through the interplay of law and chance on the one hand, and human consciousness and freedom on the other. These particular human qualities are intensely concentrated states of tendencies (purposiveness and chance) found throughout the universe in natural forms. The radical freedom of natural systems to explore and discover themselves is the condition for the possibility of the emergence of free and conscious human beings.

The capacity to form a world is there from the beginning in the fundamental constitution of matter. Chance's role is to enable matter to explore these potentialities. No chance, no evolution of the universe. If it were not such an impossible oxymoron, chance might even be called a law of nature itself. *Chance, consequently, is not an alternative to law, but the very means whereby law is creative. The two are strongly interrelated and the universe evolves through their interplay.*

On balance, the general character of the world as we know it from science calls for a more subtle notion of design, one that incorporates the occurrence of the genuinely novel and unpredictable in the context of laws that underdetermine what occurs. Great possibilities are left open.

Theological Options

This scientific view of the world, which enjoys wide allegiance and is not contingent on particular, disputed points, provides a unique context in which to discuss God's creative and providential action. The model of God as king and ruler, gifted with the attributes of omniscience and omnipotence, who in creating and sustaining the world pre-programs its development, who establishes its laws of nature but sets them aside to intervene miraculously when the occasion warrants—this monarchical model is less and less seriously imaginable. The potentiality of matter, the complexity of self-organizing systems, the potent unpredictability of evolution, the operation of chance within underdetermined laws, the presence of chaos and novelty, the multi-layered, interdependent process of the world in becoming, all are putting pressure on the classical idea of God and divine action in the world.

Engaging this new question, recent theology has itself self-organized into a range of options. In his 1989–1990 Gifford Lectures, Ian Barbour delineates eight different schools of thought on the issue, each of which has its strengths and shortcomings.[10] Classical theology understands God to be an omnipotent, omniscient, unchanging sovereign who relates to the world as ruler to kingdom. The Deist option sees God as designer of a law-abiding world to which God relates as clockmaker to clock. Neo-Thomist theology predicates God as primary cause working through secondary causes, on the analogy of an artisan with tools. The kenotic position perceives God as voluntarily self-limiting divine power in order to participate vulnerably in the life of the world, the way a parent enables a child to grow. Since existentialist theology sees God acting only in personal life, it has no model of God's relation to the world. Linguistic theology discerns God as the agent whose intention is carried out in the overall development of the cosmos, which can then be interpreted as the one, all-encompassing action of God. The option for the theme of embodiment sees the world as God's body to which God relates intimately as a person does to one's own body. Process theology sees God as a creative participant in the cosmic community, with a divine leadership role to play.

In addition to these positions, there is clearly also another view which hews literally to the biblical text, consequently seeing God as a personal agent who directly intervenes in the world, examples being the Exodus event, the resurrection of Jesus, and the answer to prayer. In dialogue with science this position argues ingeniously that, thanks to the indeterminism of reality at the quantum level, God's direct intervention in these instances does not transgress the laws of nature, for the natural system itself is "gappy" and open to outside influence without being violated.[11] The difficulty with this position, however, is that it confuses a gap, something missing in the ontological structure of natural systems, with indeterminacy, the openness of natural systems to a variety of outcomes. This openness of matter, however, is an intrinsic part of the working of nature and necessary for its creative development. In principle there are no gaps in the universe, which is complete on its own level.

Evaluating the current state of discussion in 1991, Owen Thomas, editor of a major volume on divine action, argues that while each position contributes some insight, only neo-Thomism and process theology are genuinely adequate, as only they give a philosophically satisfying and coherent account of how both divine and creaturely agents are fully active in one unified event.[12] How, in either case, can we conceive of the play of chance in the providential guidance of the world? Process theology would appear to have the advantage in this question with its understanding of how God continuously lures the world to its goal. In this process, God prehends every new event into the divine consequent nature and gives new initial aims to every on-going experience on the basis of what has already transpired. Since God and the world are in process together, not only does chance not threaten divine control over the universe, as it does in the classical model, but chance positively enriches divine experience. At the same time it provides opportunity for God's ongoing providential guidance in the giving of new initial aims to actual occasions impacted by chance.

Neo-Thomism, with its roots in a medieval and thus scientifically static view of the world, would seem less able to account for the occurrence of genuinely random events. Assessing its strengths and weaknesses, Barbour notes as a problem its difficulty in moving away from divine determinism to allow for the genuinely random to occur.[13] A closer reading of its central tenets, however, provides understanding of how chance may factor into divine creative and providential action. In fact, it seems to me that Thomism's insights into how God acts in the world fairly resonate with potential to account for the play of chance.

Aquinas and the Integrity of Created Systems

At the heart of Aquinas' vision is the evocative idea of participation. In creating, God, whose essence is the very livingness of being itself, gives a share in that being to what is other than Godself:

> Whatever is of a certain kind through its essence is the proper cause of what is of such a kind by participation. Thus, fire is the cause of all things that are afire. Now, God alone is actual being through divine essence itself, while other beings are actual beings through participation.[14]

As to ignite is the proper effect of fire, so too is the sharing of being the proper effect of the Mystery of Being. Hence, all that exists participates in its own way in divine being through the very gift of creaturely existence. It is not as if God and creatures stood as uncreated and created instantiations of "being" which is held in common by both. Rather, the mystery of God is Being itself who freely shares being while creatures participate. Nor is the gift of being given only once in the instant when a creature begins to exist, but continuously in a ceaseless act of divine creation. To cite another fiery analogy, every creature stands in relation to God as the air to the light of the sun. For as the sun is light-giving by its very nature, while the air is illuminated by it as long as the sun shines, so also God alone simply exists (divine essence is *esse*) while every creature exists insofar as it participates in being (creaturely essence is not *esse*).[15]

This notion of participation affects the understanding of both God and the world. Continuously creating and sustaining, God is in all things not as part of their essence but as the innermost source of their being, power, and action. There is, in other words, a constitutive presence of God at the heart of things. Conversely, in its own created being and doing, the world continuously participates in the livingness of the One who simply is. The universe, in other words, is a sacrament. Every excellence it exhibits is a participation in that quality in the unknowable mystery of God. Take the key example of goodness. Since "it befits divine goodness that other things should be partakers therein,"[16] every created good is a good by participation in the One who is good by essence. It follows that "in the whole sphere of creation there is no good that is not a good participatively."[17] In having their own good, creatures share in the divine. This is the basis for any speech about the transcendent mystery of God at all, for in knowing the excellence of the world we may speak analogically about the One in whose being it shares.

One of the strengths of Aquinas' vision is the autonomy he grants to created existence through its participation in divine being. He is so convinced of the transcendent mystery of God (*esse ipsum subsistens*) and so clear about the *sui generis* relation of God to the world that he sees no threat to divinity in allowing creatures the fullest measure of agency according to their nature. In fact, it is a measure of the creative power of God to raise up creatures who participate in divine being to such a degree that they are also creative and sustaining in their own right. A view to the contrary would diminish not only creatures but also their Creator: "to detract from the perfection of creatures is to detract from the perfection of divine power."[18] This is a genuinely noncompetitive view of God and the world. According to its dynamism, nearness to God and genuine creaturely autonomy grow in direct rather than inverse proportion. That is, God is not glorified by the diminishment of the creature but by the creature's flourishing. The nature of created participation in divine being is such that it grants creatures their own integrity, without reserve.[19]

This participatory relationship has strong implications for the question of agency. The power of creatures to act and cause change in the world is a created participation in the uncreated power of the One who is pure act. Conversely, God's generous goodness and wisdom are seen especially in the creation of a world with its own innate agency. As is the case with created things' participation in divine being, so too with agency. God's action is not part of the creature's essential action which has its own creaturely integrity. Rather, God's act giving creatures their very nature is what makes creaturely act possible at all in its own created autonomy. Technically, God is primary cause of the world, the unfathomable Source of being who continuously creates and sustains it, while creatures are secondary causes, moved movers who receive from God their form and power to act with independence.[20]

These two causes are not two species of the same genus, not two different types of causes united by the commonality of causing. They operate on completely different levels, one being the cause of all causes and the other participating in this power. In this system of thought it is an error to think of God as working in the world apart from secondary causes, or beside them, or in addition to them, or even in competition with them. God's act does not supply something that is missing from a creaturely act or rob it of its power so that it is only a sham cause. Rather, the mystery of God acts by divine essence, power, and presence *in and through* the acts of finite agents which have genuine causal efficacy in their own right. If divine and finite agents are not complementary, then each does not contribute distinct parts to the one outcome. Instead, God acts wholly in and through the finite agents which also act wholly in the event. As a result, the one effect issues from both primary and secondary causes simultaneously with, however, each cause standing in a fundamentally different relationship to the effect. God makes the world, in other words, in the process of things being themselves.

Working in this tradition Karl Rahner argues that even in the creation of the human soul divine causality does not insert itself into the finite causal series but, through the power given to matter to evolve toward spirit, enables the human parents to transcend themselves in the creation of a genuinely other person.[21] Rahner among others also appeals to the doctrine of incarnation, where the divine and human are united while remaining distinct, and to the doctrine of grace, where the Spirit brings wholeness to human beings without violating their freedom or responsibility, as paradigms for the God-world relationship. It is so easy to forget this, slipping God into the web of interactions as though the divine were simply a bigger and better secondary cause. But the distinction between primary and secondary causality enables thought to hold firm to the Godness of God and the integrity of creatures, seeing both acting in a unique *concursus*.

In Aquinas' discussion of divine governance of the world, this idea of double agency with respect to efficient causality is correlated with final causality to provide the grid for his understanding of providence. It would seem, he objects with a curiously modern ring, that the universe does not need to be governed by God, for the processes of the world seem to accomplish their purpose on their own and without any interference. However, he replies, this very self-direction is itself an imprint *(impressio)* from God, for in giving creatures their own being God gives them a natural inclination whereby through their own natural actions they tend toward the good. This dynamic tendency is genuinely part of their own nature, but it also expresses God's purposes. While endowing creatures with their intrinsic nature and ways of acting, God leaves them free to follow the strivings of their natural inclination which aims them toward the good. Since all good is a participation in divine goodness, we can affirm that the universe as a whole tends toward the ultimate good which is God. Biblically portrayed, Holy Wisdom reaches from one end of the world to the other, ordering all things sweetly and mightily (Wis 8:1).[22] Technically, God is immanent in the universe as final cause. It does not escape notice today that this notion has interesting similarities with process theology's idea of God as forever luring the world to its next goal.

Let us draw all of these threads together to see how they deliver an intellectual system of interpretation of how God acts providentially in the world. As Aquinas explains, the way God is governor of things matches the way God is their cause. As God is primary cause of the world as a whole, endowing all created beings with their own participation in divine being (enabling them to exist), in divine agency (empowering them to act), and in divine goodness (drawing them toward their goal), so too God graciously guides the world toward its end in and through the natural workings of the processes found in creation as a whole. Immanent in these processes, divine providential purposes come to fruition by means of purposes inherent in creatures themselves.

Why is this fitting? In a particularly insightful reply Aquinas argues that forms of governing are best that communicate a higher perfection to the governed. Now there is more excellence in a thing's being a cause in relation to others than in its not being a cause. Consequently, God governs in such a way as to empower creatures to be causes toward others. Indeed, "If God were to govern alone, the capacity to be causes would be missing from creatures," to the detriment of their flourishing and their Creator's glory.[23] Or looked at another way, if God did everything directly so that created causes did not really affect anything, this would be a *less powerful* God. For it shows more power to give others a causative capability than to do everything oneself.[24] Thus God is everywhere present and active, continuously interacting with the world to implement divine purpose while granting creatures and created systems a full measure of being and efficacy. This is a both/and sensibility that guarantees the integrity of the created causal nexus while affirming the gracious and intentional immanence of the transcendent God active within worldly purposiveness.

Divine purpose is accomplished in a *concursus,* or flowing together of divine and creaturely, act in which the latter mediates the former. This means that the world necessarily hides divine providential action from us. God's act is not a discrete object that can be isolated and known as a finite constituent of the world, for its very nature is transcendent mystery while its mode of operation transpires immanently in and through created causes. At the same time, faith affirms that the world, far from being merely a stage for divine action, is itself a sacrament of God's providential action, which is sweet and strong within every cause so that everything may truly contribute to the realization of the goal.

Providence and Chance

Bringing contemporary science's view of the role of chance into dialogue with neo-Thomism's understanding of the God-world relation yields interesting results. The latter's conviction of the integrity of natural causes, while formulated within a static scientific worldview, accommodates evolutionary science with almost surprising ease. For the basic principle remains the same: God's providential guidance is accomplished in and through the free working of secondary causes. Indeed, for Aquinas the understanding that God's providential activity is exercised in and through secondary causes includes rather than excludes chance, contingency, and freedom of choice: "It is not the function of divine providence to impose necessity on things ruled by it."[25] Rather, random occurrences themselves are secondary causes with their own integrity. Science may describe these secondary causes in different ways today, but they still function theologically as the means by which God fulfills divine purpose.

As we have seen, the process of creation is described by the natural sciences as one in which new qualities and modes of existence continuously emerge out of simpler forms of matter by the operation of natural laws. These laws of nature are ingenious and felicitous in that they enable matter and energy to self-organize in unexpectedly remarkable ways from clouds of dust and gas to galaxies and solar systems, and from non-organic matter to life to mind. Multilayered and underdetermined, these laws reflect the universe's potential to create richness and complexity spontaneously, from within, in a process whose inherent openness precludes detailed fixing in advance. As secondary causes, they realize God's purposes. In the words of astro-physicist and theologian William Stoeger, reflective of the neo-Thomistic consensus, "God is always acting through the deterministic and indeterministic interrelationships and regularities of physical reality which our models and laws imperfectly describe."[26]

Today's science has discovered that chance is an essential element in the continuous working out of these laws of nature. The Creator endows the material of this world with one set of potentialities rather than another. These are then unveiled by chance exploring their gamut in an inevitable yet indeterminate evolutionary process. Indeed, the more we think about it, this seems to be the only way in which all potentialities might eventually, given enough time and space, be actualized. *Chance, consequently, is not an alternative to law, but the very means whereby law is creative. The two are strongly interrelated and the universe evolves through their interplay.* If *this* is the kind of universe created by God, then faith can affirm that God works not only through the deep regularities of the laws of nature but also through random occurrence. God uses chance, so to speak, to ensure variety, resilience, novelty, and freedom, right up to humanity itself. Absolute Holy Mystery dwells within, encompasses, empowers the evolutionary process, making the world through the process of things being themselves, thus making the world through chance and its genuinely irregular character. If God works through chance, then the natural creativity of chance itself can be thought of as a mode of divine creativity in which it participates. And the gracious mystery of God can be glimpsed as the Source not only of deep regularities in the universe, but also of novelty. The future remains genuinely open: God does not determine chance atomic events or initial conditions of chaotic systems. Randomness is real, for God respects the structure of creation while at the same time weaving events into providential patterns toward the realization of the whole. Divine sovereignty and creaturely freedom, of which chance is one instance, do not compete.

Risk-Taking God

How does this interpretation of providence in turn influence the classical idea of divine attributes? With this question we reach a frontier where scientific insight in dialogue with Christian faith is providing the occasion for new theological wisdom about the doctrine of God. If Aquinas maintained that God governs in the same way God causes, then neo-Thomism is nuancing this with the understanding that God governs in the same way God saves. Many theologians, in fact, appeal today to the gracious action expressed in incarnation and the gift of grace as the basic paradigm of the God-world relationship.

The Creator God who is Being Itself is also the Redeemer God, whose self-emptying incarnation into the vagaries of history reveals the depths of divine Love. The Creator God is also the Sanctifier God, whose self-gift in grace brings wholeness to the brokenness of sinful hearts and situations without violating human freedom. Could it not be that the *kenosis* so typical of divine involvement in human history also characterizes God's working in the natural world? Could it not be that God's being edged out of the world and onto the cross, in Bonhoeffer's profound intuition, also refers to the cost of divine vulnerability in creation? Could it not be that since the human world is on a continuum with the micro world, only mediated by more complex biological matter, that the best way to understand God's action in the indeterminacy of the natural world is by analogy with how divine initiative relates to human freedom?

If so, divine perfection is ultimately a perfection of relationality and love rather than of self-sufficiency and control. Consequently, omnipotence unfailingly manifests itself not as coercive "power over" but as sovereign love which empowers. God's providential guidance, in other words, is not that of a puppeteer but the patient, subtle presence of a gracious Creator who achieves divine purpose through the free play of created processes. Indeed, it is quite likely that Love can only work in such a way out of respect for the beloved. Some thinkers carry this self-limitation even further to the attribute of omniscience, arguing that God does not know what will happen before it happens, since there is as yet nothing to know. It should be noted that the great difference between process theology and neo-Thomism regarding God's self-limitation is that for process thought this is a metaphysical necessity, while for Thomism it is a free and voluntary act of love.

Divine governance then involves God in waiting upon the world, so to speak, patiently acting through its natural processes including unpredictable, uncontrollable chance to bring about the emergence of the new while consistently urging the whole toward fullness of life. Since, with the development of nerves and brains, suffering in both the natural and human world is a consequence of the free play of randomness, providence also involves the gracious mystery of God in suffering with the beloved creation as new life is created through death. Not the monarch but the lover becomes the paradigm.[27]

In the course of thinking upon these things, theologians have found it helpful to imagine new metaphors to capture the nuances of God's providential relation to the workings of chance. As might be suspected, these images are drawn more from artistic creativity and parental love than from the classical model of an artisan working with tools. No one, of course, is adequate but each sheds a little light. They also point quite directly to the importance of responsible human action in cooperation with God's providential purpose. Among them: God is like a master theatrical improviser in live performance, amplifying and embroidering each theme as it presents itself; like a choreographer composing steps in tandem with the creative insights of the whole dance troupe; like a composer of a fugue, starting with a simple line of melody and weaving a complex structure by endlessly folding it back upon itself; like a jazz player, inspired by the spirit of the audience and the night to improvise riffs upon riffs; like a designer who sets the rules of the game, including wild cards, and then lets it play. In every instance the image is arrived at through the logic set out in W. Norris Clarke's evocative passage:

> what must the "personality" or "character" be like of a Creator in whose image this astounding universe of ours is made, with its prodigal abundance of energy, its mind-boggling complexity, yet simplicity, its fecundity of creative spontaneity, its ever surprising fluid mixture of law and chance, etc. Must not the "personality" of such a Creator be one charged not only with unfathomable power and energy, but also with dazzling imaginative creativity? Such a creator must be a kind of daring Cosmic Gambler who loves to work with both law and chance, a synthesis of apparent opposites—of power and gentleness, a lover of both law and order and of challenge and spontaneity.[28]

The biblical images for the Creator Spirit, namely wind, fire, and water, also express the moving, playing, unpredictable qualities of the God to whom chance is not a rival.

In dialogue with contemporary science, theology understands that the Creator God is neither a maker of clocks nor an instigator of anarchy, but the one ceaselessly at work bringing overall direction and order to the free play of the undetermined realms of matter and spirit, "an Improviser of unsurpassed ingenuity."[29] In this evolutionary world, the essential role of genuine randomness does not contradict God's providential care but somehow illumines it. To use Christopher Mooney's lovely phrasing:

> Wave packets propagate and collapse, sparrows fall to the ground, humans freely decide for good or for ill; yet hairs of the head nevertheless get numbered, elusive quantum particles eventually statistically stabilize, and "where sin increased, grace abounded all the more."[30]

The world develops in an economy of divine superabundance, gifted with its own freedoms in and through which God's gracious purpose is accomplished. Dante's vision of the "Love that moves the sun and the other stars,"[31] it now appears, is a self-emptying, self-offering, delighting, exploring, suffering, sovereign Love, transcendent source of all possibilities who acts immanently through the matrix of the freely evolving universe.

NOTES

1. For historical background of the discussion, see Ernan McMullin, "Natural Science and Belief in a Creator: Historical Notes," 49–79, and Michael Buckley, "The Newtonian Settlement and the Origins of Atheism," 81–102, in Robert Russell, William Stoeger, and George Coyne, eds., *Physics, Philosophy, and Theology: A Common Quest for Understanding* (Vatican City: Vatican Observatory Publications, 1988).

2. See papal message calling attention to the importance of this agenda, in Robert Russell, William Stoeger, and George Coyne, eds., *John Paul II on Science and Religion: Reflections on the New View from Rome* (Vatican City: Vatican Observatory Publications, 1990). Scholarly discussion is collated in such works as Ted Peters, ed., *Cosmos as Creation: Theology and Science in Consonance* (Nashville: Abingdon, 1989); David Burrell, ed., *God and Creation: An Ecumenical Symposium* (Notre Dame: University of Notre Dame Press, 1990); and Robert Russell, Nancey Murphy, and C. J. Isham, eds., *Quantum Cosmology and the Laws of Nature: Scientific Perspectives on Divine Action* (Vatican City: Vatican Observatory Publications, and Berkeley: Center for Theology and the Natural Sciences, 1993). Individuals who have scholarly credentials in both science and theology and whose works helpfully reflect this dialogue include Arthur Peacocke, *Science and the Christian Experiment* (London: Oxford University Press, 1971), and *Theology for a Scientific Age: Being and Becoming—Natural, Divine and Human* (Minneapolis: Fortress, 1993); and John Polkinghorne, *One World: The Interaction of Science and Theology* (Princeton: Princeton University Press, 1986), and *Science and Creation* (London: SPCK, 1988).

3. For general background written for the non-specialist, see John Polkinghorne, *The Quantum World* (Princeton: Princeton University Press, 1984); and C. J. Isham, "Quantum Theories of the Creation of the Universe," in Russell, Murphy, Isham, eds., *Quantum Cosmology*, 49–89.

4. For a general introduction, see James Gleick, *Chaos: Making a New Science* (New York: Penguin Books, 1987); a key refutation of the idea that chaos amounts to blind, purposeless chance is Ilya Prigogine and Isabelle Stengers, *Order Out of Chaos* (New York: Bantam Books, 1984).

5. Term used by John Polkinghorne, "The Laws of Nature and the Laws of Physics," in Russell, Murphy, Isham, eds., *Quantum Cosmology*, 437–48.

24   *Elizabeth A. Johnson, C.S.J.*

6. Helpful introductions for the lay reader are Robert Jastrow, *God and the Astronomers* (New York: Norton, 1978); Carl Sagan, *Cosmos* (New York: Ballantine Books, 1980); Paul Davies, *God and the New Physics* (New York: Simon and Schuster, 1983), and *The Cosmic Blueprint* (New York: Simon and Schuster, 1988); and Arthur Peacocke, *God and the New Biology* (San Francisco: Harper and Row, 1986).

7. Paul Davies, "The Intelligibility of Nature," in Russell, Murphy, Isham, eds., *Quantum Cosmology*, 152; see also George Ellis, "The Theology of the Anthropic Principle," in ibid., 367–405.

8. Conclusion of Davies, *The Cosmic Blueprint*, 202.

9. William Stoeger, "Contemporary Physics and the Ontological Status of the Laws of Nature," in Russell, Murphy, Isham, eds., *Quantum Cosmology*, 209–34.

10. Ian Barbour, *Religion in an Age of Science* (San Francisco: Harper and Row, 1990) 243–70, with chart on 244. See also the schema by Robert Russell, "Introduction," in Russell, Murphy, Isham, eds., *Quantum Cosmology*, 4–10.

11. Representative of this group is William Alston, "Divine Action, Human Freedom, and the Laws of Nature," in Russell, Murphy, Isham, eds., *Quantum Cosmology*, 185–207.

12. Owen Thomas, "Recent Thoughts on Divine Agency," in Brian Hebblethwaite and Edward Henderson, eds., *Divine Action* (Edinburgh: T&T Clark, 1991) 35–50. See Thomas' own edited volume, *God's Activity in the World: The Contemporary Problem* (Chico, Calif.: Scholars Press, 1983).

13. Barbour, *Religion in an Age of Science*, 249–50.

14. Thomas Aquinas, *Summa Contra Gentiles* III, 66:7; hereafter *SCG*. Edition used is translated by Vernon Bourke (Garden City, N.Y.: Doubleday, 1956). Aquinas' extended discussion of divine governance can be found in *SCG* III, especially chapters 64–77, and his *Summa Theologiae* I, qq. 103–9.

15. *Summa Theologiae* I, q. 104, a. l; hereafter cited as *ST*. Edition used is translated by the English Dominicans (New York: Benziger, 1956).

16. *ST* I, q. 19, a. 2.

17. *ST* I, q. 103, a. 2.

18. *SCG* III, 69:15.

19. For further explanation of this position, see Piet Schoonenberg, "God or Man: A False Dilemma," in his *The Christ* (New York: Seabury, 1971) 13–49.

20. For explanation of this point, see Etienne Gilson, "The Corporeal World and the Efficacy of Secondary Causes," in Thomas, ed., *God's Activity*, 213–30. Gilson stresses how strong Aquinas is on the integrity of secondary causes, using Aristotle to combat the Platonism of Avicenna. See also David Burrell, *Aquinas: God and Action* (Notre Dame: University of Notre Dame Press, 1979).

21. Karl Rahner, *Hominization: The Evolutionary Origin of Man as a Theological Problem* (New York: Herder & Herder, 1965); see also his essays "Christology within an Evolutionary View of the World," *Theological Studies* V (New York: Seabury, 1975) 157–92; and "The Unity of Spirit and Matter in the Christian Understanding of Faith," *Theological Investigations* VI (New York: Crossroad, 1982) 153–77.

22. Argument found in *ST* I, q. 103, a. 8.

23. *ST* I, q. 103, a. 6.

24. *ST* I, q. 105, a. 5.

25. *SCG* III, 72:7; see also chapters 73 and 74.

26. William Stoeger, "The Ontological Status of the Laws of Nature," in Russell, Murphy, Isham, eds., *Quantum Cosmology*, 234.

27. Peter Hodgson, *God in History: Shapes of Freedom* (Nashville: Abingdon Press, 1989) develops this idea with depth and lucidity; Sallie McFague, *Models of God: Theology for an Ecological, Nuclear Age* (Philadelphia: Fortress, 1987) gives it imaginative depth.

28. W. Norris Clarke, "Is a Natural Theology Still Possible Today?" in Russell, Stoeger, Coyne, eds., *Physics, Philosophy, and Theology*, 121. The theme of improvisation is stressed by Peter Geach, *Providence and Evil* (Cambridge: Cambridge University Press, 1977); the model of a fugue is developed by Peacocke, *Theology for a Scientific Age*, 173–7; and that of the game by Davies, *God and the New Physics*.

29. Arthur Peacocke, *Intimations of Reality* (Notre Dame: University of Notre Dame Press, 1984) 73.

30. Christopher Mooney, "Theology and the Heisenberg Uncertainty Principle," 62; paper delivered to the Catholic Theological Society of America in June 1992 and summarized in *Proceedings of the Catholic Theological Society of America* 47 (1992) 130–2; biblical reference: Rom 5:21.

31. Dante, *Paradiso*, Canto 33, 1.145 (trans. Dorothy Sayers).

THREE

The Gospel According to the Scriptures

Paul M. van Buren

This essay has grown from several papers[1] arguing that the Church's Old Testament is a distinct text of the Christian Church, as different from the Jewish people's *Tenach* as are the two communities, and that it is of the essense of each text that it exists as interpreted by that community for which it is Sacred Scripture. As the project has developed, I have become more and more fascinated by the way in which the Jews who followed Jesus of Nazareth arrived at the gospel which Paul first learned, the gospel "according to the scriptures" (1 Cor 15:3-5). I offer this preliminary attempt of a theologian to learn from and make use of the work of scholars in Gerard Sloyan's field of biblical studies, as a mark of my respect for him and his work, trusting that he will accept such a breech of disciplinary boundaries with his usual forbearance and fine sense of humor.

I

A reasonable hypothesis concerning the path taken that led to the gospel "according to the scriptures" will require that we attempt to enter into the minds of those first-century Jews who were faced with the shocking and incomprehensible event of Jesus' death as King-Messiah, and then either the (perhaps even more unsettling) subsequent event of not finding his body, or of being confronted by strange and evidently ambiguous visions/appearances of Jesus, or both. We can be almost certain that they fled for help—it must have been for them almost instinctive to do so—to the one world in which they were at home, the one they knew best, the world they could trust, one in which God's will could be surely found: the world of the Scriptures. But before we set out on that journey, we need to be clear in our own minds that the world of the "really real" was not for them where it is for us.

We seem to think that what is real is "out there" where history happens, certainly not in books. "Out there" is where we think of God as acting, if we think of God at all and of God as one who acts. And if we think there is a divine purpose at all, then we think of "out there" as where it will be or is being unfolded. That is where we think human life, and whatever meaning it has or ought to have, is "played out."[2] It is as natural for us, as it would have been foreign to those Jews, to look back to the historical life and teaching of Jesus as the key to understanding him. For us, his story is the story of one whom historians today identify variously as the Galilean healer and teacher, the Galilean holy man or Hasid,[3] or the Galilean prophet of Jewish restoration.[4]

If, however, we try to move from the gospel that Paul received back to that historical Jesus, or from Jesus to that gospel, we shall draw a blank, for that does not at all appear to have been the move made by the formulators of that gospel. Nothing of the sort was apparently in the minds of those who had developed the gospel that Paul received. They moved from the death of "the King of the Jews" and the disturbing occurrences of Easter, to the Scriptures, back and forth, until they found "the" meaning of those events, which they called the Good News, and thus also the new "meaning" of those Scriptures.

If we ignore what they did, failing to see what was for them the world of "the really real," then we may proceed with our twentieth-century minds to look for the connection between that gospel which Paul received and the history of Jesus of Nazareth detectable by critical historical research, but what we discover is just how little there is. William Nicholls, in his *Christian Antisemitism,*[5] following Geza Vermes' *Jesus the Jew,*[6] takes this route and finds, naturally, a tremendous gap. The real (in our sense) Jesus did not teach or preach the gospel that Paul received. A critical analysis of the written Gospels leads to the conclusion that the predictions of his death and resurrection found in them are almost certainly insertions, made by authors who had received the same gospel that Paul had received earlier, and who wrote their Gospels in its light. Jesus preached the imminence of the reign or rule of God, not his own death "for our sins" or his being "raised on the third day," let alone that these were "according to the scriptures." The subject of Jesus' preaching, apparently, was God and God's reign, not Jesus, let alone "Christ."

This is not to say that there are no connections at all between the Jesus of Nazareth recoverable by scholars versed in the languages, literature, customs, and practices of first-century Judaism, and the gospel that was already developed and transmitted to Paul when he joined the movement. One major commonality was the conviction that the end of this aeon and the beginning of a new one was terribly near, so near for Jesus, perhaps, that it could be grasped as present and lived by, even as the great transformation of the world approached. In the Philippians hymn, the reality of the future is to be confessed as present: "Jesus Christ *is* Lord to the glory of God the Father," and in his last letter, Paul wrote that the end was "nearer to us now than when we first believed" (Rom 13:11), making evident his conviction that the realization of Jesus' designation as Son of God in power by his resurrection from among the dead (Rom 1:4) was so imminent that its effects could be felt and lived by already (Romans 5 and 6).

Yet when we take note of the direction in which the post-Easter, pre-Pauline gospel developed, we can recognize with Nicholls and Vermes that that gospel is clearly reflected and celebrated in the Church's Eucharist (its cult of the sacrificial death of Jesus and his resurrection) and elaborated and praised in its later creeds, but it is far removed from anything Jesus said or did. On the one hand is Jesus the Jew, however exceptional, and on the other is the death and resurrection of Christ in the gospel Paul said he had received, and his humiliation and exaltation in the Philippians hymn, not to speak of the Gospel of John's "stranger from heaven."[7] To move from these variations of the gospel to the language of the Eucharist and the Second Article of the Nicene Creed is easy. To move from them back to Jesus the Jew involves a leap over insurmountable obstacles.

William Nicholls has posed the problem in the following manner. The figure of Jesus has become clearer in recent years in part because of the work of Jewish scholars, whose studies have greatly increased our knowledge of Second Temple Judaism and its Hellenistic context, and so of the historical setting of the first-century documents of early Christianity. This has made possible what has been called *die Heimholung Jesu bei seinem Volk,* to use the expression of Schalom Ben-Chorin,[8] the reclamation by Jewish scholars of Jesus, the Torah-faithful Jew, as one of his own people. Christian scholars have also taken part in this reconstruction, and their results agree with those of their Jewish colleagues: Jesus fits and can be understood within his particular time, place, and people. He was undoubtedly a remarkable Jew, but he was no anomaly. It is no historical puzzle that he attracted a devoted following and probably a few enemies, but he was certainly a first-century Jew among first-century Jews.

On the other hand, there is the Christian myth, as Nicholls calls it, using the term in its neutral, formal sense, by now standard in the study of the history of religions.[9] A myth is a story that a community fashions, tells, and believes, a story that accounts for its origins and *raison d'être*, and which gives its members a sense of their own and their community's identity. For the Christian community, that myth is the story, to which they believe Israel's Scriptures point, of the Savior from heaven, who died as Israel's awaited but rejected Messiah for the sins of the world, was raised to the presence of God, and will return in glory to establish God's dominion over creation. It is the myth celebrated in the Church's Eucharist, narrated in its canonical Gospels, and formulated for liturgical praise in its creeds.

The religion of the myth, however, is not just different from the religion of Jesus the Jew, Nicholls insists: it contradicts it, for Jesus is to be found clearly within and as a part of first-century, Second Temple Judaism. But it is precisely Judaism that is rejected in the myth, at least in its developed form, for Jesus' coming and message were understood to have made "the old law" obsolete.[10] And from the beginning, the Scriptures of Israel were taken to be no longer primarily "the story of God's choice of a people and his gift to them of a way of life"—i.e., the Torah—but as pointers to the coming crucified and risen Messiah.[11] Consequently, if anyone wishes to follow Jesus and his teaching, that person cannot properly be a Christian, for to be a Christian is to believe in the myth that negates the Jewish religious tradition of Jesus the Jew.[12]

Moreover, because Nicholls believes that the Christian myth necessarily entails a negative judgment on the Jewish people for failing to recognize and accept, indeed for rejecting their Messiah, he takes it to be the inevitable root of Christian anti-Judaism which led inexorably to the rise of modern anti-Semitism, which in turn formed the matrix of the murder of some six million Jews in the *Shoah*. He therefore concludes that a moral choice is unavoidable: either a Christian may follow Jesus the Jew, in which case he will abandon the Christian myth, or he will continue to believe the myth that led to the death of so many of the people of Jesus the Jew, and therefore live contrary to the way into which Jesus called his disciples. Morally, there is no way to have both.[13]

The choice, however, is not so neat as it appears, for the myth that we are being asked to discard is, in its root form, just the gospel that had taken shape in those first couple of years before Paul joined the movement. That gospel has two features that are distinguished by

their absence in the account of Jesus based on current historical scholarship. The first is that it was an interpretation of Jesus that began with
and centered on his end, his death on a cross. The second is that it was
an interpretation "according to the scriptures."

The interpretation of Jesus offered by Nicholls, following essentially that of Vermes, may be classified, in Donald Juel's words, as
being among "current attempts to understand Jesus that focus on his
ministry almost to the exclusion of his trial and death."[14] There appear
to have been "estimates of Jesus by his contemporaries that took little
account of his passion," such as the one made by those who, according
to Mark 8:28, took him to be a prophet. In short, "it is certainly correct
that people could regard Jesus as a religious figure of major importance with little consideration of the cross-resurrection kerygma."[15]
But the *kerygma* (the Greek New Testament's word for "proclamation")
was just that preached gospel of which we hear in 1 Corinthians 15:3-
4. We need not dispute that one may interpret Jesus quite apart from
his crucifixion as "King of the Jews," as "Contender for Israel in the
languages of the world."[16] That, however, is evidently not what was
attempted by those among his disciples who taught Paul their gospel.

The interpretation of Nicholls, Vermes, and some others appeals
selectively to the parts of the Gospels that focus on Jesus' ministry, as
well as to Jewish writings that throw light on first-century Jewish beliefs and practices. The Scriptures of Israel are of little interest in this
attempt. Or rather, biblical texts are treated as we moderns almost in-
variably treat texts: as windows through which we peer in order to see
what really happened. The appeal, therefore, is to history, insofar as it
can be recovered, for that is what moderns take to be the realm of reality. The first-century Jews who formulated the original gospel also
appealed to reality, but for them, what was real was to be found in
Israel's Scriptures.

Before we reject what those Jews did, it is well to recall why they
did what they did. I think we may assume that they were just as impressed by "Jesus the Jew" as are Vermes or Nicholls, if not more so. I
think we are safe in assuming that they were profoundly impressed by
him, and perhaps not just as "a religious figure of major importance."
It is not unreasonable to assume, to use a modern hasidic analogy, that
they saw him at least as their "Rebbe," or even thought that he was
God's quite special envoy whose presence among them was a sign that
the hopes of their people for God's rescue from Roman oppression
were soon to be realized. We cannot be at all sure of any of the precise
formulations of the hopes that centered on him, since every one of
them were at the least profoundly influenced by the gospel that the
first disciples developed after Easter, the interpretation which they

made of his death. What I think we may be reasonably sure of is that all of those hopes were dashed to pieces by the crucifixion of their leader.

I think we may be equally as sure that Jesus' followers were as shattered and confused by whatever it was that happened on Easter. Trained by the rhythm of the liturgical calendar, Christians have come to see Easter as the glorious and happy answer to Holy Week and its grim ending on Good Friday. The Cross became a symbol of hope because it was crowned by Jesus' resurrection: Good Friday can be known to be good, because of what we know we shall celebrate on the Sunday following. It takes an imaginative effort to resist reading this interpretation back into the experience of the disciples on the original Easter. It is perhaps not too difficult to imagine that they could at first have seen nothing good in the events of that Friday. What is much harder to realize, but surely far nearer to what must historically have been the only possibility for them, is that there could have been nothing obvious in which to rejoice on that first Easter. Whatever hopes they may have shared in a general resurrection in "the age to come" could hardly have helped them to rejoice over a single empty tomb or appearances of the single figure of Jesus, even had they been able to recognize him—and the often conflicting stories they came to tell of it leave even this primary recognition in doubt. Before that first day of the week could become Easter, they would have had to understand it as Christians have in fact understood it ever since. But they would first have had to come to that understanding on which ours depends, whether it took them minutes or hours or days or weeks to do so. Joy could have come only with the interpretation at which they arrived.

Assuming that Jesus was for his disciples no minor figure in their lives, what they were driven to come to terms with, what they desperately needed to understand, was not Jesus in his Galilean ministry, but that this Jesus had been publicly crucified as King of the Jews, as King-Messiah, and that his tomb had been found empty. Nothing in their experience with "Jesus the Jew," and nothing that they could have expected of a King-Messiah, accounted for such a death or explained the frightening events of Easter. This is what must have torn them to pieces and driven them in their quest to understand.

Being first-century Jews, not twentieth-century westerners, we can be fairly sure that, in order to try to understand what had happened, they turned to what they would have regarded as their most reliable guide to reality: the Scriptures. Their Jesus had been killed as Israel's King-Messiah. Had they totally misunderstood the role and destiny of the King-Messiah? It is likely that in their frantic quest for understanding, they would have turned to every passage which they as Jews had ever read concerning the Messiah. They had no answers, I am suggesting, for which they wanted confirmation from the Scriptures. What I believe was the case, with Juel, following Nils Dahl, is that they turned to the Scriptures in desperation just because they did *not* have any answers. To follow them in that turn means to do it, to the best of our abilities, as they would have done it.

II

In attempting to follow those first-century Jews, Jesus' disciples, in their terrified, frantic search into their one source of understanding, the Scriptures of Israel, we are going to have to allow Juel to remind us repeatedly that a text, specifically this text, was not for them, or for any other Jew of the time, what it is for us. For us a text is a window onto events or into certain persons having certain thoughts in certain circumstances. Our interest lies always in that which lies behind the text. First-century Jews, so scholars of the period tell us, saw reality lying directly in the text itself.[17]

The centrality of, nay the exclusive attention to, the text as the locus of divine wisdom, instructions and (to use the modern term) revelation was hardly an invention of first-century Judaism. It was the mark of Ezra's reform following the return from Babylon, and it would lead to the saying, No more prophecy after Ezra.[18] That is to say that it was well-established Jewish practice and understanding before the first century that if you wanted to know the will of God on any matter, you would never seek out a prophet or rely on the omens of a Temple priest, as would have been normal to do in ancient Israel; now you consulted the text of Torah, or, better, one versed in reading and interpreting the Torah. The word of God was no longer looked for in prophetic utterance, but, well before the first century of the Common Era, had now become the written words of the Book, the Scriptures.

For first-century Jews the Scriptures were a collection of the words of God for the benefit of his people and, through them, for that of the whole world, certainly given by God himself: oracles, we would say, and all from God. Because the individual words were understood to be inspired, so it was thought right to associate one text with another on the mere basis of finding a word common to each. If a Jew of this period found a particular word in a given text puzzling, for example, he would feel it right to search for other texts in which that same word was to be found, and those other texts could be expected to solve the puzzling aspect of the word in the first text.

A lovely example of this method, which Juel examines at length, occurs in a document that is admittedly later than the first century, but which appears to have followed well-established practice.[19] A puzzle seems to have been noticed in reading the delicious rehearsal of the Exodus in Psalm 114, where it says literally (v. 3), "The sea saw and fled." "Saw" (*raah*) calls for a direct object, a grammatical point covered up by the usual translations. What, a certain Rabbi Simon of Kitron seems to have asked himself, did the sea *see* that caused it to flee (*nus*)? Well, there was another flight in another biblical text: the righteous Joseph, resisting the seductions of his master's wife, who "caught him by his garment, saying 'Lie with me,' . . . "left his garment in her hand and fled (*nus*) . . ." (Gen 39:12), the words, "left his garment . . . and fled" being repeated three times (in vs 13, 15, and 18). Moreover, the Exodus story tells us (Exod 13:19) that Moses took the bones of Joseph with him out of Egypt, as Joseph had requested just before his death (Gen 50:25). And there is the answer! The sea saw the bones of Joseph and rewarded his righteous flight from Potiphar's wife by fleeing before the escaping children of Israel!

Another example can be taken from the same source.[20] Why did God command Moses (Exod 14:16) to stretch out his hand and *split* (*baqa*) the sea? That seems a strange thing to try to do with water. But the word is found in a foundational text which we shall not have room to consider in this essay, the *Aqedah* or the Binding of Isaac. There we read (Gen 22:3) that Abraham *split* (*baqa*) the wood for the burnt offering. The incomparable obedience of Abraham to the divine command to sacrifice his beloved son received its replicate reward in the moment of Israel's deliverance from the pursuing Egyptians, split for split!

It should be noted that these interpreters did more than satisfy their curiosity about what the sea had seen or why it had been divided so strangely. Far more importantly, they also won striking new confirmations of their trust in God's providential rule over the vast realm of Scripture. No word of the Scriptures is where it is just by chance. Three times God had caused the puzzling word of Psalm 114 to be repeated in Genesis 39, to insure that it would be found when needed, so that God's rule over the world of Joseph would be demonstrated, not only in his righteous deed, and not only in his final request to have his bones carried up to the Land of promise, but finally and above all in the Exodus itself, in which Joseph would receive in his bones the reward for his earlier righteousness, not for his sake alone, but for all his descendants after him. And the solution to the puzzle in the account of the Exodus was provided for in a text just as foundational for Israel's existence, thus insuring that it would not be missed. Thus was confirmed God's providential rule not only over the Scriptures, but also over the whole history of his people.

So it is that what at first sight might appear to be only a theology of words, even of "word-to-word," presupposing something like a theology of verbal inspiration, is at the same time a theology of Israel's identity as the people of God, and ultimately of God's sovereignty over the whole world in which Israel dwells. Israel may have enemies, but under this God, she must know that she is ultimately safe. Exegesis of this sort supported not only the faith of the exegete but also that of his whole people.[21]

I have been assuming that the starting point for the frantic and terrified search for understanding by the disciples of Jesus was the oxymoron "Crucified Messiah," derived from the fact that Jesus had been condemned and crucified as "King of the Jews." This assumption is drawn primarily from the thesis of Nils Dahl, who credits Wellhausen with its first formulation.[22] There is, however, scarcely a thesis on any point of biblical scholarship that is not contested, and this one is no exception.[23] But even were we to grant that the origin of the conviction, that Jesus was somehow the promised Messiah, antedated his arrest, conviction, and death, we would still be left with the oxymoron as our starting point: a messianic designation for one of whom only utterly non-Messianic activity, or even passivity, is reported. That designation would not turn out to be the content of the gospel—note that it is taken for granted, not confessed, in the gospel Paul tells us he received—but it seems a reasonable point of departure for the disciples' voyage into the Scriptures in search of understanding.

If that is more or less correct, then we could assume that they turned first to those texts which we know from other Jewish sources to have been understood before Easter as referring to the Messiah. In short, they would have begun with what are believed to have been recognized "Messianic texts." The scrolls from the Qumran library establish that there were such texts, of which the oracle of the prophet Nathan in 2 Samuel 7:10-14 was undoubtedly an important one. A Qumran exegete seemed to have felt that he could take for granted an eschatological rather than a historical reading of this passage, such a reading having evidently already been established.[24] A key term, as we shall see, was going to be "seed" (v. 12), David's seed whose kingdom God would establish, with the promise, "I will be his father and he shall be my son" (v. 13). Psalm 2 was also read as a messianic text, for it spoke explicitly of the LORD's *machiach*, his "anointed" (v. 2), and in verse 7 it says that the LORD "said to me" (and David was of course understood to be the author of the Psalms), "You are my son, today I have begotten you." Clearly, son of David/son of God, anointed king of Israel, was the decisive link between these passages (see chart A below, in which the linking words have been underlined). In addition,

Isaiah 11:1-3, in conjunction with some lines from Ezekiel and Jeremiah, were together read as messianic, the connection being made by swinging from branch to branch, as chart B, below, will show:

Texts read messianically by post-biblical Jews *prior to Easter:*

A: Son (Seed) of David, Son of God

2 Sam 7:11-14	Ps 2:2, 6-8	Ps 110:1
. . . the LORD will make you a house. 12 When your days are fulfilled and you lie down with your fathers, I will raise up your *seed* after you, who shall come forth from your body, and I will establish his kingdom. 13He shall build a house for my name, and I will establish his kingdom for ever. 14*I will be his father, and he shall be my son.*	2. . . "the rulers take counsel together, against the LORD and his *anointed.* . . . 6"I will set my king on Zion, my holy hill." 7I will tell of the decree of the LORD: He said to me, "*You are my son,* today I have begotten you." 8Ask of me and I will make the nations your heritage. . . .	The LORD said to my lord, "Sit at my right hand, till I make your enemies your footstool."

B: Swinging from branch to branch

Isa 11:1-3	Ezek 3:8; 6:12	Jer 23:5; 33:15
1There came forth a shoot from the stump of Jesse, and *a branch* shall grow out of his roots. 2And the spirit of the LORD shall rest upon him, the spirit of wisdom and understanding, etc. . . .	8. . . "I will bring *my servant the Branch.* . . ." 12. . . says the LORD: "Behold, *the man whose name is the Branch:* for he shall grow up in his place, and he shall build the temple of the LORD."	5"Behold, the days are coming," says the LORD, "when I shall raise up for David a righteous *branch,* and he shall reign as king. . . ." 15"In those days and at that time I shall cause a righteous *branch* to spring forth for David."

Professor Juel, whose work we are following here, has proposed that Psalm 89 was perhaps the hinge upon which turned the whole move of the earliest search into the Scriptures with the goal of understanding Good Friday and Easter.[25] That psalm opens as a song of praise to the Lord for his steadfast love and faithfulness to David's seed (v. 30), recalling God's covenant of eternal fidelity to David, God's chosen one (v. 3), God's servant (vs. 3 and 20), and God's anointed (v. 20). In the LORD's name "his horn shall be *exalted*" (v. 24). He shall cry to God as his father (v. 26), and, since he "*belongs to the LORD*" (v. 18), God will make of him God's "*first-born,* the highest of the Kings of the earth" (v. 27).

But then in verse 38, this psalm of praise changes into one of ago-nized lament over the situation in which the earlier song of praise is set, for now it appears that God has "*rejected*" and is "full of *wrath against* thy anointed" (v. 38). Covered with *shame* (v. 45), the LORD's "servant is *scorned*" (v. 50), and "the anointed" of the Lord is *taunted and mocked* (v. 51). In spite of the humiliations just recited, a conclud-ing verse blesses the LORD, returning to the tone of the first thirty-seven verses.

I have underlined the words that might have been easily picked up by a Jewish exegete of the Scriptures in the first century, words al-ready important in established messianic texts. These are words that might explain how it came about that this psalm became so important at a very early stage of Christian messianic exegesis, being alluded to over twenty times in the New Testament.[26] But I have also put in ital-ics some other words which could have provided a vocabulary with which to speak of the humiliation of God's anointed, God's *machiach,* the Christ. Here was a text, then, which could have made it possible to speak of a crucifed King of the Jews, and yet speak of him as God's beloved "first-born," one ultimately "exalted." That the Psalm pro-vided words to say that this crucified king "belongs to the LORD" and is God's "first-born" would have been of the first importance for the development of the gospel that would be transmitted to Paul, for they echo the language and themes of the *Aqedah* and the Exodus story.

As Juel points out, Psalm 89 would have been a rich discovery for opening the road to understanding the humiliation of the "king of the Jews," and also (p. 149) for beginning to understand Easter as his exaltation. In part this could come by way of learning from Psalm 89 to regard the speaker of other psalms as the Messiah. Certainly later Jewish interpreters took this psalm to be messianic, and Juel's argu-ment for its centrality in the initial framing of the gospel seems con-vincing. With this psalm, both the humiliation and the exaltation of the King-Messiah could begin to be seen and proclaimed as a part of God's reality, understood and proclaimed, that is, "according to the Scriptures."

At one point (p. 150), Juel expresses some puzzlement about the origin of speaking of Jesus' exaltation, since neither Philippians 2 nor the opening verses of Romans has any reference to Psalm 110. "Where else might we look for scriptural ways of expressing exaltation and vindication?" he asks, and answers, "The question must be left for another occasion." I believe that Jon Levenson has now provided us with an answer in his study *The Death and Resurrection of the Beloved Son: The Transformation of Child Sacrifice in Judaism and Christianity*.[27] But that is also for another occasion.[28]

With the help of several biblical scholars we have traced a possible path by which the Jews who followed Jesus were led, after his death, to the gospel that was handed on to Paul. If the hypothesis to which those scholars have led us is even near to the truth, then we should realize how fundamentally that path was an exegetical one: the events of Jesus' crucifixion as "King of the Jews" and the events of Easter forced them to a fresh reading of the Scriptures, such that the events received an interpretation "according to the scriptures," and the Scriptures received a new and distinctive interpretation, turning them into what has been for the Church ever since its Old Testament.

From this, a few tentative consequences would seem to follow:

> 1. The Jewishness of Jesus that must matter to the Church may be less that found in his Galilean ministry and more that found in those Jewish Scriptures according to which his death and exaltation were understood from the first.
>
> 2. The "myth" of Christ crucified for us and raised up by God is drawn from the same source as is the "myth" of God the Creator and of Israel's election and calling.
>
> 3. "Old Testament typology" and the "Christological exegesis of the Old Testament" call for careful reconsideration.
>
> 4. The problem of Jewish-Christian relations, being grounded in our different self-defining interpretations of the "same" Scriptures, is deeper and more difficult than is usually recognized in "Jewish-Christian dialogue."
>
> 5. The above four consequences all suggest a fifth: that the Old Testament remains and should be regarded as the primary and absolutely essential Sacred Writ for the Christian Church.

NOTES

1. "On Reading Someone Else's Mail: The Church and Israel's Scriptures," in a *Festschrift* for Rolf Rendtorff, E. Blum et al., eds., *Die Hebräische Bible und ihre zweifache Nachgeschichte* (Neukirchen-Vluyn: Neukirchener Verlag, 1990);

"Acts 2:1-13—The Truth of an Unlikely Tale," in P. Ochs, ed., *The Return to Scripture in Judaism and Christianity* (New York: Paulist Press, 1993); "Old Testament, Tenach, Hebrew Bible," in a volume being published by the Shalom Hartman Institute, Jerusalem.

2. What I am saying that "we" think could perhaps better be called a pagan vision or understanding, as the implied figure of the playing field reveals. On the role of sports in paganism, past and present, and its total absence in the biblical world and in post-biblical Judaism, see especially Book One of Maurice Samuel's *The Gentleman and the Jew* (New York: Behrman House, 1977).

3. As in many articles by D. Flusser and G. Vermes.

4. E. P. Sanders, Neill Hamilton, and also my *Christ in Context*, 168f.

5. Northvale, N.J.: Jason Aronson Inc., 1993.

6. Philadelphia: Fortress, 1981. First published in 1973. Also subsequent articles and books.

7. The expression, repeated by Paula Fredriksen, *From Jesus to Christ* (Yale, 1988) was coined by W. A. Meeks, "The Stranger from Heaven in Johannine Sectarianism," *JBL*, 91, 1972.

8. *Bruder Jesus* (München, 1967).

9. Op. cit., xxviii, 3.

10. Cf., e.g., Heb 3:3-6; 8:6-8, 13. Nicholls, 45.

11. Ibid., 124.

12. Ibid., 431ff.

13. Ibid., 428.

14. D. Juel, *Messianic Exegesis* (Philadelphia: Fortress, 1988) 176, n. 9.

15. Juel, 176, referring to Helmut Koester's "One Jesus and Four Primitive Gospels," in H. Koester and J. M. Robinson, *Trajectories Through Early Christianity* (Philadelphia: Fortress, 1971).

16. My translation of F. W. Marquardt's, *"Streiter für Israel in den Sprachen der Weltvölker,"* in his "Was heisst: Sich zum Christus bekennen?" in B. Klappert, H. J. Kraus, F. W. Marquardt, M. Stöhr, eds., *Jesusbekenntnis und Christusnachfolge* (Munchen: KT 115, 1992) 55.

17. For this and what follows, see Juel, op. cit., especially ch. 2.

18. I have not been able to track down the source of the phrase, "No more prophecy after Ezra," however many times I have heard it from Jews, but cf. G. F. Moore, *Judaism* (New York: Schocken, 1971) I, 239, 358. First published in 1927.

19. Juel, 43ff., found this in J. Z. Lauterbach's translation of the *Mekilta* (Philadelphia: JPS, 1976 [1933]) vol. I, 220.

20. I found this in *Mekilta* I, 218.

21. A note of caution, however, may be gathered from a reminder by another scholar: It is "useful to remember," we are told, "that the relevance of a verse often extends beyond the words that the midrashist cites." J. Levenson, *The Death and Resurrection of the Beloved Son* (New Haven, Conn.: Yale University Press, 1993) 207.

22. N. Dahl, *Jesus the Christ* (Minneapolis: Fortress, 1991) 228, 238.

23. D. Juel has called my attention to the remark of B. Childs that he finds Dahl's hypothesis "unconvincing." *Biblical Theology*, 229.

24. Juel, 76, discussing 4QFlor. A modern reading of the text, by contrast, would almost certainly be historical: David is promised a biological son and heir who will rule after him and build the Temple, and such indeed was Solomon.

25. Juel, 104ff.

26. Juel, 107.

27. See note 21.

28. But see my review of Levenson's book. *JES*, 32/1 (1995) 137.

FOUR

On Rescuing the Humanity of Jesus: Implications for Catholicism

Monika K. Hellwig

It is no secret that in the history of the Christian churches there has been an insidious tendency to move Jesus out of the realm of the truly and substantially human into the safe distance of a certain divine obscurity. Whenever in history this was recognized, there were efforts to counter the trend. From Ignatius of Antioch[1] to the Council of Chalcedon[2] and beyond, we find a variety of ways, concrete and abstract, of insisting on the true humanity of Jesus. In the medieval Western Church this continues, though in an attenuated form, in the devotions centering on the passion of Jesus, on Mary as sorrowful mother, and on the birth and infancy. Among the sixteenth-century and subsequent Reformers, the return to Scripture led many to a similar re-emphasis on the humanity of Jesus.

Yet, the tendency to distance the mystery by placing it outside the ordinary ambit of life, in an ahistorical, politically and culturally neutral setting, has remained. This is, perhaps, particularly so in the Catholic Church, among the churches of the Western tradition.[3] Indeed, there are devout and thoughtful believers who see no problem in an almost exclusive focus on the divinity of Jesus. But the implications are far-reaching. They include the way in which believers think about their own relationship to God—whether they see the more perfect creaturehood as essentially passive before the unfinished universe with its many social, economic, and political problems of injustices, oppression, and exclusion. Inasmuch as Jesus is acclaimed as Savior, as the one who makes the critical difference in the human situation, to present him as living out and patiently enduring a predetermined divine plan, without human question, discernment, decision, or initiative, without trial and error and regrets, is to offer a model of perfection which is less than human rather that more so.

This is perhaps most clearly illustrated in sacramental piety. An understanding of baptism which sees it as being gathered into the safety zone where grace and salvation are assured to those who do not step out of line reflects a savior whose humanity exists only as a passive instrument. The same is true of a eucharist piety which dwells in the presence of a timeless and rather abstract Jesus, without reference to the tradition on which he drew when interpreting his deliberate confrontation with death in the parameters of the national liberation feast. A similar reflection of a humanly passive savior can be seen in certain attitudes to priestly ordination in which the designation from above seems to render the human qualities of the person almost irrelevant.

It is the claim of this essay that the twentieth-century scholarly efforts to retrieve the humanity of Jesus in biblical and theological studies have challenged and will continue to challenge many aspects of church life and of the broader scope of the Christian life in the world at large. The nineteenth-century liberal Protestant quest for the historical Jesus and its twentieth-century sequel are too well known and too frequently documented to need another rehearsal here. The process of theological retrieval of the humanity of Jesus and its implications has been given less attention, and may be less familiar to many readers. But the theological development is worthy of reflection because it has been both consequential and controversial in practical as well as theoretical contexts.

While the liberal Protestant scholars were pursuing the well-documented biblical search for the strictly historical Jesus in the nineteenth century, there was an interesting parallel development in Catholic spirituality writings. Many "lives of Christ" began to appear. They were admittedly imaginative rather than scholarly reconstructions, and they were for the most part concerned with the public ministry of Jesus as known through the Gospels of the New Testament. Often based on accurate knowledge of the geography and climate of the Holy Land and some acquaintance with the history and customs of the Jews, these lives focused more on the impact that Jesus had on his followers of that time than on any attempt to imagine what the experience of Jesus himself might have been. There were some exceptions to this in authors like Romano Guardini.[4]

This type of devout meditation on the earthly life of Jesus took a new direction with the philosophical and theological reflections of Karl Rahner. Taking the Chalcedonian definition of the true humanity of Jesus as the theological starting point and Heideggerian existential analysis as the philosophical starting point, Rahner proceeded to undertake a new kind of investigation of the humanity of Jesus. Whatever we can know introspectively to be constitutive of being human must be predicated of Jesus, and this includes a growing and developing consciousness, a process of overcoming ignorance, of shaping values and judgments, of working by trial and error from experience, of growing into relationships, of personality formation and challenges of discernment and decision. The necessity of taking the humanity of Jesus seriously in these dimensions brought Rahner and his disciples and contemporaries into some apparently insoluble conflicts with existing christological assumptions. Examination of such conflicts led in turn to the realization that a christology initiated exclusively "from above," beginning with the established dogmatic teaching on the divinity of Jesus, risks a journey into unreality inasmuch as it proceeds from the unknown to the known, distorting the latter to fit the preconceptions of the former. With this realization the new mode in christology came to be the ascending approach, or christology "from below."

Essentially this ascending approach should have been a retracing of the historical path by which christology had come to the dogmatic formulations in the first place. Yet as scholars pursued a Rahnerian line in christology, it became increasingly clear that with an existential philosophical starting point this retracing of the steps was not taking place because the method left the humanity of Jesus suspended in a kind of timeless and uncontextualized existence which does not reflect the reality of concrete human existence in time, space, and society. In short, the christology of Rahner begged for a further incarnation of our understanding of the humanity of Jesus in earthy, historical concreteness. The first notable resource for this lay in studies already well underway under other auspices concerned with the Jewishness of Jesus and what that might mean for understanding his life and actions in his own times and for understanding the relation between Christianity and its parent Judaism.[5]

There proved to be a wealth of research available into the Hebrew religious, social, cultural, and linguistic background for the life and teachings of Jesus. Sayings that most Christians had taken to be original (and often more or less incomprehensible) acquired depth and context from knowledge of contemporary scribal teachings. Actions that we had taken simply as divine intervention were shown to have parallels and precedents in the tradition of the people. Jesus emerged as one who had indeed learned prayer and interpretation and social attitudes from the customs and teachings of his Hebrew community. This development in itself already contained a considerable challenge to the largely unexamined assumptions concerning revelation in Jesus as suddenly and radically new, received from an unmediated divine origin, and containing no element of human imagination and creativity. It also challenged any easy assumption that the "new covenant" simply replaced the older (no longer necessary or useful) one. In short, the gradual and often reluctant inclusion in christology and soteriology of such research into the Jewish context affected not only the understanding of christology, but also had a more pervasive influence on the way Christian theology was drawn to reflect on the relationship between human freedom and the divine. Anyone much involved in Jewish-Christian theological exchange could not but realize that the Jewish sense of the human relationship to God was by no means as passive as conventional Christian teaching and spirituality would have it be.

From that point on it was not surprising that attention would come to focus on the realization that Jesus lived not only in a religious context, but like the rest of us, in a political and economic web of relationships and constraints. One path by which this was explored was, of course, through the studies of the trial and execution of Jesus.[6] It had become increasingly clear that the gospel accounts of the arrest, the several trials, the judgment, and the responsibility for the subsequent execution could not be seen as a straightforward factual account of what had happened but were intertwined with later events, alliances, and reinterpretations. Their purpose had not been the simple retrieval of the facts of the case. In terms of the later developments in both Jewish and Christian traditions through the centuries, it had, however, become a matter of consequence to reestablish as clearly as possible the facts of the case. What began as an issue for Jewish-Christian relations in our own time became the basis for a new understanding of the ministry of Jesus and its goals as he saw them.

The new direction was one of concern for the political relevance of the gospel of Jesus Christ in the world of our own time. The work of Juergen Moltmann and Wolfhart Pannenberg on the eschatological focus of the Christian message and on the nature of the Reign of God as envisaged by Jesus led to the more specifically political theology of J. B. Metz.[7] Metz began to interpret the meaning of the Cross of Jesus in a new perspective, relating it to the poor and oppressed of all times, not in terms of compassionate solidarity with them in suffering, but rather as prophetic denunciation and protest against values and structures of society that masquerade as law and good order but in fact disguise selfishness, violence, and cruelty on the part of the powerful. Beginning with the realization that the crucifixion of Jesus was logically linked with the impact and intent of his public ministry and preaching, and that crucifixion was not a random selection of penalty but directed at those seen as threats to the existing power structure of the society, Metz establishes the prophetically, creatively countercultural Jesus as the paradigm for the fully and appropriately human response within history. As such a paradigm, Jesus expresses and sanctions an understanding of obedience to God and of true creatureliness which is not passive and accepting before evil in the structures of society, but actively oppositional.

What was established in a rather abstract and general way in the work of J. B. Metz and other European scholars found substantial embodiment in the subsequent writings of Third World theologians generally grouped together as "liberation theologians."[8] For the liberation theologians it becomes a matter of central significance to establish the attitudes of the earthy Jesus to situations of poverty, hunger, illness, oppression, and every kind of human suffering among those around him. This is a new and more concrete way of taking the humanity of Jesus seriously as the key to a true appreciation of our own humanity and especially of the human claims of the marginated and excluded in human society. It becomes very significant that in much of the public ministry as presented in the Gospels, Jesus is preoccupied with the relief of physical suffering and of a sense of hopelessness, isolation, and social impotence. Politics in the broad and original sense is concerned with the structuring of our relationships with one another and the consequent regulation of access to material goods, opportunities, and participation. To represent Jesus as apolitical, which was certainly a consequence of dogmatic christology of the descending type, and which was not corrected in the ascending theology of Rahner and most of his disciples, has devastating consequences. It reduces his concern with the Reign of God to an exclusively other-worldly goal, not only uprooting him from his real Jewish context in life but also falsifying the testimonies we have about him. Moreover, inasmuch as Jesus is paradigmatic of the truly human, it proposes as Christian ideal an unconcern with the conditions that actually provide the possibilities and constraints of human becoming. Ultimately, therefore, such an apolitical ideal is an endorsement and living out of a radical untruth, because these human structures of society are not divinely created but are humanly made, determined, and maintained. Attempts to escape or deny responsibility for them is precisely to fail to be human and to fail to be in creaturely obedience to God.

What the liberation theologians have realized as they pursued the consequences of this insight is that it calls for an understanding of the human life and decisions and actions of Jesus far more fraught with conflict than we have usually been willing to acknowledge. Situations that call for prophetic opposition are seldom clear cut, and they seldom offer easy options. In this context Jesus appears as a complex and paradoxical figure whom apparently good people can condemn in good faith. He appears as one learning from trial and error, whose goals are not always attained and who must take many risks of being misunderstood and of failing in his relationships with others. In fact, Jesus emerges as the foundation of a Church that can err in judgments and policies and in the grasping of his vision of the Reign of God and what it entails.

The liberation theologians seem to go one step further with the claim of the hermeneutic privilege of the poor. They suggest that the most deprived and the most desperate are most likely to grasp the radical nature of the solution because the compromise efforts at partial solution are not open to them. This is linked with a way of understanding the outcome of the ministry of Jesus in terms of the dynamics of tragedy. The more desperate the situation, the clearer the logic of the radical solution. It is in ultimate impoverishment that the truth of the human situation before God becomes clearest, but this is not the realization of impotence but that of dependence and particularly of interdependence. The reflections of Paul in the New Testament on the Christian call to imitate Christ in his death seem to revolve on the necessity of abandoning a false isolation in self-assertion in favor of acknowledgment of interdependence and commitment to the common good. In this context, the actual experiences, struggles, and decisions of the earthly Jesus become an immediate and critical foundation for understanding the demands and promises of redemption in the concrete circumstances of Christian life in our own time. It is in the inexorable pursuit of the concrete and particular that the liberation theologians point in an especially urgent way to the implications of our approaches to christology. They demonstrate the all too ready possibility of falsifying the message of redemption by the approaches we take in our academic christology when it proceeds bloodlessly outside the context of the real experience of human beings in the world of his time as of our time.

The history of this twentieth-century effort to rescue the humanity of Jesus in our ways of thinking and worshiping and discipleship has, of course, been controversial in the extreme. It raises in the first place, in the Catholic context, the question of the relationship between historical and biblical studies on the one hand and the doctrinal authority of the hierarchic *magisterium* on the other. It calls into question, for instance, the post-Chalcedonian tendency to insist that the "one person" of Chalcedon is necessarily a divine person, and that Jesus is therefore not properly considered a human person. The more one pursues seriously and practically the central assertion of Chalcedon that Jesus is fully human, the more subsequent developments are challenged by the very formula of Chalcedon. It has, of course, routinely been acknowledged by theologians through the ages that the term "person" in christology and trinitarian doctrine is not to be understood in the usual modern sense, and that to speak of God in personal terms is justified only by analogy. Yet it is clear that, even while making such acknowledgment explicitly, conventional Catholic theology and Catholic doctrine as expressed in official church documents at many levels has tended to empty the acknowledgment of meaning by maintaining such a high christology that the humanity of Jesus is reduced to mere passivity.

Beyond raising questions of relationship between scholarship and hierarchic teaching tradition, the recovery of the humanity of Jesus has raised serious conflicts among scholars. Liberation theologians' perspective has been accused as partisan, only to raise the response that the conventional theology of the established academy is blind to its own hermeneutic circle. What we have discovered is that the pursuit of the humanity of Jesus brings the frailty, incompleteness, and interdependence of our own humanity into play in unexpected clarity, questioning the objectivity and certainty of our scholarship, bringing scholars we most respect into debate with one another.[9]

This, in turn, is a far more than scholarly concern. It questions the nature of authority in the world that we know. All social structures including Church and state, education and accepted aesthetic norms, economic relationships and culturally sanctioned codes of conduct, present themselves as "given." Western society moved beyond Greece and Rome with their particular acknowledgments of divine sanctions and based itself on a Christian worldview. Our divine sanction was in the person of the divine Jesus, giving us apparently a greater certainty, great enough to set the Christian West marching across the world "correcting" the cultures of other peoples and subduing them in the name of Christ. Mainstream Christian communities have generally assumed that their "Christian civilization" carries this great certainty because it was founded on Christ, and because the patterns of Christian societies are assumed to be Christ-sanctioned patterns, and therefore God-sanctioned, and therefore in some sense inevitable.

A Jesus who is not passively executing a plan which was in all its particulars blue-printed in heaven is a serious threat to Christendom thinking. He emerges as growing, learning and assessing what is going on around him, gradually both assimilating the culture in which he was raised and finding his critical distance from it, spending long periods in prayer, discerning what is to be understood as "the Father's will" and what is to be seen as quite contrary to it, disentangling what is given in nature and human existence and what is product of human decision and voluntary action. The more we try to recover the Jesus of history in his own setting, the more radical he seems to become about questions of human authority. Almost everything that structures our human lives and societies can be seen as the product of people just like ourselves. Hence, with the resources given us by the Creator, human life on earth could be structured quite differently. And, just as Jesus in his lifetime does not seem to accept the patterns of his society as simply the will of the Father, so he does not seem to hand over to his followers ready-made patterns to be implemented forever because of their coming from him. Rather, he seems to communicate to his followers his own heuristic methods in the quest for the Reign of God. This has far-reaching implications for Catholicism, as the quest to know and understand Jesus better continues its scholarly path.

NOTES

1. Letters to the Churches, e.g., Eph 7:2; 18:2; 20:1. See *Fathers of the Church: The Apostolic Fathers* (Washington, D.C.: The Catholic University of America Press, 1947) 90, 94, 95.

2. *DS* 301–2. For full translation see J. Neuner and J. Dupuis, *The Christian Faith* (Westminster, Md.: Christian Classics, 1975) 147–8.

3. This is well illustrated in the manual tradition, for instance in the persistence into mid-twentieth century of Anselm's soteriology as set out in *Cur Deus homo.*

4. Romano Guardini, *The Lord* (Chicago: Regnery, 1954).

5. For both bibliography and comment on the impact of such scholarship, see John T. Pawlikowski, *Christ in the Light of the Jewish-Christian Dialogue* (New York: Paulist, 1982). For an updated and comprehensive account see E. P. Sanders, *The Historical Figure of Jesus* (New York: Allen Lane/Penguin, 1993). And see other more recent perspectives in *Jews and Christians Speak of Jesus,* ed., Arthur E. Zannoni (Minneapolis: Fortress, 1994).

6. See Gerard Sloyan, *Jesus on Trial* (Philadephia: Fortress, 1973) and bibliography therein.

7. See especially the essay, "The Future in the Memory of Suffering," in *New Questions on God* (New York: Herder, 1972) 9–25.

8. Among Latin American liberation theologies, see for instance Jon Sobrino, *Christology at the Crossroads* (New York: Orbis, 1978), and *Jesus in Latin*

America (New York: Orbis, 1987). Also Leonardo Boff, *Jesus Christ Liberator* (New York: Orbis, 1978).

9. The human and epistemological dimensions of scholarly discourse as an important factor in the quest to know and understand Jesus are discussed by Frans Jozef van Beeck in *Christ Proclaimed* (New York: Paulist, 1979). Far-reaching issues of interaction of scholarship and sources are raised in the trilogy of Edward Schillebeeckx, *Jesus, Christ,* and *Church* (New York: Crossroad, 1979, 1981, and 1991). Also important for content and analysis of available testimonies is John Dominic Crossan, *The Historical Jesus* (San Francisco: Harper, 1991).

FIVE

A Call for a Catholic Constitutional Convention: The Beginning of the Third Millennium

Leonard Swidler

Concern for Catholic Church renewal and needed structural reform in the spirit of Vatican II is beginning once again to swell on the grass-roots level both in North America and Europe. This is not a revolutionary wave like the one which poured forth from the sixteenth-century Protestant Reformation, nor is it an enthusiastic wave like the one which sprang from the dam-burst-like release after Vatican II. It is a much more sober, chastened swell which on the one hand has no illusions that the situation in the Church will be quickly and radically transformed, but on the other hand so treasures values in Catholicism that energies are being recommitted to making those values truly available to a society living now at the edge of the third millennium. Moreover, those energies are today being expended in increasingly "savvy" and coordinated ways.

In these pages I will sketch briefly a picture of this re-energized church-renewal movement, focusing on how it developed, what it looks like now, and what it is trying to accomplish. Concerning the latter I will also be at some pains to provide the justifications offered by its participants. My final section will deal with the effort to *"re-democratize"* the Church—for the ancient Church was for many a "limited democracy"—climaxing in the call for a "Catholic Constitutional Convention" to usher in the third millennium after the birth of Jesus.

I. Vatican II Mandate for Church Renewal

"Christ summons the Church, as she goes her pilgrim way, to that *continual reformation of which she always has need.*" Those are not the words of Luther, Calvin, or some other sixteenth-century Reformer, but those of all the Catholic bishops of the world, including the pope, at Vatican II. Indeed, the pope and bishops were even more insistent when they said: "All are led . . . *wherever necessary,* to undertake with vigor the task of renewal and reform." Notice, the pope and bishops did not say all bishops, all priests, all religious, but simply, "all," that is, all those to whom that decree was addressed, namely, all the Catholic faithful.

Moreover, this mandate to renewal and reform was not conceived as a luxury for those Catholics who have nothing else to do. Rather, it is a *duty* that is incumbent on all Catholics, as the pope and bishops made clear: "Catholics' . . . *primary* duty is to make a careful and honest appraisal of whatever needs to be renewed and done in the Catholic household" (all three citations from the Vatican II Decree on Ecumenism, sections 4 and 5; italics added).

II. Vatican II Implementation

Many in the Catholic laity, religious, clergy, and even hierarchy responded positively to the charge to renew and reform the Church to make it relevant to today's world (Pope John XXIII spoke of *aggiornamento,* that is, "bringing up to date," when he explained the need to call Vatican II). Renewal moved ahead with great elan for the first few years after the end of the council in 1965. It received its first major setback in 1968, however, with Paul VI's encyclical against birth control, *Humanae vitae.*

Another heavy blow came in negative fashion in connection with the recommendation to change the electors of the pope from the papal-appointed cardinals to delegates elected by the national bishops' councils around the world. This decree sat on Pope Paul's desk already in 1970, but he was dissuaded from signing it by conservative curial elements who seemed to have whispered in his ear the prediction of a catastrophe that would result if he did sign it. The only catastrophe, of course, would have been only for certain Church power-holders. Had he made this momentous decision, the whole subsequent history of Catholic Church renewal would have been radically different. Every new pope would necessarily have had a sense of responsibility to, and more collegiality with, his "constituents," the representatives of the world Church. But most importantly, this structural change at the top would have released an irresistible movement for bishops in some substantial way to be elected by their "constituents," and then also for pastors in turn to be elected. As the Church moved further into the 1970s Pope Paul became increasingly indecisive, wanting on the one hand to carry out the Vatican II mandate of renewal and reform, while on the other fearing the specter of error and anarchy that was constantly whispered in his ear. Then came Pope Paul's death in 1978 and his replacement first by the briefly reigning John Paul I and then the long-reigning John Paul II, beginning late in 1978.

III. Pope John Paul II and Restorationism

It was a bad year, 1979. It had started bad—and was ending worse. 3:00 A.M. on December 18, my phone rang insistently, and I eventually answered it, groggily. An American theologian-journalist in Rome, Ed Grace, said breathlessly: "The Vatican just condemned Hans Küng!" Obviously shortly after John Paul II took power the headhunters at the Holy Office ("of the Inquisition" had been struck from the title earlier in the century, but apparently not from the reality) had been quickly unleashed for the following sequence of events occurred:

1. Already in the spring of 1979 the French theologian Jacques Pohier was silenced for his book *When I Speak of God*[1];

2. In July the book on sexuality by a team of four American theologians of the Catholic Theology Society of America was condemned;

3. In September the Jesuit General in Rome, Fr. Pedro Arrupe, was forced to send a letter to all Jesuits warning them that they could not publicly dissent from any papal position;

4. All autumn severe accusations of heresy against Edward Schillebeeckx were recurrently issued in drum-beat fashion; December 13–15 Schillebeeckx was "interrogated" by the Holy Office in Rome;[2]

5. That same month writings of Brazilian liberation theologian Leonardo Boff were "condemned" (he was later silenced)[3];

6. Then on December 18—at exactly the same time Pope John Paul II said, "Truth is the power of peace. . . . What should one say of the practice of combatting or silencing those who do not share the same views?" *(Washington Post*, December 19, 1979)—the Holy Office issued a declaration on Hans Küng saying he "can no longer be considered a Catholic theologian."

A few hours later I was on the phone with Fr. Charles Curran of The Catholic University of America and Fr. David Tracy of the University of Chicago—the former one of the foremost American

Catholic moral theologians (and later given the same inquisitorial treatment as Küng) and the latter clearly the most creative American Catholic systematic theologian.

We moved to quickly issue a press statement by U.S. Catholic theologians stating that "Küng was indeed a Catholic theologian." We decided to resist Rome with earlier Roman tactics, and took a leaf from Caesar's writings: "All Gaul [America] is divided into three parts" *(Omnis America in tres partes divisa est).* For the next twenty-four hours each of us got on the phone to our third of America. As I spoke with people, time and again the refrain recurred: This can't go on! Who will be next? We cannot allow Rome simply to continue to "Divide and conquer!" We have got to organize!

IV. Founding of the Association for the Rights of Catholics in the Church—ARCC

In the following days I drew up a proposal to organize what became the Association for the Rights of Catholics in the Church (ARCC) and sent it around to all interested contacts. The response was overwhelmingly positive, and on March 7–9, 1980, the Founding Convention of ARCC was held in Milwaukee, with thirty delegates from nine cities, with organizing groups from another eight cities indicating support without sending a delegate.

The ARCC was thus founded in 1980 "to institutionalize a collegial [shared decision-making] understanding of Church in which decision-making is shared and accountability is realized among Catholics of every kind and condition. It affirms that there are *fundamental rights* which are rooted in the humanity and baptism of all Catholics." It sees its particular contribution to the Church and world in the area of the rights of Catholics in the Church. This is in keeping with the urging of the 1971 "International Synod of Bishops," which stated that "within the Church rights must be preserved. No one should be deprived of his ordinary rights because he is associated with the Church."

ARCC rejects all divisive dualisms in Christian life, whether they take the form of dividing Church and world, men and women, clergy and laity, or others. This is in line with the *Charter of the Rights of Catholics in the Church* issued by ARCC in 1983, after worldwide consultation, and with Canon 208 of the 1983 Code of Canon Law, which states that "there exists among all the Christian faithful, in virtue of their rebirth in Christ, a true equality," and likewise with a widespread sense among the majority of the Catholic laity. All these pairs, springing from one source and seeking ultimately one goal, must mutually interpenetrate and cooperate. On this unity the rights of all Catholics are based: "The rights of Catholics in the Church derive both from our basic humanity as persons and from our baptism as Christians" (Preamble, *Charter*).

V. Restorationism Continues

The subsequent years of the pontificate of Pope John Paul II have been characterized by an extraordinary *Wanderlust* on the part of the Pope which allowed him, among other things, to stress the implementation of human rights in the secular sphere. In this he has been indefatigable. At the same time, however, he also used his world travels as an instrument of massive centralization of power within the Church, simultaneous with what must be described as an insistent repression of rights within the Church—projecting in the world a credibility-damaging image (and reality) of an ethical double-standard.

There has been an alternating rhythm of severe repression, as in 1979–1980, followed by a certain relenting in the face of mounting protest and resistance. All during this period Pope John Paul has been appointing conservative and ultra-conservative bishops and launching one conservative or reactionary project after another, such as the loyalty oath and the world catechism, in moves to consolidate his centralizing conservative power.

VI. The Maturation of American Catholicism

However, all this "Restoration" activity has had less than the desired result, especially in American Catholicism, as far as the Neo-Integrists [reactionary Catholics] are concerned—and this is most encouraging. The profile of American Catholicism that emerged from the Gallup survey taken in the summer of 1987 just before the Pope's September 1987 visit to the U.S. portrayed a rapidly maturing Church.

Sunday church attendance had dropped from a pre-*Humanae vitae* (1968) 65% to 50% by 1975, but has remained steady ever since. Before Vatican II American Catholics were characterized by a stress on doctrinal orthodoxy, ritual regularity, and obedience to clerical authorities.[4]

That docility has dramatically diminished. Now 70% of American Catholics surveyed think one can be a good Catholic and not necessarily go to church every Sunday. In a 1987 survey 79% of American Catholics opposed the Vatican prohibition on artificial birth control, and by 1992 that disagreement percentage reached 87%. In 1992, 74%

of American Catholics believed divorced and remarried Catholics should be able to remain Catholics in good standing.

In 1971, 49% of American Catholics were in favor of married priests; by 1983, the percentage reached 58% and remained stable through 1987, but by five years later the figure leaped to 70%.

A very clear connection between power and sex can be seen in the fact that statistics consistently show that every time the Vatican publicly condemns the idea of women priests the percentage of support for it among American Catholics rises. Recordkeeping started with the 29% of American Catholics recorded being in favor of ordaining women priests at the time of the Vatican Declaration against women priests in 1977 *(Inter insignores)*[5] to 36% shortly after the Vatican prohibition to 40% in 1979, 44% in 1982, 47% in 1985, and then a sharp jump to 60% in 1987 and 67% in 1992 (in 1992 80% also favored ordaining women deacons). Perhaps even more interesting is the fact that of American Catholics under 35 in 1992, 80% are in favor of ordaining women priests.

Ninety percent (90%) of American Catholics said that a person could dissent from Church doctrine and remain a good Catholic; and only 26% thought belief in papal infallibility was necessary to be a good Catholic.

But American Catholics have not abandoned the Church in large numbers, as the drop in docility might suggest would happen. Rather, they are staying in. As sociologist Teresa A. Sullivan says, "There is something American Catholics find in Catholicism that is deep and nurturing and doesn't have very much to do with the Vatican and the bishops and all the rest."[6] At the same time, sociologist Ruth A. Wallace notes that the Gallup survey finds among American Catholics an "eagerness with which the laity seem to want to participate in a lot of policy questions, no matter what age or level of education."[7] The survey further strengthens what Joseph Fichter, S.J., found a decade earlier:

> The church is being modernized in spite of itself. It appears that the changes are occurring at the bottom of the structure. American Catholicism is experiencing adaptation at the grass roots. The most significant aspect of this change is the switch of emphasis in the basis of moral and religious guidance. Dependence on legislation from above has largely switched to dependence on the conscience of the people.[8]

Even more interesting in Gallup survey figures are those reflecting the attitudes of the large bulge in the American population, the so-called "baby-boomers," those born between 1948 and 1957. They represent not only a disproportionately large segment of the American population, but because the Catholic "baby-boom" was even larger than the general American one they are really the trend-setters for the future of the American Catholic Church. And they are much more liberal than the average, much more pro-democracy, pro-reform in the Church. The same is also true of educated Catholics: the more educated the Catholics, the greater the likelihood of their being liberal, pro-renewal and reform, more mature—and American Catholics are rapidly becoming increasingly more educated.

ARCC is by no means the only grass-roots Catholic church-renewal organization to spring up in the United States since Vatican II. Many have emerged, and continue to emerge with each passing year. What is even more interesting is that many of these renewal movements have begun to coalesce and coordinate. In the fall of 1991 an initial grouping of them formed an umbrella coordinating organization entitled "Catholics Organizing Renewal" (COR). COR is a coalition of grass-roots Catholic organizations working on various aspects of renewal in the Church which are banding together to reinforce each other's compatible renewal efforts, and when appropriate launch joint projects.

At present COR has thirty-one organizations of various goals and sizes. The national level groups include the following: (1) "Catholics Speak Out" [founded in 1987, concerned with democracy in the Church], (2) "New Ways Ministry" [concerned with ministry to homosexuals], (3) "Call to Action" [concerned with general Church renewal; grew out of the 1976 National Conference of Catholic Bishops' "Call To Action"], (4) "Catholics for Free Choice" [concerned with reproductive issues], (5) "CORPUS" [concerned with married priests], (6) "Dignity" [organization of Catholic homosexuals], (7) "NETWORK" [a national political lobby], (8) "Federation of Christian Ministries" [focused on diverse faith communities and alternative ministries], (9) "Women's Ordination Conference" [concerned with equality for Catholic women], (10) "Coalition of Concerned Canadian Catholics" [a national level organization concerned with general Church renewal].

This burgeoning cooperation on the national level of grass-roots Catholic church-renewal organizations is another sign on the national level—simply mirroring what is happening on the grass-roots level—of the maturation of American Catholicism. American Catholics are increasingly deciding that Catholicism is not only their nostalgic childhood home, but also their adult home—and they are more and more going about the task of making it into a home not just for children, intellectually and spiritually, but also for adults.

VII. European Church Renewal Movements

The rise of grass-roots Catholic church-renewal movements in Europe easily matches, if not surpasses, that of North America. The December 18, 1979, Vatican attack on Hans Küng served as a galvanizing event for Catholics in Europe just as in the United States. In its immediate aftermath two organizations concerned with rights *inside* the Church were formed, one in Germany, *Christenrechte in der Kirche,* and one in France, *"Droits et Libertés dans les Eglises."* Those two organizations have continued to be active and have in the following years been joined by other Catholic rights-in-the-Church organizations, so that now there are eight such national organizations who have banded together in a "European Conference for Human Rights in the Church." One major reason there are different national organizations is the plurality of languages, but of course even just the existence of separate states provides its own momentum for separate organizations.

1. Holland

In addition to these organizations which focus specifically on rights in the Catholic Church, there is also a plethora of other grass-roots Catholic church-renewal organizations in several European countries. For example, Holland has redeveloped in recent years a strong and broad-based grass-roots Catholic church-renewal movement known as the "Eighth of May Movement." It was inadvertently launched in 1985 by Pope John Paul II when he refused to meet with a number of progressive Dutch Catholic organizations. The response to his refusal was to set up a Demonstration in eleven tents, which drew some 13,000 people. Although it was supposed to be a one-time affair, it was quickly decided to hold the Demonstration annually.

ARCC National Board member Terry Dosh attended the May 8, 1989, Demonstration and after a lengthy interview with leaders and participants described one aspect of it as follows:

> People can speak [at the annual Demonstration] only if a special committee says OK; this applies to bishops too. Theme for '89: Women and Men in the Image of God. There were more gray hairs the first two years; many young people (in their 20s and 30s) in the last three years; they have programs for children. Much bonding occurs. Many of the groups create huge banners; the process begins the previous November and the banner becomes a symbol of commitment and an occasion for regular bonding.[9]

Further, according to Dosh, at that 1989 Demonstration 104 groups, including all seven Diocesan Pastoral Councils, the Catholic

Women of The Netherlands (30,000 members), the married priests' group, and the organization of Gay Pastors (100) participated. "One comes as a member of a group, which is the Dutch way. This time 15,000 (out of 6 million Dutch Catholics—which would be the equivalent of 140,000 in the U.S.) came." The numbers participating in the annual Demonstration continue to stay high; in 1992, 11,000 participated, in 1993, 12,000, and in 1994, 10,000.

The "Eighth of May Movement" in fact immediately became a year-round organization with a national Coordinator and series of ongoing projects pursued through nine Standing Committees. These include "International Affairs," "Inequality Between Men and Women," "Human Rights in the Church," and "Democracy in the Church." It likewise puts out regular publications, including an English-language newsletter.[10]

2. Germany

In just the Germanic-speaking lands there is a growing networking of organizations, e.g., Switzerland has an umbrella organization entitled *Aufbruch-Bewegung* ["The Breaking Forth Movement"], which coordinates a large number of member grass-roots Catholic church-renewal organizations.[11] Austria likewise has an umbrella organization—also called *Aufbruch*—which loosely coordinates at least eight regional grass-roots Catholic church-renewal organizations.[12]

In Germany many of the grass-roots Catholic church-renewal groups, but by no means all, coordinate some of their activities through the umbrella organization *Initiative Kirche von unten*, ["Movement of the Church from Below"] which has forty-five member organizations throughout Germany.[13] Related to but not identical with it is another German movement entitled *Katholikentag von unten* ["The Catholic Congress from Below"].

In the middle of the nineteenth century, the German Catholic Church began the custom of sponsoring a huge (usually over 150,000 attendees) *Katholikentag* ["Catholic Congress"] every two years. The custom was reestablished after hiatuses during World Wars I and II; it is funded and organized by the official Catholic Church of Germany.

Starting in 1982 a group of progressive Catholics began to sponsor the *Katholikentag von unten* ["Catholic Congress from Below"] parallel to the *Katholikentag* at the same location and time—at times drawing even larger audiences than the official Congress. They have successfully continued this practice every two years to the present. Not only has the "Congress from Below" featured speakers who are more liberal than those at the official Congress and dealt with subjects that were taboo there, but its continued success has also significantly affected the official Congress's programs, moving them in a more progressive direction.

One dramatic manifestation of this renewal-oriented influence is the very extensive "Statement for Discussion" issued by the "Central Committee of German Catholics" (*Zentralkomitee deutschen Katholiken*, ZDK), the body responsible for the *Katholikentag*. This Statement, issued in October 1991, was entitled: "Dialogue Instead of the Avoidance of Dialogue. How Should We in the Church Deal with One Another?"[14] The Statement, coming as it does from an official organ of the German Catholic Church, is extraordinarily strong, speaking very concretely of the need of dialogue within the Church, the elimination of clericalism, sexism, and authoritarianism. It was widely distributed and responses were solicited.

In all these movements throughout the Germanic-speaking nations of Europe many causes are promoted, such as liberation theology/social justice concerns, equality of women and men, peace activities, and ecumenism. But the theme which appears most often is the "Need for the Democratization of the Catholic Church." That idea and term surfaces time and again.

On April 24, 1994, the Plenary Assembly of the *Bund der Deutschen Katholischen Jugend* (BDKJ—"Association of German Catholic Youth," an official organization of the Catholic Church in Germany with over 500,000 members) formulated and approved a "Plan to Promote Democracy" in the Catholic Church. It too is very strong, laying out in detail the current dissatisfaction among many Catholics: "For a long time there has been an increase of voices—and even precisely of the committed Christians of the Catholic Church—which have been expressing their dissatisfaction with the still dominant clericalism, centralism and patriarchalism and demand a change in the Church."[15] The plan goes on to claim that:

> Instead of experiencing themselves as equally valuable and acknowledged partners in the Church, they time and again are treated as incompetent objects of clerical tutelage. Especially girls and women dramatically encounter the current ecclesiastical legal situation and practice in which they are confronted with an experience of structural and personal disparagement and injustice.
>
> Instead of trust in the liveliness of Christian groups, communities and local churches, Christians most of the time experience the centralizing measures of an *angst*-filled Church which more and more values uniformity rather than variety and is suspicious of every pluralism of opinion, expression and form of life within the Church.
>
> The concentration of power within the Church in the hands of the clergy excludes the laity in most questions (and precisely in those

which affect them) from co-responsibility and decision. A decision which provides the laity with equal possibilities in decision-making is not foreseen, and in the best of cases would carry only non-binding advisory weight.

These contradictions between Church and cultural-societal reality bring more and more Christians into personal difficulties and conflicts, make their personal witness of faith and their Christian involvement in society unnecessarily more difficult and massively endangers the credibility of the Church in general.[16]

The document then produces a number of concrete demands, including the following:

In decision-making questions of Church life the laity can participate, if at all, only in an advising capacity. The faithful, however, are to be taken seriously as subjects of their faith, as bearers of the Church's life as *Communio,* with equal rights. This, therefore, is not accomplished with the possibilities of giving advice alone without real shared working and shaping plenary power. The BDJK demands, therefore, access to and the creation of decision-making structures in which all—including the laity—can appropriately participate:

The calling to Church offices, the ordering to Church responsibility and the staffing of leadership bodies must result from votes by the Christians concerned, which may not be restricted by a veto power by a Church officer. . . . Decisions should take place only when those concerned have been heard and have participated in the decision-making process. . . . The BDKJ demands a participation of women in all Church functions. This demand of course includes—though not only—the office of Church ordination. This presumes that the Church sets in motion a discussion of the concept of office that has prevailed until now. . . . The BDKJ demands that women participate in the formation of priests. . . .

The understanding of office which long has characterized the structure of the Church leads to a monopolizing in the hands of office holders the powers of setting norms, making decisions and carrying them out. Church office is often law-giver, judge and executive body all in one. This concentration of power burdens a dialogical collaboration of laity and clergy. In disputed issues a nonpartisan mediating and judging agency is lacking by way of both substantive differences and formal ambiguities. In such instances the laity lacks the possibility of calling upon an independent agency. . . . The BDKJ demands the establishment of independent arbitration and mediation agencies.[17]

The executive director of the BDKJ, Mr. Michael Kröselberg, in the spirit of that document, took a vigorous part as a panelist, along with

Professor Norbert Greinacher of the Catholic Theology Faculty of the University of Tübingen, Germany, on "A Constitution for the Catholic Church," responding to a paper on the topic by Leonard Swidler at the *Katholikentag von unten,* June 30, 1994, in Dresden, Germany.

3. Western and Central Europe

In addition, there are more than fourteen other Catholic church-renewal organizations in as many European countries which have formed a federation under the German name *Kirche im Aufbruch* ("The Church Breaking Forth"). The countries and organizations involved are: (1) The Netherlands (*Acht Mei Beweging—Commissie Mensenrechte* ["Eighth of May Movement—Human Rights Committee"]), (2) Belgium (*Priesters en Religieuzen voor Gerechtiggheid en Vrede* ["Priests and Religious for Justice and Freedom"]), (3) France (*Femmes et Hommes en l'Eglise—Section française* ["Women and Men in the Church—French Section"]), (4) Luxemburg (*Luxemburg Gruppe* ["Luxemburg Group"]), (5) Germany (*Maria von Magdala—Initiative Gleichberechtigung* ["Mary Magdalene—Movement for Equal Rights"]), (6) Switzerland (*Aufbruch-Bewegung* ["The Breaking Forth Movement"]), (7) Austria (*Aufbruch* ["Breaking Forth"]), (8) Italy (*Secretaria Tecnica delle Communità Christiane de Base* ["Technical Secretariat of the Christian Base Communities"]), (9) United Kingdom ("Catholics for a Changing Church"), (10) Ireland ("Vatican II Laity Alliance"), (11) Spain (*Communidades cristianas populares españolas* ["Spanish Christian Popular Communities"]), (12) Poland (*Nasza Droga* ["Our Way"]), (13) Hungary (Hungarian Catholic Base Communities—BOKOR), (14) Czech Republic ("Emmaus").[18] Also part of this European Federation *Kirche im Aufbruch* are the eight national Catholic Human Rights in the Church organizations that are banded together in the "European Conference for Human Rights in the Church."

Kirche im Aufbruch held its fifth annual conference at the same time and place that the "European Conference for Human Rights in the Church" held its fourth annual conference on January 6–9, 1994, in Brussels, Belgium. There were some fifty representatives at that conference, including a representative from ARCC in the U.S. (Leonard Swidler) and representatives of the Base Communities Movement in Europe (which consists of scores of base communities in Western and Central Europe). At the conference the "Declaration of Human Rights in the Catholic Church" was issued by the "European Conference for Human Rights in the Church," and a commitment was made to work together with ARCC in the United States on "A new constitution for the

Catholic Church incorporating the spirit of the Gospel, and showing respect for human rights with an ecumenical dimension."[19]

VIII. A "Call for a Catholic Constitutional Convention"

Most recently an idea, whose time I believe has come, has surfaced—I first heard of it from Rosemary Ruether—namely, the calling of a "Catholic Constitutional Convention." The countries of Eastern Europe, which most Westerners feared would not experience the inestimable advantages of democracy in our lifetime, have burst through to freedom and have either drastically restructured their constitutions, or, like Poland, the Pope's homeland, formed them anew. Those who downgraded the human rights of freedom and democracy to secondary human values have learned that the vast majority of humankind— whenever they have a chance to express themselves freely—places them at the primary level.

Catholics are no less human than the citizens of Poland, Hungary, Czechoslovakia, and the other newly-freed countries in the valuing of and demand for human rights and democracy—within the Church. Conclusion: The time is right for Catholics too to call a "Catholic Constitutional Convention." To initiate that process all concerned Catholic organizations and individuals need to begin now to plan for the third millennium's "Ecumenical Council." In the language of the now predominant political reality, democracy, such an ecumenical council might well be called a "Catholic Constitutional Convention."

1. "New Thinking"

What must be borne in mind when focusing on the development of the modern moves for democratization in the Catholic Church is that it takes place within what Pope Paul VI called "New Thinking"[20] (This was long before Mikhail Gorbachev in the late 1980s borrowed the phrase "New Thinking" to popularize his new approach to Communism.) This "New Thinking" was characteristic of Vatican II and was likewise supposed to characterize the subsequent revision of church law, the 1917 Code of Canon Law.

Pope John Paul II described this resultant shift in thinking, this "New Thinking" of Vatican II, in the following manner when promulgating the new Code of Canon Law (1983) for the Latin Church: (1) the Church seen as the People of God, (2) hierarchical authority understood as service, (3) the Church viewed as a communion, (4) the participation by all members in the three-fold *munera* [functions] of Christ [teaching, governing, making holy], (5) the common rights and obligations of all Catholics related to this, and (6) the Church's commitment to ecumenism.[21] James Provost added further: "In addition to providing the basis for understanding the new canon law, these elements set an agenda for the church, an agenda which might be considered to form the basis for a kind of 'democratizing' of the church."[22]

2. The Term "Democracy"

Something must be said about the words "constitutional" and "convention," because for many Catholics they have such a secular political, non-Catholic-Church tone about them. But even more troublesome for some Catholics is the term, and even the concept, "democracy," within whose framework "constitution" and "convention" fall. A recent book is even entitled *The Tabu of Democracy within the Church*.[23] Talk of Catholic rights, human rights in the Church, and a "Catholic Bill of Rights" also all seem to disturb a number of intelligent, informed Catholics.

But none of that unease is warranted. In a number of instances no less a stalwart of tradition than Pope John Paul II has explicitly made that clear. Pope John Paul II has advocated (1) participation in making choices which affect the life of the community, (2) a role in the selection of leaders, (3) provision for the accountability of leaders, and (4) structures for effective participation and shared responsibilities:

> The Church values the democratic system inasmuch as it ensures the participation of citizens in making political choices, guarantees to the governed the possibilities both of electing and holding accountable those who govern them, and of replacing them through peaceful means when appropriate. . . . Authentic democracy . . . requires . . . structures of participation and shared responsibility.[24]

We Catholics should not shy away from contemporary democratic political terminology any more than our Catholic ancestors shied away from the imperial political terminology of their time, for an "Ecumenical (*Oikumenikos,* 'Universal') Council" is simply the imperial Greco-Roman political terminological equivalent of the modern democratic terminological "Catholic (*Katholos,* 'Universal') Constitutional Convention." The Church did not hesitate to meet under the protection of the then predominant civil agency, the Emperor—indeed, the Emperor, or Empress(!), called the first seven Ecumenical Councils, i.e., Catholic Constitutional Conventions. Because a freely/responsibly deciding democracy is a more fully human (and, therefore, more fully in keeping with humanity's being the "image of God," the *imago Dei*) political structure than an empire, *a fortiori* we Catholics should not hesitate to meet in the context of the verbal symbolic inspiration of constitutional democracy.

3. The Term "Convention"

Some have quivered with nervousness at the thought of using the more "political" term "convention" rather than the ecclesiastical "council" or "synod." The terms council and synod have been used largely interchangeably throughout Catholic history, both meaning a meeting of persons "gathered together." "Council" is simply the Latin form, and literally means a "calling together" *(concalare),* and "synod" is the Greek form, and literally means a "coming together" *(syn-hodos).* The term "convention" in fact is a more literal Latin translation of the earlier Greek "synod," for it also means a "coming together" *(conventio).* So, why not use the Latin cognate, "convention," which is closer to the earlier Greek? Vatican II itself does when referring to itself, terming itself a "Conventus."[25]

4. The Terms "Constitution" and "Bill of Rights"

The term "constitution" does appear in church documents, most recently in the titles of several of the documents of Vatican II, e.g., the "Constitutions" on the Church, on Revelation, etc. The term "constitution" is used because the matter treated is "constitutive" of Christianity. The term "Bill of Rights" of course does not appear in ecclesiastical documents because it is a specifically English/American phrase, but its exact equivalent does appear from the pens of both Popes Paul VI and John Paul II. During Vatican II, on November 20, 1965, Paul VI spoke of a "common and fundamental code containing the constitutive law *(ius constitutivum)* of the church" which was to underlie both the Eastern and Western (Latin) codes. It was clearly what we Americans refer to as a "constitution."[26] In his address to the Roman Rota just one month after the promulgation of the new Code of Canon Law (1983), Pope John Paul II called specific attention to the "Bill of Rights," *"carta fondamentale,"* in the Code:

> The Church has always affirmed and protected the rights of the faithful. In the new code, indeed, she has promulgated them as a *"carta fondamentale"* (confer canons 208–223). She thus offers opportune judicial guarantees for protecting and safeguarding adequately the

> desired reciprocity between the rights and duties inscribed in the dignity of the person of the "faithful Christian."[27]

American Catholics have a major precedent for the use of the terms "constitution" and "convention" in that outstanding Catholic bishop of Charleston, S.C., 1820–1842, John England. He wrote a democratic "constitution" with which his diocese was most creatively governed. He informed Rome, writing:

> The people desire to have the Constitution printed, so that they may have a standard by which they may be guided. I have learned by experience that the genius of this nation is to have written laws at hand, and to direct all their affairs according to them. If this be done, they are easily governed. If this be refused, a long and irremediable contention will ensue. By fixed laws and by reason much can be obtained, but they cannot be compelled to submit to authority which is not made manifest by law.

Following his "constitution," every year a "convention" was held to review matters and plan the coming year.[28]

Hence, there is ample precedent in church documents for using the terms "democracy," "rights," "bill of rights," "constitution," and "convention."

Thus, a third millennium international "Catholic Constitutional Convention" to decide on the fundamental constitutive structures of the Catholic Church is not a radical, new departure from tradition. Very much on the contrary. Though it is of the essence of Paul VI's and John Paul II's "New Thinking," it is also very much a return to our founding tradition, our first millennium "Constitutional Conventions." Moreover, it should be recalled that those first millennium "Catholic Constitutional Conventions" (councils) not only had lay as well as clerical participants, but were even called by the then predominant lay political agency—the emperor or empress—and were not accepted as official until promulgated by laity, the emperor/empress. Hence it is traditional and appropriate that the Third Millennium Constitutional Convention also have lay as well as clerical participants and be called by the now predominant lay political agency, the *Demos*, the people.

IX. Democracy in the Catholic Church

Democracy cannot be just a set of procedures, but must ultimately engender and depend on an attitude, a consciousness of life, which views human life both individually and communally as based on the central human characteristics of freedom and responsibility. A lack of such a consciousness cannot be simply replaced by a set of democratic procedures, any more than there can be a concrete being consisting of just "form" but no "content." At the same time, a democratic consciousness cannot effectively express itself except through a set of effective procedures. Further, it is only through the use of such procedures over time that a democratic consciousness can be fully developed.

Humankind has painfully developed through experience a number of democratic principles and procedures which have been found either essential or in some instances at least highly beneficial for the development and expression of a democratic consciousness of human nature, of freedom and responsibility. Among many, these include prominently: (1) participation in decision making, (2) election of leaders, (3) limited term of office, (4) separation of powers, (5) open dialogue as essential to achieving mutual understanding and creative decisions, (6) equal access to positions of leadership, (7) accountability of leaders, (8) the principle of subsidiarity [that is, a higher agency does not do what a lower agency can do], (9) the right to information, and (10) due process of law. I will deal briefly here with only the first five, though obviously all of them, and those not listed here as well, need to be thoroughly presented, analyzed, discussed, and acted on eventually.

Preliminary: Church Structures in Early Christianity

How was this freedom and responsibility, this democracy, first put into action in the history of the Church? From the earliest documentary evidence we have, the Christian Church operated with wide participation in decision-making. This was true not only of the more free-wheeling, charismatic churches related to Paul, but also the more "ordered" ones. Thus we find in the Acts of the Apostles that, for example, "the whole multitude elected Stephen" (Acts 6:5). Again, when a large number of people in Antioch was converted to Christianity, it was not just the apostles or the elders, but rather the *whole* Church at Jerusalem which sent Barnabas to Antioch (Acts 11:22). Still later in the Acts of the Apostles there is the statement: "Then it seemed good to the Apostles and Elders, with the whole Church, to choose men from among them and send them to Antioch with Paul and Barnabas" (Acts 15:22).

In Eusebius' *History of the Church* (A.D. 323), the major source of the post-biblical history of the Church, we find Peter not referred to as the leader or bishop of the church at Rome, either the first or subsequent. Rather, Linus was said to be the first bishop of Rome.[29] Moreover,

Peter *is* indirectly referred to by Eusebius as the first bishop of Antioch![30] (Does that mean that the "Bishop of Antioch" should be the head of the Catholic Church rather than the "Bishop of Rome"?) However, it should be noted that Ignatius of Antioch was said by Eusebius to be Peter's second successor as bishop of Antioch. Ignatius is the one who provides the earliest evidence of "monepiscopacy," that is, one bishop as head of the church in an area [a diocese, in imperial Rome's political terminology], which developed in some, but by no means all, areas of the Christian world at the beginning of the second century. Ignatius does *not* refer to a bishop at Rome. Further, the *Shepherd of Hermas*, written during the second quarter of the second century, describes the leadership of the church at Rome as a committee of presbyters. All other early documents—the New Testament Pastoral Epistles, *1 Clement, Didache, Kerygma of Peter, Apocalypse of Peter, Epistle of Barnabas,* and the *Epistle of Polycarp*—give no evidence of monepiscopacy at Rome or anywhere else. Only Ignatius points to monepiscopacy, and then only in Syria and Asia Minor.[31] It is only around the middle of the second century that we have clear evidence of monepiscopacy at Rome.[32] Concerning Peter at Rome, then, there is evidence from early tradition (and the recent digging under St. Peter's Basilica in Rome) that Peter died and was buried in Rome, but not that he was head of the Christian community, the Church, at Rome.

In sum, it is clear that from the earliest period of Christianity there were various forms of community structure, from the very charismatic Pauline community at Corinth to the more presbyterally ordered community at Jerusalem. Then later, through a long period of development, the monepiscopal structure gradually arose and slowly spread, until by the end of the second century it was generally accepted and practiced. However, even the monepiscopacy of that time and the following centuries was by no means the nearly absolutist authoritarian power center it later became. It operated much more like a limited monarchy, or just as accurately said, a limited democracy.

1. Election of Leaders

The fundamental act of choice on the part of the Christian people from the initial period of monepiscopacy and for many centuries thereafter was that of electing their own leaders, their own bishops—and priests and deacons. In this, of course, they were simply continuing the same primordial custom reflected in the New Testament documents. We find corroboration in two other first-century documents, the *Didache* and Clement of Rome's First Letter: "You must, then, elect for yourselves bishops and deacons. . . ."[33]; bishops should be chosen "with the consent of the whole Church. . . ."[34]

Early in the third century Hippolytus made it clear that it was an "apostolic tradition," which was still practiced, for the entire local community along with its leaders to choose its own deacons, presbyters, and bishop.[35] His testimony is closely followed by that of St. Cyprian of Carthage (d. A.D. 258), who often referred to the election of bishops by the presbyters and people. He himself was so elected and consequently made it his rule never to administer ordination without first having consulted both the clergy and the laity about the candidates: "From Cyprian to the presbyterium, deacons, and all the people, greetings! In the ordaining of clerics, most beloved brethren, it is our custom to take your advice beforehand and with common deliberations weigh the character and qualifications of each individual."[36] Cyprian also reported a similar democratic custom prevailing in the church of Rome: "Cornelius was made bishop by the . . . testimony of almost all the people, who were then present, and by the assembly of ancient priests and good men."[37]

Cyprian also bore witness to the custom of the people having the right not only to elect, but also to reject and even recall bishops: "The people themselves most especially have the power to chose worthy bishops or to reject unworthy ones."[38] Optatus, a successor to Cyprian as bishop of Carthage, attests to the continuance of the practice of electing bishops into the fourth century when he reports: "Then Caecilianus was elected by the suffrage of all the people,"[39] and over in Asia Minor the Council of Ancyra (314) confirmed the right of election and rejection of bishops by the people.[40] Every Catholic schoolgirl and schoolboy knows the stories of the elections of St. Ambrose as bishop of Milan and St. Augustine as bishop of Hippo (fourth and fifth centuries) by the acclamation of the people: "We elect him!" *(Nos elegimus eum!)* A little later Pope St. Celestine (d. A.D. 432) said: "No one is given the episcopate uninvited. The consent and desire of the clerics, the people and leadership are required."[41] That redoubtable Pope St. Leo the Great (d. A.D. 461) who faced down Attila the Hun and saved Rome from the sack wrote: "Let him who will stand before all be elected by all."[42] These principles from the early centuries of Christian practice were reiterated in various synods until at least as late as the Council of Paris in A.D. 829.[43]

Basically the election of bishops by the clergy and people remained in effect until the twelfth century—over half the present span of Christianity. Even at the beginning of the United States of America, our first bishop, John Carroll, was, with the full approval of Rome, elected at least by all of the priests of the United States; he then proposed a similar election of all subsequent bishops in America—only to be blocked by Rome.[44] In fact, as late as the beginning of the twentieth century less than half of the bishops of the world were directly named by the pope. Thus it is only in our lifetime that the right of choosing our own bishops has been almost completely taken away from the priests and people— contrary to almost the whole history of the Catholic tradition.

2. Participatory Decision-making

It was not only in the election of their deacons, priests, and bishops that the laity of the ancient Church were involved in Church decision-making. Eusebius reports that already in the second century the *"faithful . . . examined the new doctrines and condemned the heresy."*[45] Cyprian noted that he himself often convoked councils: *Concilio frequenter acto.*[46] On the burning Church issues of the day he wrote to the laity: "This business should be examined in all its parts in your presence and with your counsel."[47] And again: "It is a subject which must be considered . . . with the whole body of the laity."[48] And again: "From the beginning of my episcopate I have been determined to undertake nothing . . . without gaining the assent of the people."[49] Furthermore, this custom of participatory decision-making was also prevalent in the Roman Church of the time, for the Roman clergy wrote: "Thus by the collaborative counsels of bishops, presbyters, deacons, confessors and likewise a substantial number of the laity . . . for no decree can be established which does not appear to be ratified by the consent of the plurality."[50]

Even outside the reach of the law-oriented culture of the Roman Empire the principle of participatory decision-making flourished in the ancient Christian Church. For example, in the East Syrian Church the Synod of Joseph (A.D. 554) stated that "The patriarch must do all that he does with the advice of the community. Whatever he arranged will have all the more authority the more it is submitted for examination."[51]

It was not only on the local and regional levels that the laity were actively involved in ecclesiastical decision-making; from the beginning that was also true on the Church Universal level as well. In the fourth century the great worldwide ecumenical councils began, the first of course being held in 325 at Nicea—called and presided over by a layman, the Emperor Constantine. In fact, all the ecumenical councils from the beginning until well into the Middle Ages were always, with one exception, called by the emperors. That one exception was Nicea II in the eighth century, which was called by the Empress Irene. Moreover, the emperors and empress called the councils on their own authority, not necessarily with prior consultation and approval of the papacy—not even, for that matter, necessarily with the subsequent approval of the papacy. That is, the decrees of the ecumenical councils were promulgated and published by the emperor without always waiting for the approbation of the papacy.

Laity were also present at the ecumenical councils, as well as the large regional councils, such as the ones at Cyprian's Carthage in the third century, the Council of Elvira in the fourth century, and again the (fourth) Council of Toledo in the sixth century, and on down through the centuries, reaching a high point in some ways at the ecumenical councils of Constance and Basel in the first half of the fifteenth century. Even at the sixteenth-century Council of Trent, laity were present and active. Only with the First Vatican Council in 1870 did the participation of the laity in ecumenical councils shrivel to almost nothing.

In very many ways the Vatican II (1962–1965) was a return to the spirit and form of the first "Constitutional Conventions" (Councils) of the Church—even though the influence of the laity came only largely through the massive power of the free press. One of the democratizing moves Vatican II made, however, was to inspire the total revision of the 1917 Code of Canon Law in the spirit of democracy and constitutionalism. Shortly after Vatican II, work was begun on the writing of this Catholic "Constitution of Fundamental Rights," the *Lex Ecclesiae Fundamentalis.*

Drafts of the *Lex Fundamentalis* were created at the Vatican, widely circulated, discussed, and revised over several years. Then, unfortunately, shortly after John Paul II became pope "The whole *Lex* project was put to death, without explanation, in 1981 after it had been approved by a specially convened international commission earlier in the year."[52] Nevertheless, a number of the canons of the *Lex Fundamentalis* were transferred to the new 1983 Code of Canon Law and became its canons 208–23, providing a contemporary beginning of a "Catholic Constitution."

It was not only on the international level that the movement toward "participatory democracy" gained momentum in the aftermath of Vatican Council II; it also happened in a number of instances on the national level, especially in the Germanic-speaking countries and the United States, namely, in The Netherlands, West Germany, East Germany, Austria, Switzerland, and Luxemburg.[53]

The Dutch Pastoral Council ran in several phases from 1968 to 1979. The West German Synod went from 1971 to 1975; the East German Pastoral Synod was shorter during the same period. The Austrian Synod held three sessions, two in 1973 and one in 1974. The Swiss Synod was held in 1972 and provisions were made for subsequent national level "Interdiocesan Pastoral Forums" from 1978 onward. The

Luxemburg Synod was the longest running, lasting from 1972 to 1981. In almost all these instances the surveys which were stimulated and the discussions which were held were extremely responsible and progressive.

The attempt to call a National Pastoral Council in the United States got as far as a committee being set up, but no further. However, the equivalent emerged under the leadership of Cardinal John Dearden of Detroit, who spearheaded the organization of the 1976 "Call to Action," as the National Conference of Catholic Bishops' contribution to the American Bicentennial Celebration. Besides employing clerical and lay representation and majority rule voting at the 1976 assembly, the "Call to Action" stimulated widespread grass-roots consultation, including travelling "hearings" by a committee of bishops. Finally a large number of very responsible and progressive resolutions were democratically passed at the Detroit assembly.

However, in the end, Rome was so resistant to serious democratizing developments, whether stemming from Europe or from America, that the initial general enthusiasm flowing from Vatican II progressively waned. As the French priest/theologian Bernard Franck put it, it gave way to a "general moroseness characteristic of the Western countries and the discouragement of a great many laity, who, here as elsewhere, watch helplessly as the church is again taken over by clergy who, as always, are jealous of their prerogatives and find it difficult to share responsibilities."[54] This was written in 1991. Now, however, chastened progressive Catholics are beginning to strive once again for participatory democratization of the Catholic Church.

3. Limited Term of Office

There is nothing in either Scripture or theology which necessitates an unlimited term of office for any position in the Catholic Church. Every position, including that of pope, is "resignable"—in fact, Pope St. Celestine V resigned as pope in A.D. 1294. On the positive side, it should be noted that there are many positions which have had time limitations set to them in a variety of ways. Various positions within a diocese, e.g., vicar general, dean, pastor, all depend for their longevity on the will of the presiding bishop. The temporal limitation of office in these cases is known only "after the fact," not "before the fact." Bishops and cardinals now have a specific "before the fact" temporal limitation, namely, they must retire from their posts at age seventy-five. Further, the position of a bishop as an "Ordinary" in a particular diocese is not infrequently temporally also limited by his leaving that diocese and going to another.

There has not been a tradition of diocesan bishops being selected for their positions for a specific period of time. However, there has been the tradition for many, many centuries in the Catholic Church of the superiors of religious orders—including abbots and abbesses who often held ecclesiastical geographical jurisdiction powers comparable to that of bishops—of being elected for specific limited terms of office. And all this has been duly approved by Rome.

Suffice it to recall the immense benefits of a limited term of office in the modern civil experience. The prospect of soon or at least eventually being "among" those about whom one is now making decisions is a healthy tempering thought for the decision-maker. Unfettered power, with the best of will, tempts the realization of the famous saying of Lord Acton: "Power corrupts, and absolute power corrupts absolutely." Hence, it is no surprise to note that in the wake of the liberating winds of Vatican II the Catholic Theological Faculty of the University of Tübingen in Germany produced a special issue of their periodical, the *Tübinger Theologische Quartalschrift,* 2 (1969), devoted to the questions of the election and limited term of office of bishops and that the whole faculty signed a careful argument in favor of the notion of a limited term of office of eight years for resident bishops. What is perhaps surprising, however, is not that Hans Küng was one of the signers of that document (which he was) but that Joseph Ratzinger (now cardinal and head of the Congregation for the Doctrine of the Faith) was also![55]

4. Separation of Powers

When we think of the modern democratic principle of the "separation of powers," from the time of Montesquieu's *De l'Esprit des Lois* (1734), we normally think of the legislative, executive, and judicial powers being separated. In the ancient and medieval Catholic Church there was for long stretches of time a similar separation of powers, though the terms used were not precisely those of Montesquieu nor of today. The holders of powers were: (1) bishops, (2) teachers, and, in the Middle Ages, (3) canon lawyers. I will deal briefly only with the first two.

It will probably come as somewhat of a shock for many Catholics to learn that in the history of the Roman Catholic Church the pope and bishops were not always the supreme teachers of what was true Catholic doctrine. For well over nine centuries of Catholic history it was the "teachers," the theologians, who were the supreme arbiters in deciding what was correct Catholic teaching. This occurred in the first three centuries of the Christian era and again from the thirteenth through the eighteenth centuries. Concerning the first three centuries one need only remember such outstanding "teachers," who were not even priests, let alone bishops, as Clement of Alexandria (150–215) and his successor Origen (185–254). It is clear that there were lay teachers in the Roman Church as well in this early period, for we find the Roman priest Hippolytus (170–236) stating such in his *Apostolic Tradition:* "When the teacher . . . whether the one who teaches be cleric or lay, he will do so."[56]

Concerning the Middle Ages from the thirteenth century on, no less a person than Aquinas clearly distinguishes between the professorial chair, *cathedra magistralis,* and the episcopal throne, the *cathedra pontificalis vel pastoralis.* "The first conferred the authority to teach, *auctoritas docendi;* the second, the power to govern and, if necessary, to punish, *eminentia potestatis."*[57] There was no subordination of the *magisterium* of the teacher to that of the bishop; they were on an equal plane: "Teachers of sacred Scripture adhere to the ministry of the word as do also prelates."[58]

In the fourteenth century we find the French theologian Godefroid de Fontaines posing the following question (and note how he poses it): "Whether the theologian *must* contradict the statement of the bishop if he believes it to be opposed to the truth?" He answers that if the matter is not concerned with faith or morals, then he should dissent only in private, but if it is a matter of faith or morals, "the teacher must take a stand, regardless of the episcopal decree . . . even though some will be scandalized by this action. It is better to preserve the truth, even at the cost of a scandal, than to let it be suppressed through fear of a scandal." And, Godefroid pointed out, this would be true even if the bishop in question were the pope, "for in this situation the pope can be doubted."[59]

Thus from the medieval scholastic perspective the theologians were supposed to determine truth and error and it was then up to the bishops to punish the offenders. That is why from the thirteenth century onward episcopal decrees were often issued "with the counsel of teachers" *(de consilio doctorum).* For example the bishop of Paris, Etienne I, condemned several propositions as heretical "with the counsel of the teachers of theology" *(de consilio magistrorum theologiae).*[60] The Western Schism (late fourteenth/early fifteenth centuries when there were two and even three popes simultaneously!) further reinforced the prestige and authority of the theologians, so that at the two Ecumenical Councils which resolved the Western Schism, Constance (A.D. 1314–1318) and especially Basel (A.D. 1431–1449), there were often hundreds of theologians present and only a handful of ignorant bishops and abbots.

Hence, as Roger Gryson put it, "one can not find any question on which the universal Church's ultimate criterion of truth did not come around to the unanimous opinion of the Scholastics [theologians], through faith in their authority *(eorum auctoritate mota)."* And by the middle of the sixteenth century the famous Spanish Dominican theologian Melchior Cano applied to theologians the words of Jesus, "Whoever hears you hears me, who rejects you rejects me": "When the Lord said: 'Who hears you hears me, and who rejects you rejects me,' he did not refer with these words to the first theologians, i.e., the apostles, but to the future teachers in the Church so long as the sheep need to be pastured in knowledge and doctrine."[61]

This "separation of powers" wherein the theologians exercised the teaching power and, as St. Thomas described it, the bishops' *Regimen* or "management" continued through the end of the "Old Regimen" the French *Ancien Régime,* at the beginning of the last century.

5. Dialogue—The Means to Mutual Understanding and Creative Decisions

Question: Can there not be, indeed, ought there not be different opinions, followed by possible dissent, then dialogue, and only thereafter decision in the Church, even on matters of the greatest religious significance? Indeed, should not this sequence of actions be adhered to especially in matters of the greatest religious significance?

Response: "The Christian faithful . . . have the right and even at times *a duty* to manifest to the sacred pastors their opinion on matters which pertain to the good of the Church." "Those who are engaged in the sacred disciplines enjoy a lawful freedom of inquiry and of prudently expressing their opinions on matters in which they have expertise." These are not the wild words of a radical group of non-Catholics, or even of a group of liberal Catholics. They are the canons 212,3 and 218 of the new Code of Canon Law. This might seem to some to seal the argument, but there is more:

> Christ summons the Church, as she goes her pilgrim way, to that continual reformation of which she always has need. . . . Let everyone in the Church . . . preserve a proper freedom . . . even in the theological elaborations of revealed truth. . . . All are led . . . wherever necessary, to undertake with vigor the task of renewal and reform. . . . [All] Catholics' . . . primary *duty* is to make a careful and honest appraisal of whatever needs to be renewed and done in the Catholic household itself.

Who this time are the radical advocates of freedom and reformation "even in the theological elaborations of revealed truth"? All the Catholic bishops of the world gathered together in Vatican II (Decree on Ecumenism, no. 4).

The same council also firmly declared that "the human person has a right to religious freedom. This freedom means that all human beings are to be immune from coercion on the part of individuals, social groups and every human power. . . . *Nobody is forced to act against his convictions in religious matters in private or in public.* . . . Truth can impose itself on the mind of humans only in virtue of its own truth" (Declaration on Religious Liberty, nos. 1, 2). The council further stated that the "search for truth" should be carried out "by free enquiry . . . and dialogue. . . . Human beings are bound to follow their consciences faithfully in all their activity. . . . They must not be forced to act contrary to their conscience, *especially in religious matters*" (ibid., no. 3).

There is still more: In 1973 the Congregation of the Doctrine of the Faith stated that the "conceptions" by which Church teaching is expressed are changeable: "The truths which the Church intends to teach through her dogmatic formulas are distinct from the changeable conceptions of a given epoch and can be expressed without them" (the Congregation of the Doctrine of the Faith's 1973 Declaration *Mysterium ecclesiae*). But how can these "conceptions" be changed unless someone points out that they might be improved, might even be defective, that is, unless there is deliberation, possibly dissent, and then dialogue leading to a new decision on how to express the matter?

And a real mind boggler: "Doctrinal discussion requires perceptiveness, both in honestly setting out one's own opinion and in recognizing the truth everywhere, even if the truth demolishes one so that one is forced to reconsider one's own position, in theory and in practice." Words of the Vatican Curia(!) in 1968 (Vatican Secretariat for Unbelievers' Document *Humanae personae dignitatem*).

Even Pope John Paul II encouraged responsible dissent and supported theologians in their invaluable service done in freedom. In 1969, then archbishop of Cracow, he said: "Conformity means death for any community. A loyal opposition is a necessity in any community." A decade later, as pope, he declared that, "The Church needs her theologians, particularly in this time and age. . . . We desire to listen to you and we are eager to receive the valued assistance of your responsible scholarship. . . . We will never tire of insisting on the eminent role of the university . . . a place of scientific research, constantly updating its methods and working instruments . . . *in freedom of investigation*" ("Address to Catholic Theologians and Scholars at The Catholic University of America," October 7, 1979—emphasis added). A little later he even went so far as to remark: "Truth is the power of peace. . . . What should one say of the practice of combatting or silencing those who do not share the same views?" (More than ironically, even as a countersign, that statement was issued on

December 18, 1979, three days after the close of the "interrogation" of
Schillebeeckx in Rome and on the very day of the quasi-silencing of
Hans Küng.)

One of the main functions of the Magisterium, and especially the
Congregation of the Doctrine of the Faith, therefore, ought not be to
put a stop to deliberation, dissent, and dialogue, but instead precisely
to encourage, promote, and direct it in the most creative possible channels. As a 1979 petition in support of Father Schillebeeckx signed by
hundreds of theologians urged:

> The function of the Congregation of the Doctrine of the Faith
> should be to *promote dialogue* among theologians of varying method-
> ologies and approaches so that the most enlightening, helpful, and
> authentic expressions of theology could ultimately find acceptance.
> Hence, we call upon the Congregation of the Doctrine of the Faith to
> eliminate from its procedures "hearings," and the like, substituting
> for them dialogues that would be either issue-oriented, or if it is
> deemed important to focus on the work of a particular theologian,
> would bring together not only the theologian in question and the
> consultors of the Congregation of the Doctrine of the Faith, but also a
> worldwide selection of the best pertinent theological scholars of
> varying methodologies and approaches. These dialogues could well
> be conducted with the collaboration of the International Theological
> Commission, the Pontifical Biblical Commission, universities, theo-
> logical faculties, and theological organizations. Thus, the best experts
> on the issues concerned would work until acceptable resolutions
> were arrived at. Such a procedure of course is by no means new; it is
> precisely the procedure utilized at the Second Vatican Council.[62]

Indeed, even the pope and the Curia wrote of the absolute necessity of dialogue and sketched out how it should be conducted. Pope
Paul VI in his first encyclical, *Ecclesiam suam* (1964), wrote that dialogue "is *demanded* nowadays. . . . It is *demanded* by the dynamic
course of action which is changing the face of modern society. It is *demanded* by the . . . maturity humanity has reached in this day and
age." Then in 1968 the Vatican declared that "the willingness to engage
in dialogue is the measure and strength of that general renewal which
must be carried out in the Church, which *implies a still greater appreciation of liberty.* . . . Doctrinal dialogue should be initiated with courage
and sincerity, *with the greatest freedom . . .* recognizing the truth
everywhere, even if the truth demolishes one so that one is forced to
reconsider one's own position. . . . Therefore the *liberty of the participants* must be ensured by law and reverenced in practice" (*Humanae
personae dignitatem,* emphasis added).

6. Summary

Thus, in summary, one can say that of course in the beginning the Church was the people, who naturally chose their leaders out of their midst; they also took an active role in deciding about a whole range of things, including doctrinal matters. It is only in the late Middle Ages and the modern period of history that the rights of the laity to choose their own Church leaders and actively to participate in Church decision making was eroded to the tiny remnant which we experienced growing up. We were told, however, that the way things were in our childhood was the way they had always been! This erosion of democratic rights of the laity reached its low point in the middle of this century just before Vatican II. That council, of course, started the process of restoring the ancient tradition of shared responsibility and in fact was followed up in this regard by the 1971 Synod of Bishops when it stated: "The members of the Church should have some share in the drawing up of decisions, in accordance with the rules given by the Second Vatican Ecumenical Council and the Holy See, for instance with regard to the setting up of councils at all levels."[63] Unfortunately for almost three decades thereafter we appeared more and more to be returning to a pre-conciliar mode.

Nevertheless, we must conclude that the Catholic Church not only could be a democracy; it in fact *was* a limited democracy—which has been dismantled. It needs to be reestablished.

X. Suggestions for the Organization and Action of the Catholic Constitutional Convention—A.D. 2000/1

The beginning of not just a new century but of a new millennium provides an opportune psychological moment to call for a dramatic breakthrough. Further, the goal of a convention in the year 2000 or 2001 provides both adequate time to build momentum for such a momentous project while at the same time not so much time that ennui would set in. In brief, the time is ripe now to launch the calling of a "Catholic Constitutional Convention." The beginning of the third millennium should be viewed as a *kairos*, a special moment of "salvation" (i.e., of full "health," "[w]holiness," as the Latin root *salus* means).

A. Considerations of a Catholic Constitutional Convention Committee

A Catholic Constitutional Convention Committee has been formed by the National Board of ARCC in conjunction with COR and the European reform movements, as well as African and Asian groups, to strategize on the steps to be taken in launching the project. These groups are considering at least the following:

1) The Catholic Constitutional Convention is not being called in opposition to the pope, bishops, or priests. Every effort has been made from the very beginning and all along the way to include every element of the Church in the shaping of the Catholic Constitution and the structure and spirit of the Church flowing from it. All Catholic organizations, papal, episcopal, presbyteral, religious and lay, local, national and international, are invited and urged to participate in the project. As at Vatican II, observers from other Christian churches and other religions are also invited to assist—this dimension of Vatican II proved to be extremely helpful and creative.

2) The tone of the whole project is totally positive. For example, a formal invitation might read as follows: "As the civil world at large is dramatically moving toward democracy, framing anew the fundamental principles of humanity, which is 'created in the image of God,' in constitutions, so too is the Catholic Church. . . . Following the inspiration of Vatican II and Popes John XXIII, Paul VI, and John Paul II in their vigorous advocacy throughout the world of Human Rights, we committed Catholics are issuing a call to a 'Catholic Constitutional Convention'. . . ."

3) Also as in Vatican II, full utilization of theological and other experts is vital. Hence, specific invitations have gone out to the organizations of the various theological disciplines (e.g., the Catholic Historical Society, Catholic Biblical Society, Catholic Theological Society of America, Canon Law Society of America, and the many parallels in other countries) to join in the project at least by focusing a portion of their programs on research into the various aspects of the question of democracy and the Catholic Church and related renewal/reform issues and by responding to a tentative proposed draft of a Catholic Constitution. The Catholic organizations, national and international, of other disciplines and professions are likewise being invited to contribute their charisms.

4) Following the example of the National Conference of Catholic Bishops (U.S.) in preparing for the 1976 "Call to Action" and the Pastoral Letter on Economics, a series of "hearings" around the country (and in other countries) might be organized at a later phase.

5) A focused plan is being developed for the writing and publishing of not only scholarly articles and books on various aspects of the question of democracy and the Catholic Church and related renewal/reform issues, but also popular-level ones.

6) The groups listed above have been distributing, as widely as possible, a tentative proposed draft of a Catholic Constitution, inviting all Catholic groups and individuals to respond and make further

suggestions, written and oral, on how the Constitution should be formed, with specifics on its form and contents. The purpose of the "Proposed Catholic Constitution" is to provide a possible structure into which to fit suggestions. The text of the "Proposed Catholic Constitution" as well as a book-length expansion of this essay can be found in Leonard Swidler, *Toward a Catholic Constitution* (New York: Crossroad, 1996), as well as from ARCC and on the world wide web: http:11 astro.temple. edu/~ARCC. (For ARCC's address, see n. 63, below.)

7) The "Proposed Catholic Constitution," of course, is subject not only to revision but even complete rejection by the participants. Ultimately an International Drafting Committee will be responsible to assimilate submitted responses and materials and begin to draft the "Revised Catholic Constitution" on their basis, to be submitted to the convention for debate, revision, and eventual adoption.

B. Suggestions from the "Association for the Rights of Catholics in the Church" and "Catholics Organizing Renewal"

The project of a "Catholic Constitutional Convention" was first developed in the "Association for the Rights of Catholics in the Church" (ARCC) and was then laid before a national meeting in Washington, D.C., on June 25, 1993, of "Catholics Organizing Renewal" (COR), where it won unanimous support and encouragement for ARCC to take the lead in launching the project. The German "Organization of Catholic Academics" *(Neudeutschland)* also gave strong support *(nachdrückliche Zustimmung),*[64] as did also the "Fourth Annual Assembly of the 'European Conference on Human Rights in the Church' in Brussels."[65] Therefore ARCC, mindful of it own stated purpose ("to institutionalize a collegial understanding of Church in which decision-making is shared and accountability is realized among Catholics of every kind and condition"), offers the following suggestions as an initial stimulus for all Catholics to think creatively about, discuss widely—and then send ideas back to ARCC for processing:

1. The *Charter of the Rights of Catholics in the Church,* along with the full *Lex Ecclesiae Fundamentalis* already approved but then mysteriously set aside in 1981, and the residue from the *Lex* imbedded in canons 208–23 of the 1983 Code of Canon Law are obvious sources for the Constitution of the Catholic Church.

2. Mindful of the 1971 Bishops' Synod's statement that "the members of the Church should have some share in the drawing up of decisions . . . for instance, with regard to the setting up of *councils at all levels,*" and its own charter, ARCC claims that "all Catholics have the right to a voice in decisions that affect them" (*Charter,* Rt. 5), "the right

to be dealt with fairly" (*Charter,* Rt. 9), and "the right to timely redress of grievances" (*Charter,* Rt. 10).

Structures that could support many of the above rights already exist, but are inadequately developed and, for millions of Catholics, they do not exist in actuality because of the lack of adequate structures to make them real.[66] Hence, whatever structures for the governance of the Church are arrived at, they should include these principles:

> a) Election of leaders, including pastors, bishops, and pope, through an appropriate structure giving serious voice to all respective "constituents."
>
> b) A limited term of office for such leaders, as has been the case for centuries in religious orders.
>
> c) A separation of powers, along with a system of checks and balances, including parish, diocesan, national and international councils, and a separate judicial system, to share the responsibility in appropriate ways with pastors, bishops, and pope.
>
> d) Establishment of the principle of dialogue to arrive at the most helpful formulations and applications of the teachings of the tradition from the local through to the highest universal level.
>
> e) Equitable representation of all elements of the faithful, including women and minorities, in all positions of leadership and decision-making.

3. Just as there were "state" level constitutional conventions during the American colonial period which led up to and contributed significantly to the national constitutional conventions in Philadelphia (the first "constitution," the "Articles of Federation," turned out to be a failure), so too would it be wise to hold various "Regional Catholic Constitutional Conventions." These would lead up to "National Catholic Constitutional Conventions," climaxing on the world level in the "*Katholos* Constitutional Convention" (and beyond that, an "*Oikumenikos* Constitutional Convention" including all the Christian churches?). Hence, ARCC:

> a) Calls upon its members, in conjunction with other Catholic Church-reform organizations, to launch one or more "Regional Catholic Constitutional Conventions" (on April 10, 1994, ARCC-Philadelphia committed itself to work concertedly on the drafting of a Catholic Constitution—in essence, a Regional Catholic Constitutional Convention being in constant session, starting in the fall of 1994).

b) Calls upon other Catholic Church-reform organizations, regionally and nationally, to begin to promote "Regional Catholic Constitutional Conventions" and to continue to co-operate in the organization of "National," and ultimately, an "International Catholic Constitutional Convention."

c) Has taken the lead in setting up a "Catholic Constitutional Convention Coordinating Committee" to plan for the "National Catholic Constitutional Convention." It is also encouraging similar national level "Catholic Constitutional Conventions" abroad.

d) Recommends that Philadelphia be a possible site of the "National Catholic Constitutional Convention." Philadelphia was the locus of both the U.S. Declaration of Independence and the Constitution—the latter of course is particularly pertinent here. In terms of facilities, Philadelphia now has a new convention center, which is just a stone's throw from Independence Hall and other historical monuments of constitutional democracy.

e) Recommends that an International Coordinating Committee be set up in the near future to begin long-range planning for the "International Constitutional Convention" to be held in the year A.D. 2000 or 2001—in Rome? Washington? Jerusalem?

XI. ARCC Suggestions of *Immediate* Steps to Be Taken

Without waiting for a Constitution to be approved and implemented, ARCC recommends that the following steps be taken now:

A. Structures for Decision Making and Due Process

1. That in every parish and diocese

a) the establishment of pastoral councils (and not just finance councils) be made mandatory,

b) that these councils be representatively elected, and

c) that they have real decision-making power so that responsibility for the welfare of the community and its mission will be truly shared among clergy, religious, and laity. (Note: such councils must work closely with the finance councils, which must be equally active, responsible, and accountable.)

2. That every diocese have courts to redress grievances of all types according to due process (following specific recommendations of the Canon Law Society of America); this might be handled by

a) extending the scope of existing marriage tribunals, contemplated by the 1983 Code or

b) new administrative tribunals, also allowed and even recommended by the 1983 Code.

In any case, a truly just and effective system must be made mandatory, widely promulgated, and implemented.

3. That there be set up on both the national and international levels representatively elected synods of clergy and laity with real decision-making responsibility along with the national bishops conferences, Synod of Bishops, and the Papacy as ongoing constitutive parts of the collegial governance of the national and universal Church.

B. The Status of Women

The most widespread and pervasive example of divisive dualism in the Catholic Church, and in society at large, is that between women and men, which operates in such a way that women are discriminated against. This clearly contradicts Christian baptism, which initiates equally all, women and men, into the community of the followers of Jesus: "There is neither male nor female . . . but all are one in Christ Jesus" (Gal 3:28).

Thus, although all people have the right to define themselves, women regularly cannot exercise this right in the Church; the 1971 Bishops' Synod saw this when it felt the need to state: "We also urge that women should have their own share of responsibility and participation in the community life of society and likewise of the Church." Unfortunately that recommendation has not yet been effectively implemented; until it is and until sufficient and adequate role models of women in leadership in the Church are provided, many women will not be able, or willing, to join actively in Church life. Therefore, ARCC urges:

4. That every parish, diocese, national, international, and other appropriate organizational unit move immediately within the present possibilities of canon law to place competent women in positions of leadership and decision-making in numbers proportional to their membership: "All Catholic women have an equal right with men to the resources and the exercise of all the powers of the Church" (*Charter*, Rt. 26).

5. That every parish, diocese, national, international, and other appropriate organizational unit move immediately to appoint competent women in all liturgical offices within the present possibilities of canon law in numbers proportional to their membership. This includes readers,

commentators, cantors, leaders of prayers, ministers of baptism and Communion, and Mass servers.[67]

6. That laity, priests, and bishops through every appropriate agency urge the Vatican to move to bring competent women as quickly as possible into the diaconate, presbyterate, and episcopacy: "All Catholics, regardless of . . . sex . . . have the right to exercise all ministries in the Church for which they are adequately prepared, according to the needs and with the approval of the community" (*Charter*, Rt. 16).

7. That every parish, diocese, national, and international unit move immediately to eliminate all sexist and other non-inclusive language in its documents: "All Catholics have the right to expect that Church documents and materials will avoid sexist language and that symbols and imagery of God will not be exclusively masculine" (*Charter*, Rt. 32).

8. That every unit of the Church, and particularly the bishop, adopt a prophetic stance in the local, regional, national, and international communities on issues of social justice, especially concerning what is usually the most voiceless element of society—women.

XII. Conclusion

Let this suffice for an initial stimulus for launching us on the road to the "Catholic Constitutional Convention." Of course it will not happen without an immense effort by large numbers of Catholics on all levels, nor will the Establishment initially move to bring it about. But, thinking about it, discussing and debating it and its possible content will raise it and all it stands for—a mature, free, and responsible democratic Catholic Church—in the consciousness of Catholics throughout the world. Then, holding the "Catholic Constitutional Convention" (and what better target date than the beginning of the third millennium?), even if it is not participated in and recognized by the official structures of the Catholic Church, will nevertheless debate and develop creative, responsible ideas and projects for further democratizing and renewing the Church, which eventually are bound to have a significant effect on the Establishment.

Would this lead to a schism in the Catholic Church? No, no one is interested in starting a *new* church or anything like it, but hundreds of millions of Catholics *are* interested in a *re-newed* Church!

Impossible? Who in 1958 would have thought the Vatican II Revolution of 1962-65 was remotely possible, or the Eastern Europe Revolution of 1989? We need to have what is a paraphrase of one of the mottos on the American penny, that is, "Trust in God," and then work with all the creativity and energy we can muster to realize in a contemporary democratic manner the other motto on the penny: "A unity flowing from the many," *E pluribus unum!*

NOTES

1. See Jean-Pierre Jossua, "Jacques Pohier: A Theologian Destroyed," in Hans Küng and Leonard Swidler, eds., *The Church in Anguish: Has the Vatican Betrayed Vatican II?* (San Francisco: Harper & Row, 1987) 205–11.
2. See Ad Willems, "The Endless Case of Edward Schillebeeckx," in ibid., 212–22.
3. See Leonardo Boff and Clodovis Boff, "Summons to Rome," in ibid., 223–34.
4. See Gerhard Lenski, "The Religious Factor, 1961, referred to in *"NCR* Gallup Poll," *National Catholic Reporter* (September 11, 1987) 10.
5. Cf. Leonard Swidler, *"Roma Locuta, Causa Finita?"* in Leonard Swidler and Arlene Swidler, eds., *Women Priests: A Catholic Commentary on the Vatican Declaration* (New York: Paulist, 1977) 3.
6. *"NCR* Gallup Poll," 10.
7. Ibid.
8. Joseph H. Fichter, "Restructuring Catholicism: Symposium on Thomas O'Dea," *Sociological Analysis* 38 (1977) 163f.
9. November 28, 1990, typed notes from a European trip by Terry Dosh.
10. *Eighth of May Newsletter,* Acht Mei Beweging, Brigittenstraat 15; NL-3512 KJ Utrecht, Netherlands.
11. "Aufbruch-Bewegung" publishes (in German) an impressive newspaper six times a year with a circulation of 34,000. It is entitled: *Aufbruch. Forum für eine offene Kirche,* Postfach 169, 1700 Fribourg 7, Switzerland.
12. At least one of the regional organizations publishes a newsletter, whose address is: "KIRCHE SIND WIR ALLE," Postfach 107, 6800 Feldkirch, Austria. A progressive Catholic monthly periodical in Austria which regularly reports on the activities of these and other renewal movements is *Kirche Intern. Forum für eine offene Kirche,* whose address is Floriangasse 1; A-2440 Reisenberg, Austria.
13. The Ikvu also puts out a quarterly periodical, entitled: *Rundbriefe Initiative Kirche von unten,* whose address is: Heerstr. 205; 5300 Bonn 1, Germany.
14. *Dialog statt Dialogverweigerung. Wie in der Kirche miteinander umgehen?* The committee was made up of 33 members, including men and women, laity, clergy, religious, and a bishop. Copies can be obtained from the Generalsekretariat des ZDK. Hochkreuzallee 246; 5300 Bonn 2, Germany.
15. *Macht teilen, Gleichheit anerkennen. Ein Demokratieförderplan für die katholische Kirche in Deutschland* (Düsseldorf: BDKJ-Bundesstelle, 1994) 3.
16. Ibid., 6.
17. Ibid., 12–5.
18. Up-to-date information on the addresses of the various organizations

can be obtained from Gerd Wild, Christenrechte in der Kirche; Commission for International Contacts; Mithrasstr. 45; 6000 Frankfurt 50, Germany; Tel.: 011-49-69-586-516; Fax: 49-6173-65220.

19. *The Tablet* (London), (January 15, 1994) 56. See also *Euronews. Informationsblatt für das "Europäische Netzwerk Kirche im Aufbruch,"* no. 3 (June 1994), ed. Josée Reichling, 12, rue des champs, L-5953 Itzig, Luxembourg, Tel./Fax: 352-369-743.

20. Paul VI used the phrase *novus habitus mentis:* Paul VI, allocution of November 20, 1965, *Communicationes,* I (1969) 38–42.

21. James Provost, "Prospects for a More 'Democratized' Church," in James Provost and Knut Walf, eds., *The Tabu of Democracy within the Church, Concilium,* 1992/5 (London: SCM Press, 1992) 132. See John Paul II's Apostolic Constitution *Sacrae disciplinae leges,* January 25, 1983; *Acta Apostolicae Sedis,* 75/2 (1983) xii.

22. Provost, ibid.

23. Provost and Walf, eds., *The Tabu of Democracy.*

24. *Centesimus annus,* no. 46, in James Provost, "Prospects for a More 'Democratized' Church," in Provost and Walf, eds., *The Tabu of Democracy within the Church,* 141.

25. "Message to Humanity," issued at the beginning of the Second Vatican Council by its Fathers, with the endorsement of the Supreme Pontiff, cited in Walter Abbott, ed., *The Documents of Vatican II* (New York: Herder & Herder/Association Press, 1966) 6.

26. *Acta Apostolicae Sedis,* 57 (1965) 988.

27. *Acta Apostolicae Sedis,* 75 (1983) 556; *Origins* 12 (1983) 631.

28. See Peter Clarke, *A Free Church in a Free Society* (Greenwood, S.C.: Attic Press, 1982).

29. Eusebius, *History of the Church,* 3, 2.

30. Ibid., 3, 36.

31. Cf. T. Patrick Burke, "The Monarchical Episcopate at the End of the First Century," *Journal of Ecumenical Studies* 11 (1970) 499–518.

32. Eusebius' account of the Easter controversy describes Anicetus in a monepiscopal role in Rome shortly before the death of Polycarp in 155—*History of the Church,* 4.22.1–3 . Cf. James F. McCue, "The Roman Primacy in the Patristic Era. The Beginnings through Nicea, " in Paul Empie and T. Austin Murphy, eds., *Papal Primacy and the Universal Church. Lutherans and Catholics in Dialogue V* (Minneapolis: Augsburg, 1943) 44–72.

33. *Didache,* 15:1-2.

34. *1 Clement,* 44, 5.

35. Hippolytus, *Traditio Apostolica,* 2, 7, 8.

36. Migne, *Patrologia Latina,* 4, 317–8. *Cyprianus presbyterio et diaconibus et plebi universae salutem. In ordinationibus clericis, fratres charissimi, solemus vos ante consulere, et mores ac merita singulorum communi consilia ponderare.*

37. Ibid., 3, 796–7.

38. Cyprian, Epistle, 67, 3, *Corpus Scriptorum Ecclesiasticorum Latinorum (CSEL),* 3.2.737. *Plebs . . . ipsa maxime habeat potestatem uel eligendi dignos sacerdotes uel indignos recusandi.*

39. Optaus, *CSEL,* 34.2.407. *Tunc suffragio totius populi Caecilianus elegitur et manum imponente Felice Autumnitano episcopus ordinatur.*

40. Canon 18. Cf. C. J. von Hefele, *Conciliengeschichte,* I (Freiburg, 1873) 237.

41. Celestine, Epistle, iv, 5; *PL,* 50, 431. *Nullus invitis detur episcopus. Cleri, plebis, et ordinis, consensus ac desiderium requiratur.*

42. Leo, Epistle, x, 4; *PL,* 54, 634. *Qui praefuturus est onmibus ab onmibus eligatur.*

43. Cf. Jean Harduin, *Acta Conciliorum et Epistolae Decretales ac Constitutiones Summorum Pontificum,* IV, 1289ff.

44. Cf. Leonard Swidler, "People, Priests, and Bishops in U.S. Catholic History," in Leonard Swidler and Arlene Swidler, eds., *Bishops and People* (Philadelphia: Westminster, 1970) 113-5.

45. Eusebius, *History of the Church, Patrologia Graeca,* 20, 468.

46. Cyprian, Epistle, xxvi.

47. Cyprian, *PL,* 4, 256–7 *Cyprianus fratribus in plebe consistentibus salutem . . . examinabuntur singula praesentibus et judicantibus vobis.*

48. Cyprian, Epistle, liv, quoted in Johann Baptist Hirscher, *Sympathies of the Continent,* trans. of *Die kirchlichen Zustände der Gegenwart,* 1849, by Arthur C. Coxe (Oxford, 1852) 123. *Singulorum tractanda ratio, non tantum cum collegis meis, sed cum plebe ipsa universa.*

49. Cyprian, *PL,* 4, 234. *Quando a primordio episcopatus mei statuerim, nihil sine consilio vestro, et sine consensu plebis, mea privatim, sententia genere.*

50. Cyprian, *PL,* 4, 312. *Sic collatione consiliorum cum episcopis, presbyteris, diaconis, confessoribus pariter ac stantibus laicis facta, lapsorum tractare rationem . . . quoniam nec firmum decretum potest esse quod non plurimorum videbitur habuisse consensum.*

51. Canon 7, in J. B. Chabot, *Synodicon Orientale* (Paris, 1902) 358.

52. Both citations are from James A. Coriden, "A Challenge: Making the Rights Real," in Leonard Swidler and Herbert O'Brien, *A Catholic Bill of Rights* (Kansas City: Sheed & Ward, 1988) 11; also in *The Jurist* 45, 1 (1985).

53. For information on the "national" synods in the Germanic-speaking countries see the detailed essay by the priest/theologian Bernard Franck, "Experiences of National Synods in Europe After the Council," in Provost and Walf, eds., *The Tabu of Democracy,* 82–97. For further analysis of the West German Synod and its aftermath, as well as the U.S. equivalent, the 1976 "Call to Action," see Heinrich Fries, *Suffering from the Church,* introduction and translation by Leonard and Arlene Swidler (Collegeville: The Liturgical Press, 1994).

54. Ibid., 92.

55. See the expanded English translation, Leonard and Arlene Swidler, eds. and trans., *Bishops and People* (Philadelphia: Westminster Press, 1970).

56. *Apostolic Tradition* (Hippolytus), XIX.

57. Roger Gryson, "The Authority of the Teacher in the Ancient and Medieval Church," in Leonard Swidler and Piet Fransen, eds., *Authority in the Church and the Schillebeeckx Case* (New York: Crossroad, 1982) 184.

58. Thomas Aquinas, *Quodlibitales,* q. 3, a. 9. *Doctores sacrae scripturae adhibentur ministerio uerbi Dei, sicut et praelati.*

59. References and fuller discussion in Gryson, *The Authority of the Teacher,* 176–87.

60. Ibid., 186.

61. Citation found in ibid., 186f. The original reads: *Cum Dominus dixit: Qui vos audit me audit, et qui vos spernit me spernit, non modo ad primos theologos, i.e. apostolos verba illa referebat, sed ad doctores etiam in Ecclesia futuros, quamdiu pascendae essent oves in scientia et doctrina.*

62. Reprinted in Leonard Swidler, *Küng in Conflict* (New York: Doubleday, 1981) 516f.

63. Reprinted in part in the *Charter of the Rights of Catholics in the Church of the Association for the Rights of Catholics in the Church* (ARCC), 2nd edition (January 1985) 17; P.O. Box 912, Delran, NJ 08075.

64. This was a result of the presentation of the idea of a Catholic Constitutional Convention in an article: Leonard Swidler, "Aufruf zur einer Katholischen Verfassunggebenden Versammlung," *Diakonia,* 24, 2 (March 1993) 133–9.

65. *The Tablet* (London), (January 15, 1994) 56.

66. See the excellent introductory essay on the realization of rights already existing in the new 1983 Code of Canon Law by Professor James Coriden in Leonard Swidler and Patrick Connor, eds., *A Catholic Bill of Rights* (Kansas City, Mo.: Sheed & Ward, 1988); *Alle Katholiken haben das Recht . . . Freiheitsrechte in der Kirche* (Munich: Kösel Verlag, 1990).

67. On the latter see the respected *The Code of Canon Law. A Text and Commentary,* commissioned by the Canon Law Society of America (Paulist Press, 1985): "The revised Code, unlike the 1917 Code, does not prohibit females from serving Mass. . . . There is no solid legal basis for excluding female altar servers" (648). This matter was finally satisfactorily resolved by the Vatican in 1994.

SIX

The Conciliar Constitution
of the Church: Nicholas of Cusa's
"Catholic Concordance"

James E. Biechler

The experience of the Second Vatican Council, with its astonishingly eu-
phoric effect upon Catholic life and thought, reopened the question of
the conciliar nature of ecclesiastical governance. A growing body of
theological, canonical, and historical work suggests that the hierarchical
understanding of power in the Church, if it is to be truly faithful to
gospel values and Christian experience, must be qualified by a weight-
ier emphasis on the communion of all the local churches, on the collegiality of bishops and indeed of all the People of God. These notions
played an important and positive role in Vatican II. The movement away
from these conciliar values during the pontificate of Pope John Paul II
has been too obvious to require documentation. The so-called "restoration" papacy has set up a striking pattern of contrasts for those who remember the pre-Vatican II Church, who followed the events of Vatican
II, and then witnessed the departure of a kind of ecclesial *élan vital* and
the growth of a sense of malaise during the past several decades. It is not
necessary to list the number of closed seminaries, religious houses of
study, and colleges, the declining number of priests and religious, or the
decrease in Sunday Mass attendance to support the observation that the
vigor and enthusiasm of the 60s and early 70s has given way to a kind
of lethargy in some, indifference or apathy in others.

Reluctance to follow the progressive leads emerging from Vatican
II was not really surprising given the tensions at the council and the

curial opposition to the very project itself. But it is the *persistent* character of the opposition to reform which has proven so ennervating and demoralizing as the Church approaches its third millennium. The People of God looked for a Church that would be liturgically alive and meaningful, that would practice justice and establish equality, that would institutionalize collegiality and subsidiarity. The ecclesial experience of the second half of the twentieth century has instead been characterized by inquisitions, demands for oaths of fidelity, suspicion of episcopal initiatives, refusal to admit women to positions of leadership, and attempts to limit academic freedom in Catholic institutions of higher learning. Sad to say, these are not offset by a few productive overtures to Protestants, Jews, and Muslims, the admission of girls as Mass servers, and papal statements condemning violence, war, and moral relativism but approving of democracy (but not for the Church!) and capitalism.

Vatican II and Pope Paul VI clearly wanted the post-conciliar Church to be a collegial Church, rather than the heavily monarchical Church canonized by Vatican I in the previous century. The episcopal Synod of 1967 reflected the collegial understanding of its members and gave substantial impetus to the conciliar agenda.[1] Despite his approval of the conciliar teaching on collegiality, Paul VI found it personally difficult to implement. His anti-collegial prohibition of the discussion of birth control by the council and his later promulgation of *Humanae vitae* against the overwhelming recommendation of the commission he had appointed to study the issue shows how ambivalent was his acceptance of collegiality. Commentators were not slow to discern that *Humanae vitae* marked a turning point in the post-conciliar Church. Priests and theologians found it necessary to express in public their inability to accept the central apodictic claim of the encyclical that each and every act of marital intercourse must remain open to the possibility of conception; laypeople found its tenor foreign to their experience of marriage and, by ignoring its demands, rejected its authority. Some analysts attribute to the encyclical a decline in contributions to the Church, a slackening attendance at Sunday Mass, and a general erosion of Catholic identity.[2] Already in 1969 Francis Oakley could write that "there is developing a growing unease about the very possibility of institutional reform, an unease deepening in some circles into a more fundamental disenchantment with the very church-institution itself—a shift, as it were, from the accommodating categories of gradualism to the bleak perspectives of abolitionism."[3] Despite substantial contrary advice and well-reasoned scholarly recommendations the Vatican promulgated a revised Code of Canon Law patterned on the much-criticized 1917 Code. The recently-won insight that the Church was a historically conditioned institution was all but ignored in an attempt to canonize a mostly pre-conciliar and non-collegial conception of the Church. William Bassett asserted that "the new code of canon law . . . dilutes and . . . betrays the expectation the Council gave to the Christian people. [It] will end the work of the Council by institutionalizing the most minimal interpretation of its principles."[4] Ladislas Örsy agrees that "we have a *Code* that does not go the whole way in applying Vatican II."[5]

The insight of the council fathers that collegiality, along with the development of workable collegial structures in the Church, is an appropriate response to the problems of modern times, was warmly greeted as one of the most promising developments of Vatican II. "Collegiality" had a modern ring for it responded to contemporary notions of individual responsibility, shared decision-making, the need for broad-based information sources, as well as the new understanding of the laity as contributors to ecclesial governance processes. Unfortunately, collegiality has its enemies in the Roman curia. From that pinnacle of power we learn that the curia itself is the permanent embodiment of collegiality.[6] Since the council, several national groups of bishops have been "put in their place" by the present pontiff, one (or more?) even scolded by his shaking finger.

History and Conciliar Theology

With the death of collegiality the Church seems to be at a dead end. Several sympathetic scholars have suggested that new attention ought to be given to the theology of conciliarism as a possible way out of our present dilemma. Their studies have made it clear that medieval conciliar theology was not the product of radical reformers or of antipapal activism. Brian Tierney has shown that the roots of the conciliar theory go back to the great popes of the Middle Ages and has pointed to Innocent III's Lateran Council IV as a model of the ideal council to which all constituent elements of the Church were invited.[7] Conciliar theology reached its apogee and finest expression in the fifteenth century in Nicholas of Cusa's *De concordantia catholica* (1433). Presented to the fathers of the Council of Basel, the work is a comprehensive treatment based on Scripture, the writings of the Church Fathers, the ecumenical councils, canon law, history, and philosophy. Although it is the optimistic and idealistic work of a young canonist, its conclusions are balanced, sober, and highly respectful of the papal office. Because it makes use of some of the best religious resources of the Catholic tradition its positions should be re-examined for possible rehabilitation by the wise householder "who brings out from his storeroom things both new and old" (Matt 13:52).[8]

It was precisely this looking back through Church history that the German canonist-theologian adopted as his principle method in reconstructing the Church's constitution. The De concordantia catholica is a veritable treasure house of historical evidence. As Cusanus explains in its Preface: "I have collected many original sources that have long been lost in the armories of ancient cloisters. Those who read these things therefore should be aware that they have been quoted here from the ancient originals rather than from some abbreviated collection."[9]

Cusanus shared some of the elements of Renaissance humanism's program for the moral reconstruction of society, and he had himself participated in the search for manuscripts containing the writings of classical authors. The Italian humanists, some as members of the Roman curia, looked to classical antiquity for rhetorical models and images which might help bring about a rebirth of society and culture. Cusanus used the new historical-critical method to discover the actual relationships which had existed between the several constituent and jurisdictional elements of the Church.[10] It is interesting to note that one of the more important results of Vatican II involved a new appreciation of the radical historicity of human events and institutions, including the Church. Thus relativized, structures and norms can be "reformed" and adapted to modern conditions. Although there are substantial differences between the views of Vatican II theologians and Renaissance thinkers like Cusanus, an appreciation of the "discontinuity of history" is very evident in the latter's work.[11]

Erich Meuthen has given some attention to Cusanus's use of the historical method in arriving at a conception of the Church's constitution and has correctly pointed to the paradox at the root of this approach. The paradigmatic, normative nature of events in Christian history all but dissolved when the Church moved beyond the apostolic age. Subsequent events, in their radical historicity, were human products and as such lacked dogmatic finality. History and the canon law enshrined in historical documents are filled with contradictions and divergent practices and so can serve the cause of constitutional reform only if brought to some sort of harmonization, a *concordantia*. Gratian himself is the classic example of this dynamic. Cusanus was certainly imitating the *magister* whose *Concordantia discordantium canonum* formed the basis of the *Corpus iuris canonici*, a work which Cusanus himself had mastered as a *doctor decretorum*. But even a harmonization of historical documents does not deliver them from their inherent conditionedness, from their radical relativity. So Meuthen leaves Cusanus mired in the essential relativities of history and canon law even while admitting the importance of his work for the history of the political thought in the era succeeding him.[12]

While it is true that harmonized or not, historical events remain historical and no mere assertions that they are "inspired" or are "infallible" can raise them to a meta-historical level, O'Malley's work reminds us that the task of de-absolutizing the status quo is basic to any reform movement.[13] So Cusanus's reformist instinct was correct. By showing that ecclesiastical structures, especially the papacy and the general council, have taken different forms over the ages, he was able to disabuse his contemporaries of that peculiarly Catholic misconception that the Church always was as it is today, that "as it was in the beginning, is now, and ever shall be, world without end." Cusanus did, in fact, attempt to derive more from "concordance" than that. He believed that concord was a sign of the work of the Holy Spirit so that where there was harmony and agreement there was truth and God. This is a beautiful Christian sentiment, but its fragility as a foundation for reform is revealed as soon as an opponent shows the discord that is the shadow side of all concord.

We cannot leave Cusanus in the mere relativities of the historical record, for he was not just a canonist-historian. As we shall see, for all its use of historical documents and the records of ancient councils, the *De concordantia catholica* does not base its central argument on these. Cusanus seems himself to have realized something of his dilemma. He knew from experience that the council fathers could use the evidence of history to defend divergent causes. This may partly account for the "overkill" of the *De concordantia catholica*—as if the sheer number of authorities on his side might be conclusive. This marshalling of authorities has always characterized the lawyer's approach. The importance of Cusanus's work lies not so much in its canonistic impressiveness as in its deeper basis in the divine and natural law. And it is precisely this natural law root-system which delivered his theory from the mere relativities of history and made it useful in subsequent centuries as political theorists went on to forge the foundations of modern democratic society.[14]

Natural Equality and Human Freedom

Nicholas of Cusa's conception of the structure of the Church is startling in its grasp of Christian ideals. More than three centuries before the democratic movements in America and France, our German canonist enunciated the truths that by nature all human beings are free, that government must therefore be based on the consent of the governed and this requires the election of all those who represent them, and that law is binding only to the extent that it is received by those subject to it. These ideals flow from the heart of the Christian gospel and were inherent, though often latent, in Christ's Church from its inception. Though they have been articulated and practiced in an incomplete or imperfect fashion over the centuries they nonetheless belong to the very essence of the Christian faith. It is therefore not surprising that ecclesiastical reformers throughout the centuries have hearkened to these truths as they called for their more perfect embodiment at all levels of the Church's organization.

The bedrock upon which the Cusan conception of society rests is the natural, divinely given equality of all human beings. According to Paul Sigmund, "the first orthodox writer to use the doctrine of original equality in a meaningful political way was Nicholas of Cusa." He was the only conciliarist who "based his consent theory on the doctrine of the original natural equality and freedom of all mankind."[15] As Cusanus states it:

> For since all are by nature free, every governance whether it consists in a written law or is living law in the person of a prince—by which subjects are compelled to abstain from evil deeds and their freedom directed towards the good through fear of punishment—can only come from the agreement and consent of the subjects. For if by nature men are equal in power and equally free, the true properly ordered authority of one common ruler who is their equal in power cannot be naturally established except by the election and consent of the others and law is also established by consent.[16]

When Cusanus says that human beings are "by nature free" he is quite aware that he is speaking of the divine law, there being no distinction for him between the law of nature and the law of God. In some sense, indeed, the term "law of nature" suggests a firmer basis than "law of God," a term somewhat weakened by overuse in the ecclesiastical sphere. The law of nature is known to human beings by reason: "All legislation is based on natural law and any law which contradicts it cannot be valid. . . . Hence since natural law is naturally based on reason, all law is rooted by nature in the reason of man."[17] Upon a firm basis in the natural law of human equality and freedom Cusanus goes on to erect his system of representative and consensual government. These principles, consent and representation, are the cornerstones of Cusanus's conciliar theology and are inherent to his conception of the Church as a corporation.[18] He saw them underlying the Church's law and operative throughout its history.

Rooted as it is in the law of nature itself, human equality and therefore the human liberty, which is its corollary, really need no further buttressing. But Cusanus gives them additional and incontrovertible support by showing that Christ himself recognizes and respects this natural liberty: "Only one who comes of his own free will and not under compulsion is acceptable to Christ. Therefore in its basis from Christ all spiritual power is properly founded in freedom and not in coercion."[19] Cusanus made frequent reference, as did many conciliar canonists, to the doctrine of the Mystical Body of Christ and the Pauline notion of the Church as the "spouse" of Christ. The spiritual marriage of Christ and his church requires free consent:

> On this point for one body to be established in a harmony of subjects and ruler, reason and natural and divine law all require that there be mutual consent in this spiritual marriage which is demonstrated by the election by all and the consent of the one elected, just as a spiritual marriage is rightly established by consent between Christ and his church. . . . Thus although the sacraments can be given to someone against his will, this is not the case with matrimony since consent is of the essence there.[20]

Here we also see the indebtedness of the canon lawyer to classical Roman law which applied its well-elaborated notions of *consensus* to the contract of marriage in the maxim *"consensus facit nuptias"* (D. 50.17.30). Consent is of the essence in the entire relationship between Christ and his followers:

> I discussed first the freedom of Christ's law to which one adheres voluntarily and without coercion. Hence since Christ himself is the Way of our faith, the only thing necessary for salvation is Christ and free access to him. Therefore in the church which is descended from Christ there should be no coercion but rather grace flowing from the fullness of the source, the Head, down to the mystical Body of Christ.[21]

The radical equality and freedom of human beings did not mean for Cusanus that there were no distinctions among them. He knew that people were not equally wise or equally good; that is why they freely choose to have one who is wiser rule over them. But their choice and consent is necessary to establish a basis for law and government. This is true in the Church as in the empire. In fact, Nicholas's conception of society is of an elaborately structured, twofold hierarchical system embracing both Church and empire. As Sigmund put it, "the principle of hierarchy was one of the central organizing conceptions of Cusanus's political theory, as it was of medieval society."[22] At first glance it might appear that hierarchy and equality are incompatible partners as indeed they are in traditional societies. What delivers hierarchy from a socially unproductive dominance or superiority, in the conception of Cusanus, are the principles of consent and representation. Free and equal human beings choose or elect other individuals to exercise rulership over them. Without such choice rulership is tyranny and laws are invalid: "They are called tyrants as usurpers of authority who are neither asked to rule nor elected" and "The binding force of every law consists in concord and tacit or express consent. . . ."[23]

So, the core argument upon which Cusanus's conciliar doctrine of the Church is based flows directly from the law of nature and its creator: all human beings are by nature equal. No person or persons may claim natural power or authority over another, i.e., human beings are by nature not only equal but therefore free. By choice and consent human beings may subject themselves to rulers and to law. They do this by choosing their rulers and by accepting law. They may exercise this choice either directly or through their freely chosen representatives. This is, in short, the essential argument of the *De concordantia catholica*. It remains to examine its implications for such structures as the papacy, the episcopacy, and ecclesiastical councils.

The Papacy in a Conciliar Church

Studies in the history of conciliar thought now agree that there was no one "conciliarism." Rather, there were many positions on the relationship between the papacy and the general council which held that under certain conditions the general council exercises supreme power in the Church. There were conciliarists, especially at the Council of Basel, who saw in the general council even executive and administrative jurisdiction over the day-to-day affairs of the Church. On the other side of the spectrum were those who allowed to the general council only emergency oversight in the specific case of a pope who defected from the faith. The latter refers to the classic canonical position, discussed in Gratian's *Decretum*, that the pope "can be judged by no one unless he is discovered straying from the faith."[24] On this spectrum, Nicholas of Cusa holds what he himself termed an "intermediate" position:

> And thus it was necessary to ask what was the authority of the Roman pontiff both as to rulership and as to the power to command and to legislate. And although I have used many arguments, I have emphasized this one—that although according to the writings of many of the holy Fathers the power of the Roman pontiff is from God

and according to others it comes from man and the universal council, it seems that in fact the intermediate position demonstrable in the Scriptures finally comes to this, that the power of the Roman pontiff as to preeminence, priority, and rulership, is from God by way of man and the councils; namely by means of elective consent.[25]

The *De concordantia catholica* is extremely respectful of the papal office and sees in it the true primacy and rulership over all members of the Church. "Just as Peter was prince of the apostles, the Roman pontiff is prince of the bishops since the bishops succeeded the apostles."[26] Whoever does not adhere to the unity of the chair of Peter is outside the unity of the Church:

> There is but one *cathedra* by succession to Peter upon whom the church was founded, and we are certain that the gates of hell will not prevail against it. From this we should conclude that whoever says that he is a Christian must of necessity say that his chair is joined to the chair of the successors of St. Peter and is united in association with that chair. Otherwise he is not a Christian.[27]

Cusanus is careful to emphasize that the primacy belongs not to an individual person as such but to the see of Rome. This see became primatial because of the rank of the city of Rome. If the primacy of a see depended upon the sanctity of the first one to exercise authority there, or because of reverence for the location, Jerusalem would be the first, Cusanus says. If the Church so wishes it could transfer the primacy to another location because "rulership would not cease in the Church even if the episcopal see of the city of Rome ceased to exist."[28]

Cusanus's "intermediate" position reconciles the theological position that papal primacy, and spiritual rulership of any kind, comes from God, with the natural law—and historically confirmed—position that governance requires the consent of the governed:

> And so I adhere to the conclusion that the primacy in the church is established in its reality by Christ through the church for the purpose of church unity and is intended by God as a ministry for its service. And in my judgment the arguments on the one side that coercive rulership in the church comes only from God, and on the other side that it exists only by the election and consent of men and the church, are correctly harmonized in this intermediate position.[29]

The position may be "intermediate" with respect to those who hold differing views, but in no sense does Cusanus think it is intermediate with respect to its truth. He finds it firmly anchored in reason, revelation, and in the tradition of the Church. It was corroborated by the dynamics of the incarnation itself:

> Therefore all rulership is sacred and spiritual and comes from God. Rulership also comes from man, just as Christ was the true son of the Virgin Mary. Hence Christ was born, God and man, of the uncorrupted and unstained Virgin by her own free consent when she said, "Be it done unto me according to thy word." On this model true rule over the one uncorrupted church or congregation of men should result from the purest consent, not from violence, or ambition, or criminal simony, but from the purity with which Christ deigned to come into the world out of love for the salvation of the people.[30]

This marriage of the divine and human in establishing the supreme rulership of the Church marks a decisive break in the Neoplatonic economy of power. Ecclesiastical hierarchy and papal primacy is no simple movement from God, through Christ, to the pope, and on downward. While continuing to yield to the understandable allure of a comprehensive hierarchy, Nicholas's insistence that consent or election is an essential component in the establishment of all human rulership, really does irreparable, indeed fatal, damage to the hierarchical structure of the world.[31]

The pope is, of course, not the bishop of the whole Church, the universal bishop. He is the one member of the Church who, more than any other member, represents the Church. But, like Peter his predecessor, his representation is "obscure" and "subject to error." He represents the Church "in a very uncertain way."[32] There are other "figures" of the Church which represent it in a more comprehensive way, representations which are "more certain and true." The entire episcopacy throughout the world obviously represents the Church more truly and if one adds the entire priesthood the representation would be still more complete. And if all these were actually elected by their people, representation would be ideal.

Conciliarists were generally agreed that the Church could never be without its supreme spiritual authority, in view of the promise and endowment of Christ. They did not all agree on the precise locus of this power under ordinary circumstances, i.e., when a validly elected, orthodox pope was in office. Nicholas's friend at Basel, John of Segovia, held that power is an accident inhering in the Church as subject. It is intrinsic to the Church but not to the pope, the latter holding power only because the Church has conferred it. Nor can the Church ever alienate this power from itself for it pertains to its very essence, much less vest it in a single person, for "the very nature of ecclesiastical power is such that it cannot reside in a single person."[33] Nicholas does not use the subject-accident language but does agree that because it is a *congregatio* of many members, no one person can possess its legislative power. With Segovia he agreed that "supreme authority must belong to an entity composed of many members."[34]

On the matter of the hierarchical structure of the Church, Cusanus made the observation that the various ranks of the hierarchy do not pertain to the essence of the Church, only the priesthood, which is as "one soul, having the power to govern and vivify, from the obedience and consent of the faithful, but above all from the legation of Christ" enjoys this status. As he put it in his treatise on the conciliar presidency:

> We then conclude that the administrations and ranks, from the episcopacy to the papacy inclusive, were ordained by Christ, through the mediation of the church, in order to avoid schism. Nevertheless, they are not essential to the existence of the church, but to its well-being. The priesthood, however, is essential. And since the administrative ranks in the church are accidental, they add nothing in themselves to the basis of the sacerdotal power of binding and loosing, because all priests are equal in this.[35]

Cusanus knew enough Scripture and history carefully to note that though the various ranks were "ordained by Christ" it was "through the mediation of the church." The implication seems clear that should the Church itself determine, for its own well-being, to modify the "administrative ranks" this would seem to be well within its mandate from Christ. Cusanus is careful not to confuse ecclesiastical jurisdiction with the Church's role in the divine economy of salvation.

Representation and the Councils

From his study of the sources, Nicholas was very much aware of a Church that was made up of distinct provinces and dioceses and that over the centuries their synods and councils had forged the great body of canons and norms governing the Church:

> But there are different conciliar gatherings ranking from the lowest through various intermediate grades up to the highest universal synod. A curate gathers a synod of his parish, and there is a diocesan synod above him, above which is the metropolitan synod, and above that the provincial synod in the kingdom or nation, over which is the patriarchal [council] and the greatest of all is the council of the universal Catholic church.[36]

The right to call such assemblies belongs to the authority presiding over that body or to his representative. In the case of the general council that right belongs to the pope and "ordinarily it is not legitimate to hold a universal council without him or his authorization."[37] Although all eight of the ecumenical councils were called by the emperor and not by the reigning pope, the pope or his representative was always present. This remains the norm: the pope or his representative must be present at the general council "provided that he is at least willing and able to be present. Otherwise, if the council waits for him and he does not send anyone or does not come or does not wish to do so, the council ought to provide for its needs and for the welfare of the church."[38]

When matters of faith are involved there is no doubt that these fall properly under the purview of the Roman pontiff, "so his council is first in matters of faith among all the patriarchal councils." He lamented the fact that in his day "the universal council of the Catholic Church and the patriarchal council of the Roman see are the same, since the whole Church has been reduced to a single patriarchate"[39] for he believed that the more comprehensive of the entire Church was the representative character of the general council, the more certain its decrees and the more likely its legislation would find acceptance. On the matter of who should be present at a general council the *De concordantia catholica* is completely practical: "I do not think that the laity or clergy should be admitted indiscriminately, but I think that qualified learned churchmen should be included in making decisions since the common good of the church is being sought and it does not matter from what source it came, providing only that it is found."[40]

A principle which finds repeated statement in the *De concordantia catholica* is that the force of the canons of a general council derives "not from the pope nor from the head of the council but only from a single concordant consent."[41] Other statements of the same general principle are:

> The obligatory force of the statutes also requires consent through use and acceptance. . . . And it is frequently found in all councils that the canons of past councils are confirmed in order to renew their force, to show that they are agreed to and accepted and to renew any canons that may have [been] abrogated through non-observance.[42]
>
> The binding force of particular statutes as they apply to subjects depends on usage and acceptance. . . . And it is also true of the statutes of the Roman pontiff that they lose their force through non-usage.[43]
>
> In order for his [the pope's] statute to be binding it is not sufficient for it to be publicly promulgated but it should also be accepted and approved in usage. . . .[44]

The authority to adopt canons does not depend solely on the pope but on universal consent. And against this conclusion no prescriptive right or custom can have any validity, just as it cannot do so against divine or natural law from which this is drawn as a conclusion.[45]

The binding power of the canons is derived from consent, for unless we could argue validity from usage and a law could be abrogated by not being observed, there would be no salvation. Who can know in what ways our teaching has been added to, or changed from, that of the Four Councils without our incurring condemnation, or when certain sacraments were introduced in the councils, or how we could evade the numberless penalties of automatic excommunication, deposition and the like contained in the canons, if in all of these matters concord and consent, usage and non-usage, did not help us?[46]

This last point is of special application in the Church where the sanctions leveled against disobedience frequently involve consequences that have eternal significance. Cusanus knows that ignorance of the law would excuse from moral culpability but that is not always true with regard to legal consequences.

One of the most important discoveries of the *De concordantia catholica* is that in certain circumstances the general council has an authority which is broader than that of the pope: "Hence it can be said in general that a universal council that represents the Catholic Church has power directly from Christ and is in every respect over both the pope and the Apostolic See."[47] Cusanus then goes on to illustrate this conclusion with "many conciliar actions and canons and proofs from reason." History has shown that the general council has power to depose a pope, not only for heresy but for other faults including misrule. The governing principle is stated quite directly: "No rational person can doubt that a council which represents the church has power over the papacy to direct its occupant in accordance with the needs of the church which is greater than the decision of one man concerning a papal office which has been given to him in the name of the church and for its benefit."[48]

None of the conciliar thinkers surpassed Nicholas in his development of the need for elections throughout the entire Church. He even went so far as to describe a step-by-step procedure, from construction of ballots to the final tally, for elections in Church and empire. Special to his sense of representation was the provision that laypeople elect their parish priests for in his hierarchical conception of society he saw the priesthood as a kind of soul of the body of the Church; election and consent provided the unity between soul and body.[49] He outlined a kind of "hierarchy of representation" in Book II:

> Hence if right order is to be preserved . . . parish priests and cu-
> rates are [to be] elected or at least some convenient provision is [to be]
> made for consent to their appointment. . . . Then the clergy should
> elect the bishop with the consent of the laity . . . and the bishops the
> metropolitan with the consent of the clergy. The metropolitans of the
> provinces with the consent of the bishops should elect the represen-
> tatives of the provinces who assist the pope and are called cardinals
> and those cardinals should elect the pope, if possible with the consent
> of the metropolitans. . . . This would mean that the Roman pontiff
> would have with him a continuing council which legitimately repre-
> sents the whole church. With this council, there is no doubt the
> church would be ruled in the best possible fashion.[50]

Although Cusanus surely knew the Roman law principle *Quod omnes
tangit ab omnibus iudicetur* ("what affects everyone should be decided
by everyone") he does not quote it verbatim in the *De concordantia
catholica*. The closest he comes is his citation of Ivo of Chartres'
Panormia which states: "The one who is seen to be over all should be
elected and ordained by all." Cusanus goes on to explain that the word
"should" is a word of necessity, that is, "it cannot be otherwise."[51]
Whether or not the Church would be ruled "in the best possible fashion" under the system Cusanus outlined, there is little doubt that his
idea would certainly be welcomed by many voiceless Catholics in a
post-Vatican II Church who are thirsting for collegiality and a sense of
participation.

Concord and *Consensus fidelium*

It may seem surprising that the notion of *concordantia* is found last in
our considerations. After all, Nicholas had placed it first. He begins
Book I of the *De concordantia catholica* by defining the Church as "a concordance of all rational spirits united in sweet harmony with Christ,
the Way, the Truth, and the Life, who is the Spouse of the church."[52]
His description of the Church is glowing and idealistic:

> Concordance is the principle by which the Catholic Church is in
> harmony as one and many—in one lord and many subjects. Flowing
> from the one King of Peace with infinite concordance, a sweet spirit-
> ual harmony of agreement emanates in successive degrees to all its
> members who are subordinated and united to him. Thus one God is
> all things in all things. From the beginning we have been predestined
> for that marvelous harmonious peace belonging to the adopted sons
> of God through Jesus Christ who came down from heaven to bring all
> things to fulfillment.[53]

Concordance is of the very essence of the life of God: "Behold the ineffable concordance that exists in a God who is threefold and unitary."[54] Gerald Christianson has summarized the Cusan vision as one of "concord . . . undivided because God is undivided, and only God is sovereign." There is no conflict between natural equality and hierarchy because "both are given by God and are held together in harmony by the presence of the Holy Spirit."[55] *Concordantia* has the status of an ontological dynamic, not a mere desideratum, but a divine reality: "It is not human but divine that various men brought together in complete freedom of speech should come to agreement as one."[56] Where this does occur, we can be sure it is a sign of the activity of the Holy Spirit. When matters of faith are being discussed *concordantia* is all the more important for "the greater the agreement the more infallible the judgment."[57]

For Cusanus, this principle applies also to the realm of general knowledge where it also has profound social implications. Because of the very nature of finite being which is what it is because of participation in Being Itself, truth can be found only step-by-step and always imperfectly, as *coniectura*. Whenever individuals seeking knowledge come to agreement out of the differences of their opinions, it is clear that they have taken a step nearer the truth. So the very search for knowledge is a social undertaking and all knowledge attained is a social achievement.[58]

In the *De concordantia catholica* Cusanus is particularly concerned to show how the divine principle of *concordantia* applies to a general council:

> Now this is an essential requirement for a universal council at which general matters are to be discussed that a hearing be given to all in complete freedom, not in secret but publicly. If anything is then defined by general agreement it is considered to be inspired by the Holy Spirit and infallibly decided by Christ who is present among those gathered in his name.[59]

The principle of open consultation has deep roots in Christian governance and spirituality and was well established in medieval society by the fifteenth century. Paul Sigmund has given a summary description of the various bodies in which consent enjoyed an institutionalized role and shows how Cusanus's position differed in being based on the natural equality of persons.[60] Monastic institutions had long practiced forms of consultation, election, and representation. One thinks of the simple and straightforward advice to the abbot given in the *Rule of Benedict*:

> Whenever any weighty matters have to be transacted in the
> monastery let the abbot call together the community and himself pro-
> pose the matter for discussion. After hearing the advice of the
> brethren let him consider it in his own mind, and then do what he
> shall judge most expedient. We ordain that all must be called to coun-
> cil, because the Lord often reveals to a younger member what is
> best.[61]

No one mistakes this for "democracy" but we note that *all* must be
called and no distinction of persons is made. The divine presence in
the gathering is assumed from Scripture (Matt 18:20) and a spiritual
axiom about the relationship between the Lord and the lowliest member of the group provides justification for the rule. Predating the *De
concordantia catholica* by nine centuries, its principles had a gradual but
deep and widespread influence on Christian spirituality.[62] Nicholas of
Cusa's requirement that in a general council all should be able to speak
freely was certainly not novel. What was novel and indeed striking
was his view that everyone in the universal Church has a voice in determining those who would represent them in the overall governance
of the Church.

Thus, it is clear that for Cusanus *consensus fidelium* is not something which can be divined by ecclesiastical rulers if, indeed, they
cared at all to determine it. A universal system of elected representatives would provide a network of communication and consultation.
Cusanus complained that even when consultation was readily available the Roman curia seemed to have little concern to practice it:

> Today however even if they [the cardinals] are present at the
> Roman curia, as foreigners they are not summoned to the papal coun-
> cil. This is absurd, especially when a case involving the universal
> church or a matter in some way affecting the whole church is under
> consideration. Hence it seems necessary to create such representa-
> tives of the provinces as cardinals for many worthwhile reasons as
> any intelligent person who has any knowledge of the procedure of
> the Roman curia will easily recognize.[63]

For Nicholas this contact with the people was not a grudging conde-
scension. He described as a "beautiful idea" that "all power, whether
spiritual or temporal and corporeal, is potentially in the people, although
in order for the power to rule to be activated there must necessarily be
the concurrence of that formative radiance from above to establish it in
being since it is true that all power is from above."[64] The traditional notion of the *consensus fidelium* would include "that formative radiance

from above" because wherever there is concord and agreement there is the Holy Spirit.

If Nicholas of Cusa had his way, the Church would be what Peter Scharr calls a "universal community of communication." Here truth is established not by assertion or by authority but by a process of discourse and reasoned argumentation. The inter-subjectivity of the divine Trinity, the absolute of interpersonal communication, would be emulated and mirrored in the Church.[65] As an ongoing dynamic process excluding no one, this would fit Cusanus's understanding of the entire process by which humanity progresses from *coniecturae* to ever more precise and adequate *coniecturae,* approximations to truth. It is interesting that even twentieth-century scientists have come to replace objective and definitive notions of truth, so-called matters of fact, with the notion of "approximations to truth"—seeing science itself as a kind of self-correcting system of interpersonal communication.

So, even though Cusanus begins his *De concordantia catholica* with the notion of *concordantia*, it is clear that he sees it as a goal, one that must ever be transcended in more perfect concord and consensus, until the final day when all shall find final union in that concordance, which is "the highest truth itself."[66]

Conclusion

Josef Lortz described Nicholas of Cusa as "the most powerful intellectual genius of the German fifteenth century." Among those of his era he was "the only fully Catholic expression of the liberty of the Christian man, of the autonomy of the human spirit within, and in allegiance to, the Church. . . ."[67] If this is true it is precisely because of the primary importance, in his ecclesiology, of the gospel principles of freedom and equality, and the concomitant need for consent and representation, at all levels of Christian life. Absolutism in the papacy as in the empire is simply tyranny, understandable among the Gentiles but not among the followers of Christ (Matt 20:25).

The contemporary call for a more democratic Church, for a constitutional council which would give formal expression to the principles of freedom and equality, consent and representation, is an echo of a call made over five centuries ago by Nicholas of Cusa and his fellow conciliarists. It was clear to them as it is to many thinkers today that Christ's Church is a conciliar Church. As E. F. Jacob put it:

> Is not the Church at its finest . . . not when it is presenting an ironclad unity to its critics, but when it is applying its dialectic to the choice between conflicting ideas and cannot yet clarify its mind in its

> internal differences? In other words, when the possible intellect is
> being exercised to the utmost in a supremely spiritual cause?[68]

Cusanus himself seems to have realized only at the end of his life what a fateful step he took when he gave up hope in the Council of Basel and yielded to the allure of papal monarchy. Even then he had wished that a kind of council of cardinals would represent the Church in papal decision-making. He found out that he had been wrong, that monarchs need not take advice.

Contemporary scholarship and the ecclesiastical experience of the last century make us ever more appreciative of the truth and indeed of the wisdom of Nicholas of Cusa's *De concordantia catholica*. Elements of his vision seem nearly made-to-order as a solution for the present impasse in the Church, a means to bridge the "frightening gulf" which "separates the Church of today from the original constitution of the Church."[69] His work makes it clear that whatever the current Code of Canon Law may say about the general council, about its convocation and its structure, and about its total subordination to the Roman pontiff, the facts of history tell a different story. As Nicholas explained, convocation by the pope is not required for the validity of the general council; otherwise the first seven ecumenical councils would be invalid. Furthermore, he makes it clear that matters once decided by a general council may fall into desuetude thus losing their normative character, or they may be rejected, modified, or qualified by later councils—much the way the First Vatican Council treated the decrees of the Council of Constance. The views of the Fathers of the Church, of the great theologians and canonists, of the general councils themselves, which support the positive and definitive role of the general council in the life of the Church, cannot be dismissed as aberrations or as subversive of Christian principles. Certainly in their more moderate expression, in a thinker like Cusanus, they are rather illustrative of a *consensus fidelium*. The *consensus fidelium*, always considered a norm of Christian truth, is not located in the papacy or in the Vatican curia. It can only find true expression in a general council that most adequately represents the whole Church.

So, the conciliar constitution of the Church is no novel idea. It is, in fact, a very old idea. Nicholas of Cusa found it gathering dust in the archives of ancient monasteries. He did not construct a new theory: the old, classical Christian sources, when examined carefully, yield the image of a church that is, quite simply, a conciliar Church from New Testament times onward. Cusanus's contribution was to delve beneath the surface to expose the radical human freedom and equality presupposed by the gospel and to show some of the implications of that freedom and equality for the governance of the Church. History is on the side of Cusanus. It has shown that whenever the Church has found itself in deepest difficulty it was the general council which gave it a new lease on life. This is surely not cause for surprise. What is surprising is that there are still those who find the emphasis on the conciliar nature of the Church—sheer common sense to most Christians today—to be subversive, even heretical. But common sense and historical evidence are, perhaps, no match for institutional inertia and entrenched power.

NOTES

1. Peter Hebblethwaite, "The Synod of Bishops," in Adrian Hastings, ed., *Modern Catholicism: Vatican II and After* (London: SPCK; New York: Oxford University Press, 1991) 203.

2. "Weekly church attendance rates among the 53 million members [of the American Catholic Church] declined almost immediately from around 70 percent to approximately 50 percent after Pope Paul VI issued the birth control encyclical in 1968." Andrew Greeley and Mary Greeley Durkin, *How to Save the Catholic Church* (New York: Viking, 1984) 3–4.

3. *Council Over Pope? Towards a Provisional Ecclesiology* (New York: Herder & Herder, 1969) 16–7.

4. "Canon Law and Reform: An Agenda for a New Beginning," in David Tracy, et al., eds., *Toward Vatican III: The Work That Needs to Be Done* (New York: Seabury Press, 1978) 196.

5. "The Revision of Canon Law," in *Modern Catholicism: Vatican II and After,* Adrian Hastings, ed. (London: SPCK; New York: Oxford University Press, 1991) 211. Eugenio Corecco, "Aspects of the Reception of Vatican II in the Code of Canon Law," in *The Reception of Vatican II,* G. Alberigo, J.-P. Jossua, and J. A. Komonchak, eds. (Washington, D.C.: The Catholic University of America Press, 1987) 249–96, offers impressive arguments revealing the failure of the revised Code to reflect the teaching of the council in such fundamental areas as the *sensus fidelium,* the need for dejuridicizing the Church, and the synodal structure of the universal Church.

6. Jan Grootaers, "The Collegiality of the Synod of Bishops: An Unresolved Problem," in *Collegiality Put to the Test,* James Provost and Knut Walf, eds., *Concilium* 1990/4 (London: SCM Press; Philadelphia: Trinity Press International, 1990) 27.

7. *Foundations of the Conciliar Theory: The Contribution of the Medieval Canonists from Gratian to the Great Schism* (Cambridge: Cambridge University Press, 1955) 47.

8. Paul Sigmund, *Nicholas of Cusa and Medieval Political Thought* (Cambridge, Mass.: Harvard University Press, 1963) 11, called the *De concordantia catholica* "the last and most nearly complete expression" of the theories of the conciliar movement. Brian Tierney, *Religion, Law, and the Growth of*

Constitutional Thought 1150–1650 (Cambridge: Cambridge University Press, 1982) 66, referred to the same work as "the most impressive synthesis" of the ideas of the conciliar movement. In the present discussion the terms "conciliarism," "conciliarist," and "conciliar" will be used to refer to any position which asserts that the general council has any authority at all over a reigning pope. The attempts of some scholars to establish a clear terminological distinction between "conciliar" and "conciliarism," and to label the latter "heretical" is tendentious and idiosyncratic. For an example, cf. August Franzen, "The Council of Constance: Present State of the Problem," *Historical Problems in Church Renewal, Concilium* 7 (New York: Paulist, 1965) 45–6, 50–1.

   9. *De concordantia catholica* [hereafter *DCC*], 2 (3): "Originalia enim multa longo abusu perdita per veterum coenobiorum armaria non sine magna diligentia collegi. Credant igitur, qui legerint, quia omnia ex antiquis originalibus, non ex cuiusquam abbreviata collectione, huc attracta sunt." The critical edition of this treatise is Nicolai de Cusa, *Opera Omnia iussu et auctoritate Academiae Litterarum Heidelbergensis ad codicum fidem edita*, XIV: *De concordantia catholica*, Gerhardus Kallen, ed. (Hamburg: Felix Meiner, 1939–1969). The translation is quoted from Nicholas of Cusa, *The Catholic Concordance*, ed. and trans. by Paul E. Sigmund (Cambridge: Cambridge University Press, 1991). Citations are by *Opera Omnia* paragraph numbers with translation page number in parentheses. The present discussion will offer substantial quotations from the *De concordantia catholica* so as to allow Nicholas of Cusa to speak for himself. Many of his ideas have a surprisingly "modern" ring, lending support to John P. Dolan's characterization of Cusanus as "spokesman for a new era." Cf. his introduction to *Unity and Reform: Selected Writings of Nicholas de Cusa* (Notre Dame, Ind.: University of Notre Dame Press, 1962) 52. In addition to Paul Sigmund, *Nicholas of Cusa*, other important studies of the *De concordantia catholica* are Morimichi Watanabe, *The Political Ideas of Nicholas of Cusa with Special Reference to His De Concordantia Catholica* (Geneva, 1963); Andreas Posch, *Die 'Concordantia Catholica' des Nikolaus von Cues* (Paderborn, 1930); and Herman Josef Sieben, "Der Konzilstraktat des Nikolaus von Kues: De Concordantia Catholica," *Annuarium Historiae Conciliorum* 14, 1(1982) 171–226.

   10. Werner Krämer, *Konsens und Rezeption: Verfassungsprinzipien der Kirche im Basler Konziliarismus*, Beiträge zur Geschichte der Philosophie und Theologie des Mittelalters, 19 (Münster: Aschendorff, 1980) 259–64, discusses Cusanus and "the historical method as a new instrument in the discovery of truth."

   11. Cf. John O'Malley, S.J., "Reform, Historical Consciousness, and Vatican II's Aggiornamento," *Theological Studies* 32 (1971) 573–601. Bernard Lonergan, "The Transition from a Classicist World-View to Historical-Mindedness, " in *Law for Liberty: The Role of Law in the Church Today,* James E. Biechler, ed. (Baltimore: Helicon, 1967) 126–33, discusses the theological relevance of an appreciation of the radical historicity of the Church. Cf. also Oakley, *Council Over Pope?* 152–4.

   12. Erich Meuthen, "Kanonistik und Geschichtverständnis: Über ein neuentdecktes Werk des Nikolaus von Kues: De maioritate auctoritatis sacrorum conciliorum supra auctoritatem papae," *Von Konstanz nach Trient: Beiträge zur Geschichte der Kirche von den Reformkonzilien bis zum Tridentinum*, Festgabe

für August Franzen (Munich, Paderborn, Vienna: Verlag Ferdinand Schöningh, 1972) 147–70. For a more recent appreciation of the dilemma theology faces in light of the understanding of the historical relativity of ecclesiastical structures cf. Roger Haight, "The Structure of the Church," *Journal of Ecumenical Studies* 30 (1993) 403–14. A brilliant analysis of the dynamic interrelationship between history and the life of the Christian believer is Giuseppe Ruggieri, "Faith and History," in *The Reception of Vatican II*, 91–114.

13. O'Malley, "Reform," 598ff.

14. Historians and political scientists are not yet in agreement on the specific influence of Nicholas of Cusa in the evolution of democratic government. It is probably not possible to arrive at clear specifics. For his place in the overall story cf. Brian Tierney, *Religion, Law and the Growth of Constitutional Thought 1150–1650* (Cambridge: Cambridge University Press, 1982). Cf. also Sigmund's introduction to Nicholas of Cusa, *The Catholic Concordance*, xxxiv, where Cusanus's possible influence on John Locke's thought is mentioned.

15. "The Concept of Equality in the Political Thought of Nicholas of Cusa," in *Nicolò Cusano agli inizi del Mondo Moderno: Atti del Congresso internazionale in occasione del V centenario della morte di Nicolò Cusano, Bressanone, 6–10 settembre 1964* (Florence: G. C. Sansoni, 1970) 512–3.

16. *DCC*, 127 (98): "Unde cum natura omnes sint liberi, tunc omnis principatus, sive consistat in lege scripta sive viva apud principem, per quem principatum coercentur a malis subditi et eorum regulatur libertas ad bonum metu poenarum, est a sola concordantia et consensu subiectivo. Nam si natura aeque potentes et aeque liberi homines sunt, vera et ordinata potestas unius communis aeque potentis naturaliter non nisi electione et consensu aliorum constitui potest, sicut etiam lex ex consensu constituitur."

17. *DCC*, 127 (98): "Omnis constitutio radicatur in iure naturali, et se ei contradicit, constitutio valida esse nequit. . . . Unde cum ius naturale naturaliter rationi insit, tunc connata est omnis lex homini in radice sua."

18. The corporation theory was fundamental and common to all conciliar canonists. Sigmund, *Nicholas of Cusa*, 112, states that Francisco Zabarella, a canonist with substantial influence on Cusanus, described the Church as a "hierarchy of corporations in which the members retain certain legal rights against the head." Cusanus, quoting Hincmar of Rheims on the council as a corporate body *(universitas)*, goes on to show that conciliar meetings are graded from high to low, from general council to parish synod convened by the pastor, a veritable "hierarchy of corporations." *DCC*, 70, 71 (50–1).

19. *DCC*, 260 (201): ". . . sufficit scire volentem et acquiescentem tantum et non coactum Christo acceptum, quare omnis spiritualis potestas in libertate et non coactione quantum ad ipsam radicem qua a Christo est proprie fundatur."

20. *DCC*, 164 (124): On the significance of the doctrine of the mystical body of Christ for conciliar thought cf. Francis Oakley, "Natural Law, the *Corpus Mysticum,* and Consent in Conciliar Thought from John of Paris to Matthias Ugonis," *Speculum* 56 (1981) 786–810. In this article the author also distinguishes between "the bulk of Conciliarists of whatever period, who were by and large content to rest their case on arguments drawn from the

Scriptures, Church history, canon law, and the Romano-canonistic tradition of representation and consent, and, on the other, that small but significant sub-group of thinkers . . . who contrived to bring those arguments into contact with more universal principles . . . the universal mandates of the natural law" (804–5). The claim of Ernst Kantorowicz, *The King's Two Bodies* (Princeton: Princeton University Press, 1957) 201, that the mystical body of Christ was juridicized into a kind of "mystical corporation," a secularized mystical body, while generally plausible, does not find support in the *De concordantia catholica*. Rather, here the reverse seems true: the juridical corporation is "spiritualized."

21. *DCC*, 250 (194): "Consideravi enim primo legem Christianam liberri-mam, ad quam nullus nisi sponte absque coactione accedit. Unde cum via fidei nostrae sit ipse Christus, non est in ipsis ad salutem necessariis aliud quam ipse Christus et ad eum liberrimus accessus. Quare coactio proprie non est in ipsa ecclesia descensive a Christo, sed gratia est, quae ab ipsa plenitudine fontis capitis in ipsum corpus Christi mysticum fluit."

22. *Nicholas of Cusa*, 40. Sigmund has given a comprehensive account of the Neoplatonic, especially Dionysian, origin of the social ideas which Cusanus shared with many of his intellectual confreres.

23. *DCC*, 330 (229): "Invasores itaque dominii non vocati nec electi tyranni dicuntur"; *DCC*, 132 (101): ". . . omnium constitutionum ligandi vig-orem consistere in concordia et consensu tacito vel expresso. . . ."

24. Dist. 40 c. 6: "(Papa) a nemine est iudicandus, nisi deprehendatur a fide devius." Although this formula was generally accepted by medieval canonists the text's origin lies in the Symmachan Forgeries, c. 500, confected to support the position of Pope Symmachus in the Laurentian schism. Cf. Tierney, *Foundations*, 8, 57–62, and Appendix I. On the Symmachan Forgeries cf. Walter Ullmann, *The Growth of Papal Government in the Middle Ages: A Study in the Ideological Relation of Clerical to Lay Power*, 3d ed. (London: Methuen & Co. Ltd, 1970) 27n., 117, and 265.

25. *DCC*, 249 (194): ". . . tamen videtur in veritate medium concordantiae per scripturas investigabile ad hoc demum tendere, quod ipsius pontificis Romani potestas quoad considerationem praeeminentiae, prioratus et princi-patus sit a deo per medium hominis et conciliorum, scilicet mediante consensu electivo."

26. *DCC*, 61 (42).

27. *DCC*, 56 (39).

28. *DCC*, 262 (203).

29. *DCC*, 264 (203): "Resideo itaque in hac conclusione quod principatus ecclesiasticus ob unitatem ecclesiae et ad eius servitium et ministerium a deo ordinatus in realitate sua a Christo per ecclesiam constituitur. Et quaecumque argumenta aut pro ea parte quod principatus coactivus a deo in ecclesia sit tantum, aut ex alia parte quod ipse coactivus principatus ex electione sive con-sensu hominum seu ecclesiae tantum exsistat, ad hoc medium concordantiae meo iudicio veraciter reducuntur."

30. *DCC*, 290 (214).

31. Alexandre Koyré, in his discussion of the cosmology of Nicholas of

Cusa, saw that one of the most historically important aspects of that cosmology was "his rejection of the hierarchical structure of the universe, and . . . his denial . . . of the uniquely low and despicable position assigned to the earth by traditional cosmology." *From the Closed World to the Infinite Universe* (New York: Harper and Row, 1958) 19.

32. *DCC*, 158 (120–1): "Petrus unice et confusissime figurat ecclesiam. . . ."

33. Antony Black, *Council and Commune: The Conciliar Movement and the Council of Basle* (London: Burns & Oates, 1979) 144–5.

34. Black, *Council and Commune*, 145; *DCC*, 131 (100).

35. "Nicholas of Cusa: 'On Presidential Authority in a General Council,'" trans. H. Lawrence Bond, Gerald Christianson, and Thomas Izbicki, *Church History* 59 (1990) 28.

36. *DCC*, 71 (51).

37. *DCC*, 72 (52).

38. *DCC*, 73 (53).

39. *DCC*, 95 (72).

40. *DCC*, 139 (106).

41. *DCC*, 100 (79): ". . . vigorem statutorum canonum in concilio non ex papa nec capite concilii, sed ex unico concordanti consensu vigorem habere."

42. *DCC*, 102 (81).

43. *DCC*, 103 (82).

44. *DCC*, 105 (83).

45. *DCC*, 109 (86): ". . . quod canonum statuendorum auctoritas non solum dependet a papa, sed a communi consensu. Et contra hanc conclusionem nulla praescriptio vel consuetudo valere potest, sicut nec contra ius divinum et naturale, a quo ista conclusio dependet."

46. *DCC*, 124 (95–6).

47. *DCC*, 148 (113): "Quare universaliter dici potest universale concilium repraesentativum catholicae ecclesiae habere potestatem immediate a Christo et esse omni respectu tam supra papam quam sedem apostolicam."

48. *DCC*, 161 (123): "Et non habet aliquis ratione utens in hoc dubium, quin maior sit potestas ipsius concilii ecclesiam repraesentantis in papalitatem, ut secundum utilitatem ecclesiae materiale eius subiectum disponatur, quam in iudicio unius hominis in ipsam papalitatem sibi nomine ecclesiae et propter ipsam adiunctam."

49. *DCC*, 167 (127). As Black points out, Heimerich van der Velde, once a teacher of Nicholas at Cologne, also held a position that maintained that "everyone is inspired by the holy Spirit to choose a pastor." *Council and Commune*, 69.

50. *DCC*, 164 (125).

51. *DCC*, 233 (182): "'Oportet autem, ut ille, qui omnibus praeesse videtur, ab omnibus illis eligatur et ordinetur.' Verbum 'oportet' est verbum necessitatis, id est aliter non posse. . . ."

52. *DCC*, 4 (5).

53. Ibid.

54. *DCC*, 6 (7).

55. "Cardinal Cesarini and Cusa's 'Concordantia'," *Church History* 54 (1985) 17.

56. *DCC,* 78 (58): ". . . non est humanum varios homines in unum con-gregatos in summa libertate loquendi constitutos ex una concordantia iudi-care, sed divinum. . . ."

57. *DCC,* 79 (58): "Ecce concordantiam maxime in hiis quae fidei sunt, re-quiri, et de quanto maior concordantia, de tanto infallibilius iudicium."

58. Josef Goergen, "Die Konsenslehre des Kardinals Nikolaus von Kues und ihre Bedeutung für die Gegenwart," *Festakademie der Katholischen Erwachsenenbildung im Bistum Trier,* Schriftenreihe der K.E.B.T., 3 (Trier: Paulinus-Druckerei, 1961) 14.

59. *DCC,* 77 (56).

60. *The Catholic Concordance,* xxiv.

61. Quoted from Marshall Baldwin, ed., *Christianity Through the Thirteenth Century* (New York: Harper and Row, 1970) 73.

62. John T. McNeill, "The Relevance of Conciliarism," *The Jurist* 31 (1971) 81–112, discusses the role played by religious orders in the development of representative government. Though his concentration is on the Dominican constitution he is aware of its dependence upon earlier models and attitudes.

63. *DCC,* 166 (126).

64. *DCC,* 168 (128).

65. *Consensus fidelium: Zur Unfehlbarkeit der Kirche aus der Perspektive einer Konsenstheorie der Wahrheit.* Studien zur systematischen und spirituellen Theologie 6 (Würzburg: Echter Verlag, 1992) Parts III & IV, *passim.*

66. *DCC,* 7 (7): "Haec concordantia est ipsamet veritas summa."

67. *The Reformation in Germany,* 2 vols. (London; New York: Darton, Longman & Todd; Herder & Herder, 1968) I, 70.

68. "Reflections Upon the Study of the General Councils of the Fifteenth Century," *Studies in Church History,* vol. 1, C. W. Dugmore and Charles Duggan, eds. (London: Thomas Nelson, 1964) 97.

69. Hans Küng, *The Church* (London: Burns & Oates, 1967) 413.

SEVEN

On Becoming a Sacramental Church Again

Mary Collins, O.S.B.

Luce Irigaray was writing of matters more comprehensive than the Roman liturgy when she observed, "Most of the time, *in men's discourse*, . . . [r]eality appears as an always already cultural reality . . . cut off from its corporeal roots, its cosmic environment, its relationship to life."[1] Applied to discourse about liturgy, Irigaray's observations would be damning, since the public prayer of the Church aspires to be sacramental. It means to connect the mystery of Christ with the material world of the disciples of Jesus Christ, men, women, and children, who inhabit it generation after generation, each for a brief lifetime. Is there an "always already cultural reality" which could be so strong as to overwhelm the fundamental Catholic belief in sacramentality located in body, cosmos, and the ordinary?

The original context of Irigaray's observation is an essay reporting on what she has observed through her psychoanalytic practice in France on the ways in which men and women use language. She contrasts men's with *women's discourse,* in which "Women . . . maintain a relationship to the real environment but they don't subjectivize it as their own. They remain the locus for the experience of concrete reality, but they leave the matter of its structuration to the others." This might be translated simply into the observation that men make the rules, women know it, and maintain a certain distance from "the real world." As I read Irigaray and think about liturgy, I recall an exchange with an academic colleague years ago. He chided, "You are missing a canonical perspective in your approach to liturgy." I heard myself replying, "I may be lacking it, but I am not missing it." Repartee aside, are there two competing ways of approaching liturgy, one concerned with legality and one with sacramentality? Or are there different ways of understanding sacramentality within the Catholic community when it comes to the question of liturgical prayer? Is there some broader explanation for this apparent difference?

A second contemporary French psychoanalyst, Julia Kristeva, provides another way to think about the kind of difference that often appears in Catholic discussions about sacramentality and the liturgical tradition. In her study of human development she notes what she judges to be a necessary interplay between what she names "symbolic" and "semiotic" processes.[2] The wires of language risk getting crossed for English-speaking students of liturgy whose understanding of "symbolic" comes from reading cultural anthropologists like Victor Turner and Karl Rahner, since Kristeva's conversation partners have been linguists and psychoanalysts for whom these words commonly refer to different realms of meaning. In these conversations the *symbolic* refers to the rational and conscious structured world of public order, the realm of tradition with its established meanings, something akin to Irigaray's "always already established reality" which women tend not to "subjectivize as their own." Kristeva identifies this realm of the *symbolic* with "the Law of the Father," honoring her Freudian roots. Much about the Catholic liturgical tradition can be located in this realm of the *symbolic*. But how much?

Kristeva's psychoanalytic theory does not privilege the symbolic as much as the Freudian tradition does. She presents the effectively functioning human person as one who can negotiate between the realms of the *symbolic* and the *semiotic*. The latter is the realm of the corporeal, drive-governed, associative, preconscious. Think sensuous smells of incense and perfumes, sonorous melody, ecstatic rhythm, ululation, milk, fabric dyed red, bodies touching. Discerning liturgists recognize that the power of the Catholic liturgical tradition is just as legitimately located in Kristeva's realm of the *semiotic*. But how much?

And who negotiates the *semiotic* and the *symbolic* for the Church? In the case of the effectively functioning human person, the negotiator of the symbolic and the semiotic is Kristeva's subject-in-process, the historical person moving through a lifetime. But the liturgical tradition of the Catholic people belongs to a vast community of believers moving through history, connecting the cosmic mystery of Christ with their lives, their places, and their times. Who controls access to the semiotic in the life of a corporate subject in history?[3]

The liturgical tradition sets out ritual behaviors for the Church gathered, a people remembering Christ Jesus by solemnly playing together in designated and delineated spaces with water, oil, fire, food and drink, touch and smells, sound and rhythm, ritual speeches and ritualized speaking, stylized postures and gestures. What St. Paul names the "law of Christ," the mystery of God's design for the world, comes to expression through the body. The Catholic Church asserts an official authority over the liturgical tradition; it posits normative ways of ritualizing in its official liturgical books. So ecclesiastical law, the law of the Church, also connects through the body. But that is not the end of the matter. Even while Christian people work with water, fire, and food to remember Christ Jesus in ways authorized by the Church, they are also involved in their own daily cultural practices. Cultural practices, too, are coded in an "always already" structured world of public order that makes a local gathering of Christians also Chinese or Peruvian, Mexican-American or French. The "law of Christ," the law of the Church, and "the Law of the [local] Fathers" all connect through the body, sometimes in a single ritual transaction. So Constantinian-era bishops formed an imperial procession to approach the mystery of Christ and in doing so gave that mystery an imperial shape; the late-twentieth-century *Rite Zairois* provides for a procession of warriors.[4]

Given the negotiating that must go on in all these realms of public order—Kristeva's *symbolic* manifesting the traditions of various "Fathers"—can the Catholic Church celebrating its liturgy also protect and promote Kristeva's sensuous *semiotic*? What are the consequences of its failure to do so? At one level, voice votes have already been coming in for some time. "The modern Catholic liturgy doesn't touch me like the old liturgy." "The liturgy is stripped bare; there is nothing beautiful about it." Elsewhere people are voting with their feet. Recent sociological studies indicate that on any given Sunday in the United States between 25 and 30 percent of Roman Catholics are in attendance at the Eucharistic liturgy.[5] Seven out of ten take a pass for the week. Too much order and rationality and not enough that is carnal, beautiful, threatening?

The tendency of the disappointed lovers of the old Catholic liturgy has been to blame the liturgical reform of Vatican II for being misguided. This essay will explore that judgment. As I read the data, the aegis of our current situation is complex. But put simply, it is my thesis that the Roman liturgy has been implicated in political conflict for the last 150 years—in competing claims among symbolic realms about what constitutes "good public order." The liturgical reform of Vatican II has simply been pulled into the ongoing fray. Prosper

Guéranger and some of his contemporary French bishops, and then later Popes Pius IX, Pius X, Pius XII, and the monk-liturgist Lambert Beauduin are representative actors—but by no means the only ones— in the contestation that has led to the almost total neglect of the *semiotic* in the Roman liturgy at the end of the twentieth century.

In the Catholic Church's continuing fight against the modern world, official Roman liturgy is a major casualty. It has been enlisted to enunciate dogma and hierarchical order, when historically it had mediated so much more of an authentically Catholic sensibility. Is there hope for recovery of a genuinely sacramental liturgy that sanctions once again the play of the Christian religious imagination engaged with the demands of faith? That question will be raised again at the end of the essay.

(Re)locating Authority in the Church

One part of the larger project of Vatican II (1962–1965) was the retrieval of a more authentic understanding and exercise of the episcopal office relative to the papacy. The popes in Rome had deliberately suppressed the episcopacy during the course of the nineteenth century, as part of a larger strategy for the construction of a monarchical papacy better suited to confronting modern, i.e., post-Enlightenment European culture, a world characterized by lack of regard for traditional religious authority. Ecclesiologist Joseph Komonchak has done an extended analysis of the historical process by which an identifiable "culture of Roman Catholicism" was constructed by the papacy in the 150 years prior to Vatican II.[6] This "culture" constituted the shared world of Catholic Christians in 1959 when Pope John XXIII announced an ecumenical council for the purpose of ecclesial self-examination vis-à-vis the modern world.

Komonchak's analysis does not consider the place of the liturgical movement in the construction of "Roman Catholicism." But, as I hope to show here, the liturgy has been implicated almost from the beginning in the papal project that undergirds modern Roman Catholicism. Thirty years after Vatican II the issue of appropriate ecclesial self-presentation in the modern world is still being negotiated. Did the Council Fathers intend to replace the nineteenth-century construct, to modify it in major or minor ways, or to reinforce the construction? A brief résumé of Komonchak's account of the development of modern Roman Catholicism will establish the frame within which to reflect on the modern papacy, the liturgical movement, and the current state of Catholic liturgical practice, especially in U.S. culture.

Constructing Modern Roman Catholic Identity. As Komonchak reads the historical evidence, consolidation of church authority in the person of the bishop of Rome was a major strategic move made and sustained by successive nineteenth- and twentieth-century popes who had to contend with the spread of enlightenment and revolutionary ideals across Europe. Traditional religious authority was severely tested in Western Europe at the end of the eighteenth century, both by the widely heralded "triumph of reason" and by the democratic rejection of hierarchy and the embrace of social egalitarianism. Such characteristically modern postulates were alien to pre-modern Catholic self-understanding. As the axiom would have it, "the Church is not a democracy." The culturally alienated Catholic Church reacted to the threat of modernity by defining itself in terms of behaviors and attitudes that constituted direct confrontation with the values, beliefs, and practices of modernity. What the modern culture rejected the Roman Church would boldly claim.

Komonchak examines four characteristics of nineteenth- and early-twentieth-century "Roman Catholicism," a way of being the Catholic Church that was neither a simple retrieval of medieval Christendom nor unalloyed "tridentine" Catholicism. First, Church authorities promoted new devotions that gave Roman Catholic piety a monarchical visage. These successfully employed popular religious imagination against the secular culture's enthronement of reason and egalitarianism. Mary's heavenly and earthly queenship was promoted. Her images were publicly crowned, subverting the enthronement of Reason.[7] The Virgin Mary's humility and obedience were celebrated, and she was revered for her apocalyptic summoning of the Catholic faithful to repentance and reparation for the modern world's sins against her Son. Parallel christological devotions celebrated Christ's sovereign dominion over a Western European culture increasingly hostile to his rule through the Church. Not only Christian homes, but even nations and the whole world were consecrated to the Sacred Heart and to Christ the King.

The constructed culture of Roman Catholicism was not only monarchical, it was militant. As associations of Catholic laymen grew, many were identified through the medieval metaphor of "knighthood." These fellowships combatted modern liberal ideas publicly and committed themselves to the defense of Catholic beliefs and liberties being discounted by secular societies. Catholic women were recruited as "Catholic daughters" to strengthen the household of the faith. As such lay associations grew in number and variety, and as they gained ecclesiastical approbation and guidance under official chaplains, they contributed to the emergence of the visible Roman

Catholic subculture, especially in Western Europe and North America where enlightenment and revolutionary values had taken firm hold in public life.

It soon became evident to Roman churchmen that international coordination of diverse local initiatives fostering Catholic resistance to the alien culture of modernity would add momentum to the goal of establishing a unified Roman Catholicism. "[For] this only the papacy could be an adequate means," writes Komonchak, "so [one] of the distinctive characteristics of the history of Catholicism in the nineteenth century was the increased centralization of Catholic life upon Rome and the figure of the pope."[8] Local bishops and even national hierarchies were diminished in stature, not by secular governments but by ecclesiastical design, as papal nuncios and the Roman curia took charge of the Church's business with civil societies.

The fourth characteristic of "Roman Catholicism" was another manifestation of the same centralizing dynamic. "As the [nineteenth] century moved on, it saw an unprecedented increase in the claims of Rome over the intellectual life of the Church."[9] Catholic theologians and Catholic intellectuals were regularly censured for deviating from Roman thought and judgment and were rewarded for showing its necessity and intelligibility.

Strategic Deployment of the Liturgy. The question of whether to deploy the Church's liturgy in the nineteenth century papal project of centralizing the Church at Rome as a bulwark against modern culture first came up circumstantially. Contrary to widespread misperceptions, the sixteenth-century Council of Trent had not established uniform liturgical practice in the Western Church. Recent research on the church in France documents the continued promulgation of diocesan missals throughout the seventeenth, eighteenth, and nineteenth centuries.[10] These neo-Gallican books were not genetically tied to the ancient Gallican liturgical rites that pre-dated the eighth-century Carolingian liturgical reform, but were for the most part products of continuing liturgical development in France even after the promulgation of the 1570 "Tridentine" Missal of Pope Pius V.

The mid-nineteenth-century French liturgical advocate Prosper Guéranger, often identified as the "father of the modern liturgical movement," was intellectually and spiritually committed to the most ancient of the liturgical traditions. In his monumental and polemical *Institutions liturgiques* he faulted the neo-Gallican rites as ill-advised in comparison with the oldest traditions East and West, and with the Roman liturgy which, in his judgment, had best mediated the riches of the ancient past. Guéranger's disputes with several French diocesan bishops about the adequacy and even the legitimacy of the diocesan missals and office books did not go unnoticed in Rome, and it was not long before Roman voices entered in.

It is clear that Pope Gregory XVI recognized that responsibility for the public prayer of the Church fell to the local ordinary. He responded to letters from certain French bishops inquiring about "Rome's" attitude toward the diversity of liturgical practice in France by reporting his preference for the unity the Roman liturgy would mediate. But it is a matter of record that Gregory consciously chose—"je ne l'ordonnerai jamais"—not to impose his preference for unified liturgy on the French church.[11]

Nevertheless, the national response to Prosper Guéranger's provocation of controversy about liturgical diversity in the dioceses of France in the 1840s was carefully monitored by the papal nuncio in Paris and reported to the bishop of Rome. Gregory XVI's successor, Pope Pius IX, also took no public action in "the liturgical question," but he openly expressed his pleasure with the wake stirred by Guéranger's polemics. Momentum built in France as successive dioceses one by one acted over the next quarter century to honor "the mind of Rome" and adopt the Roman liturgy. At Guéranger's death in 1875, Pius IX would openly credit the monk liturgist's role in strengthening the unity of the Church through the consolidation of liturgical practice.[12]

Whatever discernment French bishops might have undertaken in Lyons, Orleans, or Paris in mid-century about the legitimacy of their local liturgical traditions, decisions for liturgical uniformity were made in service of the broader nineteenth-century ecclesiastical agenda. As a universal Church centered in Rome was being constructed to deal with the modern world, local liturgical practice lost its centuries-old legitimacy.

Oddly, after Guéranger's death in 1875, little further official attention was paid to the potential value of uniform liturgical practice for confronting modernity until the beginning of the twentieth century. Why? During the nineteenth century, even throughout Guéranger's imbroglio with the French bishops, the promotion of the Roman liturgy was not a major concern of diocesan clergy. The home of the liturgical movement was new Benedictine foundations in Germany and Belgium linked by direct or indirect ties to Guéranger's Solesmes Abbey. In Belgium, where Benedictine promotion had most effectively encouraged active lay participation in the liturgy, the liturgical movement was often seen as conflicting with official ecclesiastical promotion of Catholic devotions.[13] So, it is not surprising that when Pope Leo XIII promulgated his 1891 encyclical *Rerum novarum* calling for the regeneration of European society no official connection was yet being made between the Church's liturgy and the desired social transformation.[14]

It was Leo's successor Pope Pius X who first made the necessary connection, embracing and promoting the view that lay participation in the Church's liturgy was essential to the "restoration of all things in Christ."[15] Was it merely happenstance that official papal promotion of liturgical life in the first decade of the twentieth century coincided with Pius X's vigorous condemnation of modernism? Or was there some intrinsic logic linking these two moves in Pius X's papacy? Lambert Beauduin's explication of liturgical piety in his 1909 work *La piété de l'Église* suggests the latter.

In establishing an argument for liturgical promotion—now equivalent with the promotion of the Roman liturgy—Lambert Beauduin, a Benedictine monk of Mont Cesar in Belgium who had earlier been a diocesan priest, analyzed modern Western European society as he knew it. He identifies the "sad consequences" of the culture of modernity. Interestingly, his first indictment is the Church's own promotion of devotions leading to abandonment of the liturgy as the Church's school of prayer. Among the other sad consequences of modernity, he lists the widespread abandonment of prayer altogether, individualism, what he calls "an insidious secular spirit" in public life, and the lack of hierarchical life.[16] Concerning the latter, Beauduin observed "[l]iturgical piety . . . is the best weapon for combatting this evil."[17]

Beauduin's explanation for the potential effectiveness of the Roman liturgy for promoting hierarchical life pre-dates contemporary ritual theory and liturgical theology. But his explanations are congruent with late-twentieth-century theoretical analyses of the social effectiveness of ritual and with theological explanations of the ecclesial efficacy of liturgical practice.[18] As we will suggest, they are also congruent with observations about the sad consequences of not honoring other dimensions of the ritual process.

Arguing for the liturgical apostolate in 1909, Beauduin wrote that participation in the liturgy effectively "places [participants] *under* the active influence of the *priestly power of the Church.*"[19] Through liturgy "the hierarchy exercises its *spiritual fatherhood.*" Gathered at the family table and nourished there "under the presidency of *the head of the family,*" the Christian people learn *filial piety, loving obedience, and ecclesial loyalty.* Beauduin writes in summary that development of the hierarchical piety intrinsic to the liturgy will "strengthen *the necessary bonds of subordination and attachment*" between the people and the clergy. These bonds will insure that when crises of obedience come, as they inevitably will, obedience to the Church will be "complete and sincere."[20] Beauduin's discussion of liturgical piety is focused principally on its usefulness for promoting ecclesiastical order. His essay lacks the aesthetic interest of many writings about liturgy's mystery and beauty that would follow after him throughout the twentieth century.[21]

In developing his case for "the advantages of liturgical piety," Beauduin begins by attending to liturgy's social consequences. First, Catholic Christians liturgically engaged become aware of themselves as members of the Church. Drawn into its life and traditions, they are less engaged by emergent modern culture. Next, through celebration of the Roman liturgy, Catholics everywhere also learn their attachment to the Church at Rome and to the pope, a universal identity that transcends the particularity of nationalism. Finally, Beauduin argues that liturgical piety generates a corporate public identity. The Church generated through liturgy is hierarchically organized and that order is reinforced through shared symbols and acts.[22] This is an effective corrective to modern egalitarianism.

Liturgical piety as Beauduin understood and promoted it in *La piété de l'Église* was more effective than the path of devotional life for constituting and maintaining unified Roman Catholic identity within the culture of modernity. The desirable consequences Beauduin saw were necessarily limited to those who regularly participated in celebrations of the Roman liturgy, but the Sunday obligation guaranteed a gathering of Catholics. "[I]t is a practical enterprise if ever there was one!"[23] The numbers are there: "Thousands of such groups assembled every Sunday." All that was needed was official liturgical promotion, namely, the diocesan clergy's commitment to making the Roman liturgy the vehicle for constituting communities of loyal Catholics.

Pope Pius X officially began the work of reconnecting lay Catholics everywhere to the Roman liturgy when he authorized early admission to eucharistic Communion (1906) and the promotion of more frequent Communion for adults (1909). If his condemnation of modernism (1903) warned intellectuals against flirting with the enemy, the pope's liturgical promotion was a constructive moment in his aspiration to use his anti-modern papacy "to restore all things in Christ."

Papal promotion of the Roman liturgy and grass-roots liturgical movements coexisted in uneasy relationship in the decades of the twentieth century prior to Vatican II. Pope Pius XII's 1947 encyclical *Mediator Dei* stands as witness to the perceived dangerous "exaggerations" (MD 55ff.) promoted from time to time by advocates of the liturgy outside Rome.[24] Did the ecclesiastical realm of the *symbolic*, signified by the papacy, experience itself as threatened at times with subversion by the siren call of the drive-governed *semiotic*? Or was it more simply a matter of negotiating hierarchical power—pope, bishops, and clergy—within the symbolic realm? I will argue that twentieth-century contestation about the liturgy, before and after the council, has been engaged at the level of what Irigaray names *men's discourse,* what from Kristeva's analytic perspective might be seen as a struggle about correctly identifying "the Father." The subtext of the liturgical reform is ecclesiastical authority, about who has power over the liturgy. Virtually no one in ecclesiastical office has become an advocate for the vital interests of the *semiotic* in sacramental liturgy, where power comes from below.

Catholic Sensibility: Driven by Control, Seduced by Grace

What gave rise to this study was my concern to understand "The Roman Liturgy and Inculturation," further identified as "The Fourth Instruction for the Right Application of the Conciliar Constitution on the Liturgy (nos. 37–40)" issued by the Congregation for Worship and Sacraments on March 29, 1994 [hereafter FI].[25] What I perceive, in reading FI in conversation also with Irigaray and Kristeva, is that the controlling topic is not really liturgy and inculturation, despite the official title. The main text is the discourse of churchmen negotiating power in an ongoing struggle for control.

Those writing from Rome in 1994 claim that the "right interpretation" of the acts of a council now thirty years past is that all power over liturgy is located in Rome. It is as though Vatican II was a disruption of centralized power arrangements that had been agreed upon earlier, with Prosper Guéranger showing the way to the bishops of France a century ago and even to Popes Gregory XVI and Pius IX, who had held back from officially embracing such an audacious view.[26] This of course raises the question whether FI is the "right interpretation" or rather an advocacy document in support of the resumption of the modern papacy project as Komonchak had described it. One hundred and fifty years after Prosper Guéranger's voice summoned the bishops of France to uniform liturgical practice,[27] this Roman text commends to the Catholic bishops resident in cities and towns in every continent and nation on the face of the planet a centripetal reading of *Sacrosanctum Concilium.* Catholic bishops more than two thousand strong may decide for their own political reasons to concede this interpretation of the conciliar text. But it is hard to concede, upon examining the evidence—comparing Pius XII's *Mediator Dei,* Vatican II's *Sacrosanctum Concilium,* and the Roman congregation's FI—that the latter reading is the only "correct" one.

Monarchical Authority: The View of Mediator Dei. A careful examination of the three texts discloses a consistent understanding of official authority over liturgy as hierarchical. This is hardly surprising in light of overwhelming evidence for the ubiquity of hierarchies in the ordering of human relations. The noteworthy differences are in the explicit structuration of that hierarchy. Pope Pius XII's 1947 encyclical *Mediator Dei,* reflecting the momentum that built up in the previous century, teaches that "the Sovereign Pontiff alone enjoys the right to recognize any practice touching the worship of God, to introduce and approve new rites, and also to modify those he judges to require modification" (MD 58). Monarchical papal authority over the liturgy went uncontested in the pre-conciliar period. What did Pius XII judge to be the authority of the diocesan bishops in liturgical matters? He said they had "the right and duty to watch over the exact observance of the prescriptions of the sacred canons respecting divine worship" (MD 58).

Bureaucratic Authority: The View of the 1994 Instruction. Against that Pian background, a close examination of the fourth post-conciliar instruction on the liturgy is instructive. The 1994 text says, "Adaptations of the Roman rite, even in the field of inculturation, depend completely on the authority of the church" (FI 37). Lest there be any doubt about where ecclesial authority resides, the document further specifies that "[t]he authority belongs to the Apostolic See." But the 1994 text makes a significant turn Pius XII himself did not make either in *Mediator Dei* or in his own practice.[28] "The authority belongs to the Apostolic See . . . *which exercises it through the Congregation for Divine Worship and the Discipline of the Sacraments. . . .*"(FI 37).

What of the diocesan bishops' authority over liturgy? The Instruction specifies that it exists "within the limits fixed by law," (FI 37). Unexceptional in the given order of things. But the Instruction (the voice is that of the Congregation) then proceeds to lay down certain terms of the law that distinguish this voice from conciliar teaching and the *praenotanda* of the reformed Roman liturgical books.[29] It communicates an attitude of reluctant concession in discussing whatever positive response the Roman Congregation might make in the future to liturgical initiatives from diocesan bishops. The pervasive reluctance is telling. For the authoritative voice speaking in this text (echoing the perspective of *Mediator Dei,* and, incidentally, that of Prosper Guéranger), little episcopal authority relative to the Church's liturgy is properly located in the local churches. It should also be noted that while the viewpoints of the 1994 and the 1947 texts are similar, they are not identical. If Annibale Bugnini is correct that Pope Pius XII did not bind himself to work through the Roman congregations, the Roman congregational share in ecclesial authority over the liturgy has clearly grown in 1994, both in this text and in practice.[30]

Collegial Hierarchical Authority: The View of Sacrosanctum Concilium. The previous observations about just where in Vatican City authority over the liturgy is to be located in 1994 might seem unexceptionable to somnolent readers of Roman Catholic documents or to Catholics who had not yet reached their majority at the time of Vatican II, some current members of the college of bishops among them. But the line from 1841 to 1947 to 1994 passes through an uncommon time, 1962–1965, when two major constitutions on the liturgy and on the Church were given formal approval as the official teaching of the Church. *Sacrosanctum Concilium* self-consciously reformulated the prevailing understanding of the dominance of the Roman Church in the matter of the Church's public prayer. Theologically, *Sacrosanctum Concilium* located authority for the liturgical life of the local church in the episcopal office, a notion not unknown to Gregory XVI and Pius IX. The liturgical life of the diocese was declared to "center around the bishop," described in a mixed metaphor as "the high priest of the flock" guiding a priestly people (SC 41).

Two years and two sessions of the council after *Sacrosanctum Concilium*, pope and bishops gathered in council persisted in this emphasis on the liturgical authority of the local bishop. *Lumen gentium*, the 1965 Constitution on the Church, asserts, "Every legitimate celebration of the Eucharist is regulated by the bishop, to whom is committed the office of offering the worship of Christian religion . . ."(LG 26). Bishops are also said to "direct by their authority" the full sacramental and liturgical life of their dioceses." The authority of the papacy in liturgical matters is alluded to in curiously low relief in *Lumen gentium*. The text says that the diocesan bishop conducts himself "in accordance with the Lord's commandment and with the Church's laws, as further defined by his particular judgments for his diocese" (LG 26).

What were the papal/episcopal relationships liable to legal definition that *Lumen gentium* was referring to? Two notable shifts from the teaching of Pius XII in *Mediator Dei* had already appeared in the formulation of general norms for liturgical reform in *Sacrosanctum Concilium*. First, the subject of authority over the liturgy ("Sovereign Pontiff" in 1947) was named "the Apostolic See" in 1963. The movement in the text was away from the personal authority of the officeholder (the pope as monarch) to the apostolic authority vested in the Roman see, that is, to ecclesial authority. This move might seem to legitimate the 1994 relocation of authority over liturgy to the Roman

Congregation. However, practice in the 1960s and 1970s indicates that this is not the only correct interpretation of how the Apostolic See might function. Under Pope Paul VI, a post-conciliar *consilium* was established as a separate body to collaborate with the pope in implementing *Sacrosanctum Concilium*. So also groups of bishops with shared interests and concerns took the initiative to constitute themselves as collaborators in the work of preparing vernacular translations with the full endorsement of Pope Paul VI.[31]

A second shift away from the perspective of *Mediator Dei* was also written into *Sacrosanctum Concilium*. Ecclesial authority over the liturgy was characterized as collegial. It was said to be vested conjointly in *"the Apostolic See and in the bishops,* as laws may determine" (SC 22.1; emphasis added). It was presumably not anticipated that future procedural law would negate the significance of the conjunction.[32]

Bureaucracy Ascendant. Yet in the guise of instructing bishops in correct procedures to follow in the matter of liturgical inculturation, the Roman Congregation has effectively repudiated the proper episcopal authority of diocesan bishops. The procedural protocols function to cancel the theological "and" of *Sacrosanctum Concilium*. Diocesan bishops and bishops' conferences are accorded a role akin to that of petitioners seeking building permits in the office of a modern bureaucracy.

The Instruction does not formally challenge the conciliar teaching. In fact the first part of the Roman Congregation's document (FI 4–20) goes almost the whole distance in affirming contemporary theories of inculturation,[33] theories that tend to renegotiate ecclesiastical authority in the interests of making the Church more fully "catholic," incarnate in local cultures. However, later sections of the Instruction (FI 21–32 and 62–68) present episcopal conferences with highly formal operating procedure for dealing with development in the liturgy of their local churches. By making the issue a matter of procedure—one that "in [the] future . . . will be considered the only correct procedure" (FI 3)—the Roman curia bypasses intellectual engagement with the authority of bishops in theory and practice and with the fuller implications of inculturation theory. The requirement of correct procedure assures bureaucratic control.

The Roman congregation claims for itself, as a constitutive element of correct procedure, the prerogative of judging and correcting the judgment of national and regional bishops' conferences (FI 66–68). Lest procedurally careless bishops' conferences misunderstand, the text warns that episcopal initiatives for inculturating public prayer in their local churches can be negated on technical grounds, when correct procedure is neglected (FI 37). Finally, correct procedure as set out in the Instruction does not offer holders of the episcopal office any procedure for appealing the judgment of the bureaucracy. Authority over the liturgical life of the local churches, deliberately retrieved at Vatican II as apostolic authority exercised collegially, this 1994 document would reaggregate to the church at Rome. Despite some affirmations about the *semiotic* power of liturgy (FI 41–45), the Instruction registers discomfort with the introduction of any ambiguity (FI 48) and privileges the realm of law (FI 27). All of this control is judged to be for the good of the Catholic people.

Redress from the Straight and Narrow. Perhaps—just perhaps—Lambert Beauduin's 1909 analysis in La *piété de l'Église* reported above is all there really is to the Roman liturgy at the end of the twentieth century. Perhaps the liturgy only serves the Church functionally, politically. Perhaps, through liturgical prayer, the church authorities merely teach orthodoxy in the guise of addressing holy mystery (FI 27). Through Roman liturgy, bishops learn their place in relation to the Church at Rome. Through Sunday assemblies the Catholic people learn docility, their subordination to the hierarchy, and attachment to Rome. But this is too cynical an interpretation of the Catholic tradition of sacramental liturgy. The reductionism it expresses must be resisted, despite whatever developments serve to feed cynicism. How ironic it is that French post-modernist feminist psychoanalysts, themselves suspicious of official religion, offer relief from the narrow preoccupations with who is in control of ecclesiastical order and suggest a way forward for the Catholic people through the recovery of the beauty and terror that point to myster in the ritual process.

Much of this essay has been directed to assessing the political valence of recent Roman liturgical history in its service of the Church's confrontation with modern secular cultures. What has been documented concerning the preoccupations of popes, bishops, and curial congregation takes place within the realm Julia Kristeva names the *symbolic* and characterizes as "the Law of the Father." Catholics whose religious horizon is confined solely within this symbolic are likely to be few in number, although there are undoubtedly some; and some of these are likely to be drawn to contestations about what is lawful and who is in charge as moth is drawn to flame. Luce Irigaray writes of such a world as linked to the individual and collective history of the masculine subject, a world designated via "inanimate abstractions integral to the subject's world."[34] Absolute power and authority over ambiguity and meaning are such abstractions. The question whether privileging the *symbolic*, and one's own self at the center, is always and only a matter of gender difference invites more sustained reflection. As this essay has shown, however, it is an occupational hazard for some clearly zealous church office holders.

Yet I would agree with Julia Kristeva that Catholic sacramental sensibility has opened worshipers to "other meanings" than "the Law of the Father," and continues to do so. The sensuous forms of corporate public worship—the scent of beeswax candles, a stark crucified body—have effectively mediated access to the mysterious holy, a womb that contains us, a wrath that might well destroy us. The real issue for the revitalization of Catholic liturgical life after 150 years of being deployed in resistance to modernity is what sensuous forms will be publicly available to the Catholic people gathered for liturgical celebration, which will be suppressed, and who will decide.[35]

The issue is, finally, what FI claims it is, "The Roman Liturgy and Inculturation." Still, the prospect is dim for inculturation of Catholic faith, life, and worship in the world's myriad cultures at the turn of the third millennium if the terms spelled out in that document hold. The materiality of cultures is always particular. Gertrude Stein's dictum to the contrary notwithstanding, roses have different species, including tomato. For most of its history, the Catholic Church has cultivated a florid garden. When the material culture of particular local churches is suppressed as dangerous or without dignity, and the material culture familiar to, valued by, and under the control of distant hierarchical authorities is imposed on Catholic worshipers everywhere—even for high purposes, however laudable—the spiritual well-being of the Church is endangered. This is what it means to be a sacramental Church.

The official strategy now, as at the time of Pius X at the opening of the century, is to control the Church's self-understanding through control of liturgy.[36] This privileging of the *symbolic* by office holders is understandable. But it is a short-sighted view of the liturgical tradition.[37] What the times call for is regional conferences populated with a few bishops who, themselves seduced by that "beauty ever ancient, ever new," value the deep well-spring of sacramental liturgy, the *semiotic*, the ambiguous, the mysterious. The power of the aesthetic is not "power over"; so bishops cannot be in charge of it. But bishops could begin to make space for it, could risk defying correct procedure, could even risk squandering their good names in Vatican City. Such bishops would instead indulge—perhaps even trust—the spiritual genius of their Catholic people, would encourage the people—even without prior authorization—to express the mystery of Christ as redemptive grace that can be apprehended in the materiality of their peculiar cultures. The times call for bishops who cherish the artists around them, artists who can put the Church's living faith in beautiful forms with language, sound, and material things. The times call for women and men who are able to reclothe the Catholic liturgy in the beauty, terror, and ambiguity suited to the holy mystery enfolding the world.

Redress for the Catholic liturgy well begun, uncontrollable good things might follow. The Christian faithful fanned out over the globe might find healing and so cleave to the Church in love, and the world's oppressed might then be served more justly. That would be getting closer to "the restoration of all things in Christ."

NOTES

1. Luce Irigaray, *je, te, nous. Toward a Culture of Difference*, trans. Alison Martin (New York: Routledge, 1993) 35; emphasis in the original.

2. Julia Kristeva, "Revolution in Poetic Language," in *The Kristeva Reader*, ed. Toril Moi (Oxford: Basil Blackwell, 1986) 113ff. Also see the discussion by Cleo McNelly Kearns, "Kristeva and Feminist Theology," in *Transfigurations*, ed. C. W. Maggie Kim et al. (Minneapolis: Fortress Press, 1993) 65–7. Liturgical theologians have just begun exploration of Kristeva's theory and its implications for analysis of the dynamics of the liturgy.

3. Margaret Mary Kelleher discusses the Church as a collective subject engaged in self-transcendence through its liturgical practice in "Liturgy: An Ecclesial Act of Meaning," *Worship* 1985 (59:6) 482–97. Kristeva's *semiotic* refers to drive-governed, pre-conscious dimensions of the individual psyche.

4. Chris Nwaka Egbulem, *The "Rite Zairois" in the Context of Liturgical Inculturation in Middle-Belt Africa since the Second Vatican Council* (Ann Arbor: Dissertation Microfilm, 1989).

5. Mark Chaves and James C. Cavendish, "More Evidence on U.S. Catholic Church Attendance," *Journal for the Scientific Study of Religion* 33:4 (1994) 376–81.

6. Joseph A. Komonchak, "Modernity and the Construction of Roman Catholicism," in ed. George Gilmore, Hans Rollman, and Gary Lease, *Modernism as a Social Construct* (Mobile, Ala.: Spring Hill College, 1991) 11–41.

7. As recently as 1981 the Roman Congregation promulgated an official liturgical order of crowning an image of the Blessed Virgin Mary. Excerpted in *Celebrating the Marian Year* (Washington, D.C.: National Conference of Catholic Bishops, 1987).

8. Komonchak, "Modernity," 19.

9. Ibid., 21.

10. Pierre Jounel, "Les missels diocésains français du 18ᵉ siècle," *La Maison-Dieu* 141, 91–6; Gaston Fontaine, "Présentation des missels diocésains français du 17ᵉ au 19ᵉ siècle," ibid., 97–166; also Cuthbert Johnson, *Prosper Guéranger (1805–1875): A Liturgical Theologian* (Rome: Pontificio Ateneo S. Anselmo, 1984) 154–89.

11. Johnson, *Prosper Guéranger,* 210–1.

12. Ibid.

13. Olivier Rousseau, *The Progress of the Liturgy: An Historical Sketch from the Beginning of the Nineteenth Century to the Pontificate of Pius X* (Westminster, Md.: Newman Press, 1951).

14. For a discussion of the informal convergence of the social and liturgical movements see my article "Liturgical Movements, Social Influence of" in *The New Dictionary of Catholic Social Thought* (Collegeville: The Liturgical Press, 1994) 553–6.

15. For an extended discussion of this theme, see Mark Searle, "The Liturgy and Catholic Social Doctrine," in *The Future of the Catholic Church in America. Major Papers of the Virgil Michel Symposium* (Collegeville: The Liturgical Press, 1991) 43–73.

16. Lambert Beauduin, *Liturgy, the Life of the Church,* trans. Virgil Michel (Collegeville: The Liturgical Press, 1926) 12–21; emphasis added. For Virgil Michel's own, more "democratic" view, see my essay "Participation: Liturgical Renewal and the Cultural Question" in *The Future of the Catholic Church in America,* 20–42.

17. Beauduin, *Liturgy,* 20.

18. See, for example, Catherine Bell, *Ritual Theory, Ritual Practice* (New York: Oxford, 1993); Clifford Geertz, "Religion as a Cultural System," 87–125, and "Ethos, World View, and the Analysis of Sacred Symbols," 126–41, in *The Interpretation of Culture* (New York: Basic Books, 1973); Margaret Mary Kelleher, "Liturgy and the Christian Imagination," *Worship* 66:2 (1992) 125–48.

19. Beauduin, *Liturgy,* 20; emphasis added.

20. Ibid., 21.

21. For example, Romano Guardini, *Vom Geist der Liturgie* (Freiburg: Herder, 1918) (Tr.: *The Spirit of the Liturgy* [London: Sheed and Ward, 1930]); Annie Dillard, "An Expedition to the Pole," in *Teaching a Stone to Talk* (New York: Harper and Row, 1982) 17–52. For contemporary examples of a Eucharistic Prayer intentionally open to the semiotic, see *An Original Eucharistic Prayer. Text for Study and Comment* (Washington, D.C.: ICEL, 1984).

22. Beauduin, *Liturgy,* 22–32.

23. Ibid., 41.

24. Pope Pius XII, *Mediator Dei.* November 20, 1947. Citations are from *On the Sacred Liturgy,* with introduction and notes by Gerald Ellard, S.J., enlarged and revised edition (New York: America Press, 1961).

25. *Origins* 23:43 (April 14, 1994) 745, 747–56.

26. Guéranger scholar Cuthbert Johnson cites him on this point: ". . . le valeur d'une Liturgie procède de l'autorité qui la confirme." *Prosper Guéranger,* 330, n. 235.

27. Ibid. "It remains a fact that Prosper Guéranger was one of the principal causes of the ecclesiastical revolution which brought about the return of the dioceses of France to the unity of the Roman Liturgy," 243; "In the year in which Guéranger died the last of the dioceses of France which was still using its own liturgical books, Paris, returned *(sic)* to the unity of the Roman rite," 241.

28. According to Annibale Bugnini, a churchman who served three popes (Pius XII, John XXIII, and Paul VI), Pius XII set up a secret commission for liturgical reform accountable to him alone, so secret that its existence was

unknown even to the Congregation of Rites. *The Reform of the Liturgy 1948–1975* (Collegeville: The Liturgical Press, 1990) 9–10.

29. The ritual introductions, which have the status of liturgical law, are printed in each Roman liturgical book. They are collected in *The Rites* (New York: Pueblo Publishing, 1976 and 1980); see also R. Kevin Seasoltz, *New Liturgy, New Laws* (Collegeville: The Liturgical Press, 1980), on the relative canonical status of documents on the liturgy, 169–81.

30. See n. 28 above

31. Frederick R. McManus, "ICEL: The First Years," in *Shaping English Liturgy.* Eds. Peter C. Finn and James M. Schellman (Washington, D.C.: Pastoral Press, 1990) 433–59.

32. Seasoltz, *New Liturgy,* "Strictly speaking, an instruction does not have the force of universal law or definition. If by chance an instruction cannot be reconciled with a given law, the law itself is to be preferred over the instruction," 175.

33. Robert Schreiter, *Constructing Local Theologies* (Maryknoll, N.Y.: Orbis, 1985). Anscar Chupungco, *Liturgies of the Future: The Process and Methods of Inculturation* (Mahwah, N.J.: Paulist, 1989). See also n. 77 of the Fourth General Instruction, citing Pope John Paul's 1991 caution about liturgical inculturation.

34. Irigaray, *je, te, nous,* 35.

35. "Obviously *(sic)* the Christian liturgy cannot accept magic rites, superstition, spiritism, vengeance, or rites with a sexual connotation," Fourth Instruction, #48.

36. "In the liturgy the faith of the Church is expressed in a symbolic and communitarian form: this explains the need for a legislative framework for the organization of worship, the preparation of texts, and the celebration of rites. The reason for the preceptive character of this legislation . . . is to ensure the orthodoxy of worship," Fourth Instruction, #27.

37. See James C. Russell, *The Germanization of Early Medieval Christianity. A Sociohistorical Approach to Religious Transformation* (New York: Oxford, 1994).

EIGHT

Veritatis splendor and Contemporary Catholic Moral Theology

Charles E. Curran

Pope John Paul II's encyclical, *Veritatis splendor,* officially signed on August 6, 1993, has the "central theme" of the "reaffirmation of the universality and immutability of the moral commandments, particularly those which prohibit always and without exception intrinsically evil acts" (n. 115).[1]

The Pope directs his remarks primarily to the state of Catholic moral theology today, but since the Catholic approach always saw its moral teaching affecting society as a whole the encyclical makes important remarks about life in the world today. The Pope had publicly mentioned his intention of writing such an encyclical on August 1, 1987, the second centenary of the death of Alphonsus Liguori, the patron saint of moral theologians and confessors (n. 5). Rumors about the preparation, the primary authors, the central themes, and even the possible scrapping of the whole idea surfaced in the intervening years. The Pope himself refers to the encyclical as "long awaited" and proposes as one reason for the delay that the *Catechism of the Catholic Church* be published first (n. 5).

Overview of the Encyclical

The encyclical is addressed to "the venerable brothers in the episcopate who share with me the responsibility of safeguarding 'sound teaching' . . ." (n. 5).

The occasion for the new encyclical is the "new situation" within the Catholic Church itself. It is no longer a matter of limited and occasional dissent, but of an overall and systematic calling into question of traditional moral doctrines on the basis of certain anthropological and ethical presuppositions (n. 4). These dissenting positions are heard even in seminaries and theological faculties with regard to questions of the greatest importance for the life of the Church and souls (n. 4). This reality constitutes "a genuine crisis" for the Church (n. 5).

At the root of these unacceptable presuppositions causing the present crisis are currents of thought which end by detaching human freedom from its essential and constitutive relationship to truth (n. 4). This explains the whole thrust of the encyclical with its title of the "Splendor of Truth" and with the very first paragraph of the introduction citing 1 Peter 1:22 about the need for "obedience to the truth." The whole structure of the document with its three chapters follows logically and coherently from the understanding of the occasion for it and the root causes of the problem.

The first chapter involves an extended reflection on the story in Matthew 19:16ff. of the rich young man who came to Jesus with the question, "What good must I do to have eternal life?" Jesus' response is to obey the commandments and to give up all his possessions and come follow Jesus. This comparatively long biblical reflection involves a somewhat new approach in papal teachings on moral matters. Catholic moral theology is traditionally based on human reason and natural law. However, similar but shorter reflections on biblical passages can be found in other encyclicals of the Pope.[2] The Pope uses this scriptural passage to point out that God's revelation includes moral commandments and the moral life is intimately connected with faith. However, in no way does the Pope abandon the Catholic emphasis on natural law as the second chapter makes abundantly clear.

The real import of the first chapter comes from its relationship to the purpose of the entire document. "Jesus' conversation with the rich young man continues in a sense in every period of history including our own" (n. 25). The Church ("the pillar and bulwark of the truth"— 2 Tim 3:15) continues the teaching role of Jesus with the "task of authentically interpreting the word of God . . . entrusted only *(sic)* to those charged with the church's living magisterium, whose authority is exercised in the name of Jesus Christ" (n. 27).[3] These quotations come from the end of the first chapter and make the point that the Pope today continues the work of Jesus in teaching the commandments to guide the moral life of all the followers of Jesus.

The way in which Scripture is used depends on the purpose of the one using it. Here the Pope's purpose has shaped and limited the use of the Scripture. The moral life is understood primarily in terms of commandments (to the exclusion and underplaying of other elements such as the change of heart, virtues, vision, attitudes, moral imagination, goals, etc.), and the role of Jesus and consequently of the Church is reduced to teaching commandments. Jesus as exemplar or paradigm is left out. The risen Jesus through the Spirit as the enabler and empowerer of the Christian life is not mentioned. The moral life itself is understood in light of a legal model with the Pope following the role of Jesus proposing the commandments "with the reaffirmation of the universality and immutability of the moral commandments, particularly those prohibiting always and without exception intrinsically evil acts" (n. 115).

The second chapter has an entirely different feel and approach. The Pope, carrying on the moral teaching function of Jesus, points out and condemns certain interpretations of Christian morality which are not consistent with sound teaching. The Pope explicitly denies any intention "to impose upon the faithful any particular theological system, still less a philosophical one" (n. 29). However, in reality John Paul II strongly reasserts the nineteenth- and twentieth-century Neo-Scholasticism of the manuals of moral theology within his more personalistic framework.

The general error pointed out in this section fails to recognize the importance of truth in moral theology and absolutizes freedom or conscience cutting off their basic relationship to truth. The Pope specifically mentions and condemns the most important aspects of the so-called revisionist school of Catholic moral theology (he does not use that term) that has been evolving since Vatican II—an autonomous ethic, the charge of physicalism made against the accepted Catholic teaching in sexual and medical ethics, the theory of fundamental option, and the ethical theory of proportionalism. All these in their own way have called into question the existence of some intrinsically evil acts. *Veritatis splendor* in this chapter also strongly criticizes in the broader context the absolutization of freedom, false autonomy, subjectivism, individualism, and relativism.

Chapter 3 develops a number of related points. The first stresses the bond between freedom and truth. Commitment to the truth above all shows forth in the willingness of people to give their lives for the truth of the Gospel of Jesus. Although martyrdom represents the high point of witness to moral truth, and one to which few people are called, all Christians must daily be ready to make a consistent witness at the cost of suffering and sacrifice (n. 93). Second, universal and unchangeable norms are at the service of persons and of the society thus showing the necessary connection between freedom and truth. Only a morality which acknowledges certain norms and rights as valid always, everywhere, and without exception can guarantee an ethical foundation of social coexistence on both the national and international levels (nn. 95–101). Third, the chapter recalls that God's grace transforms and strengthens weak and sinful human beings to be able to obey God's law (nn. 102–5). A final section on morality and evangelization contains an important section dealing with the roles of the magisterium and of moral theologians who are called to be an example of loyal assent, both internal and external, to the magisterium's teaching (nn. 106–17).

Reaction to the encyclical has followed a somewhat predictable course.[4] Proponents of what has been called revisionism in Catholic moral theology have tended to be quite negative,[5] whereas more conservative moral theologians have been quite positive although some want the Pope to go even further to a definitive and infallible magisterial judgment on the received teaching on intrinsically evil acts and to the same kind of judgment on certain understandings of faith and revelation which are even more fundamental.[6] Some more evangelically rooted scholars have lauded the Pope's great emphasis on Scripture and the Gospel, but perhaps they do not give enough importance to how strongly the second chapter of the documents holds on to Neo-Scholastic philosophy.[7] Feminists readily find fault with the methodology involved.[8] A good number have been appreciative of the Pope's dealing with the broader societal issues.[9] All of us interpret and react to the document in the light of our own understandings and interests, but we all must be careful to try to understand precisely what the Pope is saying before entering into dialogue with him. In this spirit I recognize that I am coming from a revisionist position and have disagreed over the years with the papal teaching on intrinsically evil acts and dissent in the Church. One commentator has pointed out that the encyclical is directed at my work.[10] However, I also find myself in agreement with many points made in the encyclical.

Positive Evaluation

I find myself in agreement with many of the Pope's problems with some contemporary ethical thinking, with the positive points he makes against them, and with the applications especially in the area of social ethics. Moral truth is most important. Freedom and conscience can never be absolutized. There are many things one should not do (nn. 35–53). The Catholic tradition in the past often failed to give enough importance to freedom as exemplified in its long-standing opposition to religious freedom and the continuing problems with academic freedom. However, as the twentieth century developed, the Catholic Church in reaction to the danger of totalitarianism began to give a greater role to human freedom. A very significant development occurred in Pope John XXIII's writings within two years. In *Mater et magistra* in 1961 he claimed that the ideal social order was founded on the values of truth, justice, and love.[11] In *Pacem in terris* in 1963 he added freedom to this triad.[12] Freedom is very significant, but it must be seen in its relationship to other values. The Pope in *Veritatis splendor* is concentrating on freedom's relationship to truth, but it is fair to say he is not denying the other important relationships of freedom with justice and charity. One is not free to deny fundamental human rights.

Just as freedom cannot be absolutized, so too conscience cannot be absolutized. Conscience cannot make something right or wrong (nn. 54–64). Adolph Eichmann claimed that he only followed his conscience, but he was rightly convicted of crimes against humanity. Conscience is called to recognize and respond to moral truth.

Intimately connected with the absolutization of freedom of conscience is the false autonomy of the individual. The individual is not autonomous in the sense that the individual makes something right or wrong on her own. Here too, however, the Catholic tradition has not given enough importance to the role of creativity and the initiative of the individual. But one cannot go to the other extreme and proclaim the absolute autonomy of the individual. Any theistic morality sees the individual in relationship to and dependent on God.

The challenge is to avoid both a one-sided autonomy or a one-sided heteronomy. *Veritatis splendor* deals well with this aspect of autonomy in the first part of chapter 2 (nn. 38–42). To its credit the Catholic tradition with its emphasis on participation has been able to provide a very satisfactory approach to this question. Too often the issue is proposed in terms of a competition between the divine and the human. If you have one hundred points to assign to both, then you might assign eighty to God and twenty to the human. But maybe human beings should have more and God less. The traditional Catholic emphasis on participation and mediation as mentioned in the encyclical avoids such an either or approach. The glory of God is the human person come alive. God wants us to attain our happiness and our perfection. The basic insight of Thomas Aquinas well illustrates this approach. In the Second Part of the *Summa*, Aquinas treats of the human being. The human being is an image of God because like God she is endowed with intellect, free will, and the power of self-determination.[13] The human person imitates God by using her intellect, free will, and the power of self-determination. Traditional Catholic moral theology following the teaching of Thomas Aquinas sees the natural law as the participation of the eternal law in the rational creature. Human reason reflecting on God's created human nature can arrive at the plan of God for us which involves our own fulfillment.[14] All theists and even some nontheists would join the Catholic tradition in denying the absolute autonomy of the human being. But the Catholic tradition does not want to embrace a heteronomy which downplays the place of self-direction and human fulfillment.

Likewise the Pope properly points out the related danger of individualism in our society (n. 33). The absolutization of freedom, conscience, and autonomy logically lead to individualism. The individual becomes the center of all reality and not enough importance is given to the community in general, the various communities to which we all belong, and the relationships that tie us to other human beings. In the past again the Catholic tradition has not given enough importance to the individual, and sometimes in the name of community restricted the role and rights of the individual. Think of the acceptance of torture in some cases and the failure to recognize the right of the defendant not to incriminate oneself. Until this century it was universally held that the state could and should use capital punishment to protect itself, but now many Catholics, recognizing more the dignity of the person, strongly oppose capital punishment. A greater emphasis is being given to the rights of the individual vis-à-vis the state, but contemporary Catholic thought in keeping with the best of its own tradition rightly rejects individualism. In the United States society today many are criticizing American individualism in the name of a more communitarian understanding of human anthropology.[15] The Catholic tradition strongly supports such a communitarian critique of individualism.

Subjectivism logically follows from all the above-mentioned approaches. The Pope correctly condemns the subjectivism that makes the subject the center of right and wrong and does not give enough significance to objective reality (n. 32). Here again the Catholic tradition in the past has not given enough importance to the subject, and many recent developments in Catholic theology and philosophy have embraced the turn to the subject but this does not entail a radical moral subjectivism.

This radical subjectivism often appears in our society but without much philosophical grounding. The morality accepted by many people today proclaims that you do your thing and I'll do my thing. Just don't interfere with each other. Such subjective individualism destroys any possibility of a community of shared truths and values. To have a community one needs such shared moral values. The Pope rightly points out there are rights that are always and everywhere to be acknowledged and protected. There are actions such as torture, arbitrary imprisonment, and treating workers as mere instruments of profit that should never be done (nn. 95–7). The dangers of individualism and subjectivism are present in our contemporary American society.

Finally, John Paul II points out the danger of relativism for human social living (nn. 96–101). The Catholic tradition by definition stands opposed to relativism. Catholic means universal, and the Pope insists on the existence of universal principles and norms. The danger in the Catholic tradition has been not to give enough importance to diversity in all its different forms. Think, for example, of the insistence on the universal language for liturgical prayer before Vatican II so that almost no Catholic understood the language of the Eucharist. The Catholic emphasis on universality too easily claimed universality for what was a historically or culturally conditioned reality. Feminism reminds us how easy it was for those in power to impose patriarchy in the name of universality.

One of the most significant debates in contemporary ethics focuses on the possibility of universality in ethics with many either theoretically or practically denying the possibility of such universality.[16] However, the Catholic tradition with its emphasis on the one God who is Creator, Redeemer, and Sanctifier of all can never accept a relativism. We are brothers and sisters of all other human beings and called to live together with them in peace and harmony. In the midst of the pluralism and diversity of our world universalism is more chastened than in the past and more difficult to ground and explain. I think that the Pope tends to gloss over too easily some of the objections to universalism, too readily grounds it in Thomistic natural law, and at times claims too much for it. However, the Catholic tradition has correctly insisted on universality.

The signs of the times also demand some universality. We experience the lack of unity in many countries in the world including our own. Religious, ethnic, and tribal differences are the cause of war and disintegration in many nations. In our own United States' society the divisions based on color and economic class are evident in every one of our cities. In our world with its growing interrelatedness, we badly need to be able to communicate with one another despite religious, linguistic, ethnic, and cultural differences. In many ways the challenge to our society today is how to achieve unity in the midst of the great diversity that exists on all levels.

Negative Evaluation

My strong disagreements with the papal letter center on his understanding of and approach to contemporary Catholic moral theology and what might be described as the churchly aspect of moral theology as distinguished from Catholic social ethics. Having already identified myself as a revisionist Catholic moral theologian, one would expect such differences to be there. Naturally, I disagree with the position that condemns the revisionist developments in moral theology, but I am even more disturbed by other aspects of the papal document.

The Role and Understanding of Law. The first objection comes from the moral model which the Pope proposes in *Veritatis splendor.* Here John Paul II understands morality primarily on the basis of a legal model. Such an approach which characterized the manuals of moral theology in vogue until very recent times sees morality primarily in terms of obedience to the law or the commandments of God. No one can doubt that *Veritatis splendor* employs such a model. The very first paragraph emphasizes the need for obedience to the truth but recognizes that such obedience is not always easy. The pericope of the rich young man stresses Jesus as the teacher proposing the commandments that are to be obeyed. The first and longest of the four parts of chapter 2 deals with freedom and the law (nn. 35–53). Chapter 2 especially emphasizes the role of the natural law. Positive precepts of the natural law are "universally binding" and "unchanging." The negative precepts of the natural law oblige always and in every circumstance—*semper et pro semper* (n. 52). The third chapter continues this approach with its emphasis on laws and commands and the Church's firmness . in defending the universal and unchanging moral norms (n. 96).

In the judgment of many the legal model is not the best and most adequate model for moral theology or any ethics. At the very minimum the legal model cannot adequately cover all the moral decisions that a person makes. In fact, the vast majority of moral decisions are not made on the basis of existing laws. Law directly enters into comparatively few of the moral decisions by which we live our lives. In addition, the legal model tends to restrict moral considerations only to acts and forgets about the more important realities of change of heart, vision, attitudes, dispositions, etc. Thomas Aquinas did not follow a legal model, but rather a teleological model based on what is the ultimate end of human beings. For Aquinas the ultimate end of human beings is happiness, and actions are good if they bring one to that end and evil if they prevent one's arriving at that end. Reality of course is quite complex so there exists not only the ultimate end but also other ends which are not ultimate and interrelated with one another. In addition, Thomas Aquinas developed the moral life primarily in terms of human powers and habits and only brings in law at the end of his discussion of what we call fundamental moral theology.[17] The manuals of moral theology, the textbooks in the field before Vatican II, did adopt a legal model. Much has been said about the legal model, but for our present purposes it suffices to point out the inadequacy of the model and the fact that Thomas Aquinas himself adopted a different approach.

One might defend the legal model in *Veritatis splendor* precisely because the Pope is dealing primarily with the existence of universal and immutable moral commandments, especially those which prohibit always and without exception intrinsically evil acts. However, at the very minimum the encyclical should have pointed out that the legal model is not the most adequate model for moral theology and this document is dealing only with one aspect of moral theology. Neither explicitly nor implicitly does the Pope make such an admission. *Veritatis splendor* thus gives the impression that it is describing the model for moral theology in general.

Ironically someone in the Catholic tradition using the legal model tends to weaken the basic assertion of the entire encyclical that there is no opposition between freedom and law. Historically the manuals of moral theology with their legal model, ever since the debates over probabilism in the seventeenth century and later tended to posit an opposition between law and freedom. This assertion needs further explanation.

The Catholic tradition as illustrated in Thomas Aquinas has always insisted on an intrinsic morality. Something is commanded because it is good. For Aquinas the ultimate end of human beings is happiness. Morality involves what is good for me as a person and ultimately makes me flourish. There is no opposition between freedom and moral obligation because the moral obligation is based on what is good for the individual. This is the central point to which the Pope so frequently returns in his document. However, in the manuals of moral theology ever since the probabilism controversy a greater opposition rather than harmonious agreement exists between freedom and law. Probabilism maintains that one may follow a truly probable opinion going against the existence of a law even if the opinion favoring the existence of the law is more probable. The so-called reflex principle used to defend this position holds that a doubtful law does not oblige—an adage more attuned to human law than anything else. The individual starts out with one's freedom and this freedom can only be taken away by a certain law.[18] Ironically the law model as it was employed in the manuals of Catholic moral theology in the light of the probabilism controversy emphasized the tension and apparent opposition between freedom and law rather than the harmony which the Pope wants to emphasize.

Laws Which Always and Everywhere Oblige. The major thrust of the encyclical insists on universal, immutable moral commandments which prohibit always and without exception intrinsically evil acts. In this context note that the Pope never cites the fifth commandment, "Thou shalt not kill." Everyone recognizes that killing is not always and everywhere wrong. We have justified killing in cases of self-defense and war. In fact, after much discussion and nuancing the manuals of moral theology came to the conclusion that the intrinsically evil act which is always forbidden is the following: direct killing of the innocent on one's own authority. Thus we allowed indirect killing, killing in self-defense or in war, and capital punishment.[19]

Notice the difference between the two. Killing is a physical act which in some circumstances can be permitted. The second rule tries to account for all the possible justifying circumstances and thus states the norm that admits of no exceptions. But one has to circumscribe quite severely the generic "no killing. " The Pope himself in this document does not cite this very specific absolute norm that was developed in Catholic moral theology.

What then is the papal example of the universal, immutable condemnation of an act that is always and everywhere wrong? The answer: murder. Thus in the passage about the rich young man in Matthew, Jesus begins the commandments with, "You shall not murder" (n. 13). All would agree that murder is always wrong because by definition murder is unjustified killing. Thus we have here three different types of norms dealing with killing. The Pope cites only the very formal norm of no murder.

But there is a problem in *Veritatis splendor* from the Pope's own perspective because of a fourth formulation that is proposed. The Pope wants to illustrate the point that there are intrinsically evil acts which are always and per se such on account of their very object and quite apart from the intention of the agent and circumstances. He quotes the Pastoral Constitution on the Church in the Modern World, paragraph 27, to illustrate this thesis (n. 80). The quote begins: "Whatever is hostile to life itself such as any kind of homicide. . . ." However, homicide is not an intrinsically evil act. Homicide is the physical act of killing a human being. Our language recognizes that homicide can be justifiable in certain circumstances.

But the problem might not come primarily from the Pope. The official Latin version of the encyclical in its citation from the Pastoral Constitution on the Church in the Modern World uses the word *homicidium.*[20] *Homicidium* in the Latin can refer either to murder or homicide. As mentioned above in this case the Pope is citing a text from the Pastoral Constitution on the Church in the Modern World of Vatican II.

Two unofficial English translations of the Vatican II documents translate *homicidium* as murder.[21] However, the official translation of the papal encyclical that came from the Vatican uses the word homicide. The error might rest with the translator and the approval of that translation by the Vatican. However, at the very minimum this goes to show how intricate and difficult it is to speak about norms that are always and everywhere obliging without any exception.

In fact, the list of actions found originally in the Pastoral Constitution on the Church in the Modern World and quoted in *Veritatis splendor* contains some actions which are not always and everywhere wrong. Both documents include abortion under the category of "what is hostile to life itself." However, the Catholic tradition has always recognized the existence of some conflict situations and concluded that direct abortion is always wrong. Indirect abortion can be justified for a proportionate reason so that abortion is not always and everywhere wrong. One would have to be stretching the point beyond belief to claim that the original clause of "whatever is hostile to life itself" means that homicide is murder and abortion is direct murder. The reality is that any homicide or abortion is hostile to life itself, but in some circumstances might be justified.

The second category of those actions in both documents which are now claimed by the Pope to be always and everywhere wrong concerns "whatever violates the integrity of the human person such as mutilation. . . ." However, Catholic moral theology has consistently recognized justified mutilation. In fact, the primary precept in medical ethics justifies a mutilation of a part of the body for the sake of the whole.[22] Here again one cannot appeal to the opening clause "whatever violates the integrity of the human person" to show that the mutilation in such a context excluded medical mutilation for the good of the whole person. If the heading were the dignity or total good of the human person, then one could make such a claim. By definition all mutilation goes against the integrity of the person, but the Catholic tradition does not say that all mutilation is wrong. The Pope's efforts to uphold laws that are intrinsically or always and without exception wrong by reason of the object is fraught with difficulties. There are such actions when the act is described in merely formal terms such as murder. One could also make the case that there are such acts when the significant circumstances are included. In reality, *Veritatis splendor* itself does not succeed in making a consistent case to prove its own position about acts that are always and intrinsically evil by reason of the object alone.

Evaluation of Contemporary Moral Theology. Veritatis splendor strongly disagrees with and condemns many of the developments in Catholic moral theology since Vatican II and stands opposed to the revisionist moral theology in general.

However, *Veritatis splendor* distorts and does not accurately describe the various positions attributed to so-called revisionist moral theologians. The first part of chapter 2 disagrees with a school of autonomous ethics which first arose in Germany (nn. 36, 37). I have disagreed with the name autonomous but accept the reality proposed in the sense that the moral content for life in this world is the same for Christians as for non-Christians. In my judgment this position is in keeping with the traditional assertion that the Christian brings the human to its perfection and fulfillment. Like *Veritatis splendor* I have also disagreed with the contention that the Scripture provides only *parenesis* or exhortation as some hold.[23] However, the supporters of autonomous ethics in the Catholic tradition would strongly disagree with the following description of their position. "Such norms . . . would be the expression of a law which man *(sic)* in an autonomous manner lays down for himself and which has its source exclusively in human reason. In no way could God be considered the author of this law except in the sense that human reason exercises its autonomy in setting down laws by virtue of a primordial and total mandate given to man by God" (n. 36).

Veritatis splendor in the same first part of chapter 2 points out that some Catholic moral theologians have disagreed with the teachings of the hierarchical magisterium in the area of sexual morality because of its "physicalism" and "naturalistic" argumentation (n. 47). Such a statement is correct. In my opinion physicalism is the a priori identification of the human or the moral aspect with the physical, natural, or biological process. So far, so good. But the Pope goes on to explain this theory in this way. "A freedom which claims to be absolute ends up treating the human body as a raw datum devoid of any meaning and moral values until freedom has shaped it in accordance with its design. Consequently, human nature and the body appear as presuppositions or preambles, materially necessary for freedom to make its choice, yet extrinsic to the person, the subject, and the human act. . . . The finalities of these inclinations would be merely 'physical' goods, called by some *premoral*. To refer to them, in order to find in them rational indications with regard to the order of morality, would be to expose oneself to the accusation of physicalism or biologism. In this way of thinking, the tension between freedom and a nature conceived of in a reductive way is resolved by a division within man *(sic)* himself" (n. 48).

Those who charge the hierarchical magisterium's teaching on sexuality with physicalism do not "treat the human body as a raw datum devoid of any meaning." The physical is one aspect of the moral or the fully human. The moral or the fully human must embrace all the aspects of the human—the physical and the spiritual, the sociological and the psychological, the eugenic and the hygenic, etc. In keeping with the Catholic tradition one should never be guilty of a reductionism that reduces the fully human to just one aspect of the human no matter what that aspect is. Yes, there are times when the physical is the same as the moral and the truly human, but this needs further justification to make the point.[24] In this very citation the Pope contradicts his own assertion. *Veritatis splendor* refers to this physical aspect as physical or premoral goods. Note the word "goods. " They are not just "raw datum" or "extrinsic to the person." Those making the charge of physicalism take seriously the position of Pius XII that the physical and the bodily exist to serve the higher spiritual good of the person.[25] That one can in theory interfere with the physical or biological process because of the good of the total person as a whole seems to be very much in accord with any kind of personalism. But at the very least *Veritatis splendor* distorts the position of those who characterize hierarchical Catholic sexual teaching as guilty of physicalism. We do not absolutize freedom and we do not deny any value or meaning to the physical. In our judgment the hierarchical magisterium in this matter has absolutized the physical and the biological at the expense of the truly and the fully human.

The second part of chapter 2 deals with the relationship between conscience and truth. However, John Paul II also dealt with that question earlier in the encyclical. The Pope claims that those who invoke the criterion of conscience as "being at peace with oneself" (he puts the words in quotation marks) are guilty of absolutizing freedom, forgetting the claim of truth, and subjectivism (n. 32).

I have proposed a theory of conscience which "attempts to explain in a more systematic and reflective way the traditionally accepted notion that joy and peace mark the good conscience which is the adequate criterion of good moral judgment and decision."[26] I explicitly point out that my approach disagrees with the position of the manuals that the judgment of conscience is based on conformity with the truth "out there." I developed this theory in dialogue with the transcendental approaches of Karl Rahner and Bernard Lonergan. However, I insist that one's judgment has to attain the true and the real value. I do put great emphasis on the subject but insist that "thus we have established the radical identity between genuine objectivity and authentic subjectivity."[27] Such an approach is proposed as a theory and others might readily disagree with it, but it does not "exalt freedom to such an extent that it becomes an absolute" nor "adopt a radically subjectivistic conception of moral judgment" (n. 32).

In the second part of chapter 2 on conscience, it seems that the Pope's insistence on the relationship between conscience and truth has influenced him to take a position which at the very least is in opposition to the generally accepted position in Catholic moral theology. *Veritatis splendor* states: "It is possible that the evil done as the result of invincible ignorance or a nonculpable error of judgment may not be imputable to the agent; but even in this case it does not cease to be an evil. . . ." (n. 63). Thomas Aquinas maintained that invincible ignorance renders the act involuntary and excuses from sin. In other words, the evil act done in invincible ignorance is never imputable to the agent. The encyclical does not go as far as Aquinas and simply says that it "may not be imputable to the agent." However, St. Alphonsus Ligouri, the patron saint of moral theologians and confessors, goes even further than Aquinas. Alphonsus maintains that an act done out of invincible ignorance is not only not imputable but it is actually meritorious. This opinion of Alphonsus became the more common position among Catholic theologians.[28] Louis Vereecke, now an emeritus professor of the history of moral theology at the Academia Alfonsiana in Rome and a consultor to the Holy Office, concludes his article on conscience in Alphonsus Liguori by claiming that Alphonsus' moral doctrine on conscience embraces three values—the importance of truth, the importance of reason and conscience, and the importance of freedom.[29] By so emphasizing and perhaps even absolutizing the relationship of conscience to truth *Veritatis splendor* not only does not accept the position of Alphonsus but does not even accept the position of Thomas Aquinas that does not go as far as Alphonsus.

The third part of chapter 3 addresses the theory of the fundamental option. Here also the theory is distorted. For example, the encyclical speaks of the theory as separating "the fundamental option from concrete kinds of behavior" (n. 67, see also n. 70). The theory of fundamental option distinguishes the different levels of human freedom and of transcendental and categorical acts, but it does not separate them. As Joseph Fuchs, who has written much on the fundamental option, points out, the encyclical distorts the meaning of the theory by failing to recognize that the fundamental option and categorical acts happen on different levels and thus the fundamental option does not occur in the area of reflex consciousness.[30]

The fourth part of chapter 3 deals with the moral act, insists on acts that are intrinsically evil by reason of their object, and condemns teleological and proportionalist theories which hold "that it is impossible to qualify as morally evil according to its species—its 'object'— the deliberate choice of certain kinds of behavior or specific acts apart from a consideration of the intention for which the choice is made or the totality of the foreseeable consequences of that act for all persons concerned" (n. 79). On a number of occasions the Pope points out that a good intention is not sufficient to determine the morality of an act (n. 67, n. 78). But no Catholic moral theologian I know has ever claimed that the intention alone suffices to determine the morality of an act.[31] Above I pointed out that as a revisionist I accept some acts as always and everywhere wrong if the significant circumstances (not the totality of the forseeable consequences) are included.

I have no doubt that the Pope disagrees with all these recently developed theories in Catholic moral theology, but the encyclical tends to distort them and thus does not reflect their true meaning. In a certain sense they are made into straw people which then are much easier to reject. However, this is not the worst distortion in the encyclical about the present state of Catholic moral theology.

The Pope claims that the "root of these presuppositions [of the dissenting Catholic moral theologians] is the more or less obvious influence of currents of thought which end by detaching human freedom from its essential and constitutive relationship to truth" (n. 4). This sentence is found in the opening introduction to the entire document. The introduction to chapter 2 points out "these tendencies are at one in lessening or even denying the dependence of freedom on truth" (n. 34). Note some qualification in these statements, but the fundamental problem the Pope has with revisionist Catholic moral theologians is their tendency to detach or lessen human freedom's relationship to truth. Such an assertion itself is not accurate. I know no Catholic moral theologian who absolutizes freedom or detaches conscience from truth. The real question remains the proverbial one—what is truth?

As a result of this misreading of the present state of Catholic moral theology, the Pope apparently sees no difference between Catholic revisionist moral theologians and the proponents of absolute freedom, conscience separated from truth, individualism, subjectivism, and relativism. Non-Catholic colleagues or any fair-minded interpreter of the present state of Catholic moral theology would readily recognize that revisionist Catholic moral theologians are not absolutizing freedom or conscience and are not supporting individualism, subjectivism, and relativism. Catholic revisionist moral theologians strongly agree with the Pope in opposing these positions. That is why I made it a point earlier in this essay to stress my strong agreement with the Pope on these points.

All recognize that the Pope strongly disagrees with and condemns revisionist Catholic moral positions, but the problem here is the understanding of revisionist moral theologians. Their theories are caricatured, but even worse the Pope falsely accuses them of absolutizing freedom and separating it from truth and wrongly identifies them with subjectivists, individualists, and relativists.

What is going on here? I do not know. Some have blamed the Pope's advisors.[32] Such an approach is a familiar Catholic tactic. When Catholics disagree with the Pope, it is always easier to blame it on the advisors than on the Pope. On the other hand, I have never heard anyone who agreed with a papal statement say that they agreed with the Pope's advisors! Popes obviously have advisors, but the final document is the Pope's and not the advisors'. More worrisome is the fact that the Pope's area of expertise is ethics. Does he really think that Catholic moral theologians who dissent on some church teachings especially in the area of sexuality are subjectivists, individualists, and relativists?

A realistic assessment of the contemporary state of Catholic moral theology differs considerably from the picture painted in *Veritatis splendor*. The differences between the Pope and revisionist moral theologians are by no means as great as *Veritatis splendor* states. Yes, different methodologies are often at work, but revisionist moral theologians have generally agreed with the papal teaching in the area of social ethics. Likewise revisionist moral theologians are willing to accept some intrinsically evil acts when the object of the act is described in formal terms (murder is always wrong, stealing is always wrong) or when the act is described in terms of its significant circumstances (not telling the truth when the neighbor has no right to the truth).

The primary area of disagreement concerns the understanding of the moral object—the encyclical claims that morality is determined by the three sources of morality—the object, the end, and the circumstances and that some actions are intrinsically evil by reason of their object (nn. 71–83). The question is, how does one describe the object? As mentioned above, revisionist theologians would be willing to admit intrinsically evil acts by reason of the object if the object were described in a broad or formal way or with some significant circumstances. The earlier discussion about always obliging laws pointed out a very significant problem in the encyclical itself in describing the moral object.

Revisionists in general object to those cases in which the moral act is assumed to be identical with the physical structure of the act. These areas occur especially in the area of sexuality. As pointed out, not every killing, mutilation, taking something that belongs to another, and false speech are always wrong. Contraception, however, describes a physical act. The physical act described as depositing male semen in the vagina of the female can never be interfered with. Some people have mistakenly thought that the hierarchical teaching against contraception was based on a pronatalist position. Such is not the case. The hierarchical teaching also condemns artificial insemination with the husband's seed even for the good end of having a child. The reason why both contraception and AIH are wrong is because the physical act must always be there and one can never interfere with it no matter what the purpose.[33]

The charge of physicalism is intimately connected with the theory of proportionalism. Rather than describe the physical act or object as morally wrong this theory speaks of premoral, ontic, or physical evil that can be justified for a proportionate reason. This challenges the hierarchical teaching on contraception but also explains the existing hierarchical teaching on killing, mutilation, taking property, etc. There is no doubt that Catholic moral theologians are calling for a change in hierarchical teaching especially in the area of sexuality, but they are precisely challenging these areas in which the moral aspect has been a priori identified with the physical aspect of the act. Thus the differences between these revisionist moral theologians and the Pope are much less than the encyclical recognizes. The problem is not that dissenting moral theologians absolutize freedom and/or conscience or separate them from truth. The question remains, what is moral truth?

Hierarchical Magisterium and Theologians. The confrontation and differences within Catholic moral theology in the last few decades have centered not only on the moral issues themselves but on the ecclesiological questions of the role and functioning both of the hierarchical magisterium and of theologians. *Veritatis splendor* explicitly addresses these issues in the third chapter (nn. 106–17), although the role of the hierarchical magisterium is mentioned throughout the document.

The encyclical itself deals primarily with moral truth. The ultimate question for both the hierarchical magisterium and for moral theology is what is moral truth and how do we arrive at moral truth? *Veritatis splendor* condemns many approaches in moral theology and in the broader ethical world, but it never really explicitly addresses the question about how the hierarchical magisterium itself arrives at moral truth. In fact, the encyclical gives the impression that the hierarchical magisterium just has the truth. However, the hierarchical magisterium like everyone else has to learn the moral truth. How is this done? The most frequently used phrase in this regard in the encyclical is the "assistance of the Holy Spirit." Mention is also made of the revelational aspect of morality and the hierarchical magisterium's role as the protector, guarantor, and interpreter of revelation.

The entire second chapter with its discussion of very complex theories and positions shows that the hierarchical magisterium also uses human reason in its attempt to know and explain moral truth. The Catholic insistence on mediation means that God works in and through the human and does not provide short circuits around the human. The assistance of the Holy Spirit does not exempt the hierarchical magisterium from using all the human reason necessary to arrive at moral truth. The tradition of Catholic natural law once again affirmed and developed in this encyclical maintains that its moral theology is based on human reason and accessible to all human beings. Yes, the encyclical reminds us (correctly) that human sin affects all our reasoning processes, but sin does not take away human reason's ability to arrive at moral truth (nn. 86–7). In learning moral truth the hierarchical magisterium must use human reason like everyone else.

In the last few decades many theologians have also pointed out the experience of Christian people as a source of moral knowledge. Once again, sin affects human experience and a proper discernment is required. One cannot just work on the basis of a majority vote. However, the hierarchical magisterium itself in its Declaration on Religious Freedom of Vatican II recognized the experience of Christian people as a source of moral wisdom by saying that the fathers of the council take careful note of these desires for religious freedom in the minds of human beings and proposes to declare them to be greatly in accord with truth and justice.[34] However, *Veritatis splendor* never mentions even implicitly that the hierarchical magisterium can and should learn from the experience of Christian people. The Pope explicitly says the fact that some believers do not follow the hierarchical magisterium or consider as morally correct behavior that their pastors have condemned cannot be a valid argument for rejecting the moral norms taught by the hierarchical magisterium (n. 112).

The Thomistic moral tradition which the hierarchical magisterium claims to follow has insisted on an intrinsic morality—something is commanded because it is good and not the other way around. The hierarchical magisterium does not make something right or wrong, but the hierarchical magisterium must conform itself to the moral truth. Thus the hierarchical magisterium must use all the means available to arrive at that truth.

In addition, the Thomistic tradition recognizes that one cannot have the same degree of certitude about practical truths as about speculative truths.[35] The hierarchical magisterium has a role in guaranteeing and protecting revelation under the inspiration of the Holy Spirit but must also use all the human means available to arrive at moral truth and live with the reality that practical truths do not have the same degree of certitude as speculative truths. One cannot expect an encyclical to say everything on the subject, but a document dealing with the splendor of truth might have been expected to say something about the nature of moral truth and how the hierarchical magisterium itself learns and knows this moral truth.

History points out that the teaching of the hierarchical magisterium in moral matters has been wrong in the past and has developed or changed. John Noonan has recently documented this change in the areas of usury, marriage, slavery, and religious freedom.[36] The fact that past teachings of the hierarchical magisterium in morality have been wrong must have some influence on how one understands the pronouncements of the hierarchical magisterium today.

The Catholic tradition itself has rightly recognized a hierarchy of truths,[37] and even the pre-Vatican II theology developed a system of theological notes to determine how core and central teachings are in Catholic faith.[38] All interpreters would admit that most of the papal teaching (I would say all, as would many others) on specific moral issues involves the noninfallible teaching office of the Pope. The fact that something is noninfallible does not mean that it is necessarily wrong or that Catholics can disagree with it, but by definition it means that it is fallible. Catholic moral theologians as well as the hierarchical magisterium today must do more work to develop and talk about these different categories in the light of the general insistence on the hierarchy of truths and the older theological notes. At the very minimum the hierarchical magisterium itself must also be willing to recognize the more tentative and peripheral nature of some of its pronouncements. In addition, the hierarchical magisterium has never come to grips with the fact that some of its teachings in the past have been wrong and subsequently changed.

Veritatis splendor understands the role of the moral theologian in the light of its understanding of the hierarchical magisterium. The assumption is that the hierarchical magisterium with the assistance of the Holy Spirit has the moral truth and proclaims it. Therefore moral theologians are to give an example of loyal assent, both internal and external, to the hierarchical magisterium's teaching (n. 110).

Veritatis splendor in an adversative clause acknowledges "the possible limitations of the human arguments employed by the magisterium," but calls moral theologians to develop a deeper understanding of the reasons underlying the hierarchical magisterium's teaching and to expound the validity and obligatory nature of the precepts it proposes (n. 110). Thus there might be limitations in the arguments proposed by the hierarchical magisterium, but these in no way affect the validity of the precepts it proposes.

In condemning dissent the present document follows the approach of *Donum veritatis*, the 1990 document of the Congregation for the Doctrine of the Faith on the role of theologians.[39] Dissent, in the form of carefully orchestrated protests and polemics carried on in the media, is opposed to ecclesial communion and to a proper understanding of the hierarchical constitution of the people of God. Opposition to the teaching of the Church's pastors cannot be seen as a legitimate expression either of Christian freedom or of the diversity of the Spirit's gifts (n. 113). I know no Catholic moral theologian who dissents from Church teaching who would propose what she or he has done in those terms. One might argue that such a definition of dissent leaves the door open for a different type of dissent. However, the encyclical itself calls for moral theologians to give an example of loyal assent, both internal and external, to the magisterium's teaching (n. 110).

The consideration here of the hierarchical magisterium does not intend to be a thorough discussion of the role of the hierarchical magisterium or of the moral theologian. This discussion is sufficient to point out the differences that exist. Revisionist Catholic moral theologians recognize the role of the hierarchical magisterium, but insist that its teachings cannot claim an absolute certitude on specific moral issues, have been wrong in the past, and might in some circumstances be wrong today. In this light dissent is at times a legitimate and loyal function of the Catholic moral theologian. However, *Veritatis splendor* at the very minimum does not admit any kind of tentativeness or lack of absolute certitude about the teachings of the hierarchical magisterium, and in no way explicitly recognizes a positive role for dissent.

Ever since the Pope announced his intention in August 1987 of writing an encyclical dealing more fully with the issues regarding the foundations of moral theology in the light of certain present-day tendencies, any student of moral theology had a pretty good idea of what the encyclical would do. The Pope was certainly not going to change any of the teachings that have recently been reinforced nor was he going to abandon the reasoning process behind those teachings. As a result then no one should be surprised by those aspects found in *Veritatis splendor.*

What is surprising is the fact that the Pope caricatures the positions of Catholic revisionist moral theologians and refuses to recognize the great areas of agreement between them and himself. One can only wonder why *Veritatis splendor* proposes such an "either/or" or "all or nothing" understanding of the positions taken by Catholic revisionist moral theologians. The fundamental question remains: what is moral truth?

NOTES

1. Pope John Paul II, *Veritatis splendor, Origins* 23 (1993) 297–334. References will be given in the text to the paragraph numbers in the encyclical.

2. E.g., the parable of the prodigal son in *Dives in misericordia*, nn. 6–7. See Pope John Paul II, *"Dives in misericordia,"* in Michael Walsh and Brian Davies, eds., *Proclaiming Justice and Peace: Papal Documents from* Rerum novarum *through* Centesimus annus (Mystic, Conn: Twenty-Third Publications, 1991) 344–7.

3. This passage is a citation from *Dei Verbum*, the Constitution on Divine Revelation of the Second Vatican Council, n. 10.

4. Symposia on *Veritatis splendor* have appeared in *Commonweal* 120 (October 22, 1993) 11–18; *First Things*, n. 39 (January 1944) 14–29. *The Tablet* (London) devoted a series of eleven articles to the encyclical beginning with the October 16, 1993 issue, 1329ff.

5. E.g., Bernhard Häring, "A Distress that Wounds," *The Tablet* 247 (October 23, 1993) 1378–9; Richard A. McCormick, "Killing a Patient," *The Tablet* 247 (October 30, 1993) 1410–1; Daniel C. Maguire, "The Splendor of Control," *Conscience* 14, n. 4 (Winter 1993/1994) 26–9.

6. John Finnis, "Beyond the Encyclical," *The Tablet* 248 (January 8, 1994) 9-10; Robert P. George, "The Splendor of Truth: A Symposium," *First Things* n. 39 (January 1994) 24–5; Germain Grisez, "Revelation vs. Dissent," *The Tablet* 247 (October 16, 1993) 1329–31.

7. Stanley Hauerwas, *"Veritatis splendor,"* *Commonweal* 120 (October 22, 1993) 16–7; L. Gregory Jones, "The Splendor of Truth: A Symposium," *First Things* n. 39 (January 1994) 19–20; Oliver O'Donovan, "A Summons to Reality," *The Tablet* 247 (November 27, 1993) 1550–2.

8. Lisa Sowle Cahill, "Accent on the Masculine," *The Tablet* 247 (December 11, 1993) 1618-9.

9. E.g., Mary Tuck, "A Message in Season," *The Tablet* 247 (December 4, 1993) 1583-5.

10. Maguire, *Conscience*, 14, n. 4 (Winter 1993/94) 28.

11. Pope John XXIII, *Mater et magistra*, n. 212, in David J. O'Brien and Thomas A. Shannon, eds., *Catholic Social Thought: The Documentary Heritage* (New York: Orbis, 1992) 118.

12. Pope John XXIII, *Pacem in terris*, n. 35, in O'Brien-Shannon, *Catholic Social Thought*, 136.

13. Thomas Aquinas, *Summa Theologiae* (Rome: Marietti, 1952) $I^a II^{ae}$, Prologue.

14. Ibid., q. 91, a. 2. John Paul II cites this passage in *Veritatis splendor*, n. 43.

15. E.g., Robert Bellah et al., *The Good Society* (New York: Alfred A. Knopf, 1991); Amitai Etzioni, *The Spirit of Community* (New York: Crown Publishers, 1993).

16. For my response to this debate, see *The Church and Morality: An Ecumenical and Catholic Approach* (Minneapolis: Fortress, 1993) 96–109.

17. Thomas Aquinas, *Prima Secundae, I*^{a} *II*^{ae}.

18. See, for example, John Mahoney, *The Making of Moral Theology* (Oxford: Clarendon Press, 1987) 224–45.

19. P. Marcellinus Zalba, *Theologiae Moralis Summa II: Tractatus de Mandatis Dei et Ecclesiae* (Madrid: Biblioteca de Autores Cristianos, 1953) nn. 243–66, 255–86.

20. *Acta Apostolicae Sedis* 85, n. 12 (December 9, 1993) 1197.

21. Walter M. Abbott, ed., *The Documents of Vatican II* (New York: Guild Press, 1966) 226; Austin Flannery, ed., *Vatican Council II: The Conciliar and Post-Conciliar Documents* (Northport, N.Y.: Costello Publishing, 1975) 928.

22. Zalba, *Theologiae Moralis Summa II*, nn. 251–2; 263–8.

23. Charles E. Curran, *Toward an American Catholic Moral Theology* (Notre Dame, Ind.: University of Notre Dame Press, 1987) 57–9.

24. Charles E. Curran, *Directions in Fundamental Moral Theology* (Notre Dame, Ind: University of Notre Dame Press, 1985) 127–37, 156–61.

25. Pope Pius XII, "The Prolongation of Life" (November 24, 1957) in Kevin D. O'Rourke and Philip Boyle, eds., *Medical Ethics: Sources of Catholic Teachings* (St. Louis, Mo.: Catholic Health Association, 1989) 207.

26. *Directions in Fundamental Moral Theology,* 244.

27. Ibid., 242.

28. Louis Vereecke, *De Guillaume d'Ockham* à *Saint Alphonse de Liguori* (Rome: Collegium S. Alfonsi de Urbe, 1986) 555–60; James Keenan, "Can a Wrong Action Be Good? The Development of Theological Opinion on Erroneous Conscience," *Église et Théologie* 24 (1993) 205–19. However, Aquinas, Alphonsus, and Pope John Paul II all recognize that the external act remains an objective disorder and is wrong.

29. Vereecke, *De Guillaume d'Ockham,* 566.

30. Joseph Fuchs, "Good Acts and Good Persons," *The Tablet* 247 (November 6, 1993) 1445.

31. Richard A. McCormick, "Killing a Patient," *The Tablet* 247 (October 30, 1993) 1410, 1411.

32. Fuchs, *The Tablet* 247 (November 6, 1993) 1445; McCormick, *The Tablet* 247 (October 30, 1993) 1411.

33. See "Artificial Insemination" and "Contraception," in O'Rourke and Boyle, *Medical Ethics,* 62, 92–5.

34. Declaration on Religious Freedom, n. 1, in Abbott, *Documents of Vatican II,* 676.

35. Thomas Aquinas, *I*^{a} *II*^{ae}, q. 94, a. 4.

36. John T. Noonan, "Development in Moral Doctrine," *Theological Studies* 54 (1993) 662–77.

37. Decree on Ecumenism, n. 11, in Abbott, *Documents of Vatican II,* 354.

38. Sixtus Cartechini, *De Valore notarum theologicarum* (Rome: Gregorian University Press, 1951).

39. Vatican Congregation for the Doctrine of the Faith, "Instruction on the Ecclesial Vocation of the Theologian," *Origins* 20 (1990) 117–26.

NINE

Religious Education after Vatican II

Gabriel Moran

At the beginning of the 1960s the Catholic Church began a transformation that was almost unimaginable for an institution of its size and age. The Church's leaders sought to direct the change in orderly fashion, preserving continuity with the past while listening to the "signs of the times." Part of what was unimaginable was how traumatic and far-reaching the changes would be. Unaware of the complexity of the task, many enthusiasts of the time supposed that in a few years, or perhaps a decade at the most, the renewed Catholic Church would settle down and go on with its usual work.

Three decades after Vatican II the one thing clear is that a process of renewal will take many more decades and that the shape of the Church is still emerging. One of the main keys to the process is education: the education of all members of the Church and the education of the Church in relation to the non-church world. So far, interest in educational questions still seems confined to a small band of writers and to some hard-working but overburdened parish staffs and a small number of diocesan personnel.

Not everyone in the 1960s naively expected quick success. A group of dedicated Catholic leaders, both lay and clerical, had been struggling with the problems of education throughout the 1940s and 1950s. The North American Liturgical Conference was a gathering place for many of these people, although their interests were not exclusively liturgical. As was true earlier in Europe, liturgical reform was usually associated with biblical, catechetical, and ecumenical movements. All of these concerns continue in the 1990s to be part of an educational transformation needed within the Catholic Church.

I often imagine the Catholic Church making the precarious journey from pre-Vatican II to post-Vatican II on the backs of a few dozen of these people. They had been formed by the best elements in the old Church which they loved, but they were ready for whatever was to come in a new Church. I refer to people such as Mary Perkins Ryan, Robert Hovda, Mary Reed Newland, Godfrey Diekmann, and Gerard Sloyan. Because of his position in the 1960s at The Catholic University of America, Gerard Sloyan had a special place in the bridge between pre-conciliar and post-conciliar eras. Through his direction of the Department of Religious Education, he provided a distinctive spirit to a generation of religious educators.

What follows in this essay is inspired by the work of Gerard Sloyan and those other bridge builders referred to above. I am primarily interested in the Catholic Church, but one of the things that has changed since the 1960s is that Catholic religious education cannot be understood in isolation from the rest of religious education. The term "religious education" is problematic within the Catholic Church and elsewhere. But I know of no other term in the English language that has a chance of succeeding both in gathering educational efforts within the Catholic Church and in stimulating discussion with other religious and educational agencies.

Vatican II did not address the topic of religious education. I am aware of only one place in the council's documents where the term is used. The council did publish a document entitled A Declaration on Christian Education. That sounds at least close to my topic here. However, I think there was widespread agreement at the time, and there is no reason today to change the belief, that A Declaration on Christian Education was one of the weaker documents of Vatican II. After some introductory paragraphs, the document is mostly a plea for Catholic schools. The title of the document is therefore misleading. One should not promise a discussion of Christian education and come out with a small slice of the problem. The Catholic school, in one form or another, can be a valuable part of Christian or religious education but it needs a context.

From one point of view, therefore, religious education is absent from the council's deliberations. But if one looks at the council with a richer possible meaning of religious education, the concern is as wide as the council itself. Vatican II as a whole was an exercise in Christian or religious education. It began an educational reshaping of the Catholic Church, and it fundamentally altered the relation of Roman Catholicism to the rest of the world.

In this context, the most important council documents on religious education were those that changed authority and worship patterns within the Church. Especially important were The Constitution on the Sacred Liturgy and The Pastoral Constitution on the Church in the Modern World. In addition, several other documents suggested a change in the Catholic Church's relation to a divine plan of salvation. The Dogmatic Constitution on Divine Revelation and The Declaration on the Relation of the Church to Non-Christian Religions pointed the way to a new meaning of "religious" in religious education. Each of these four documents, whatever its limitations, did the essential thing in breaking open new possibilities. I fear that history will be kinder to the authors of these documents than it will be to the generation after the council for failing to maintain the openness, creativity, and scholarly efforts of the first half of the 1960s.

The Dual Nature of Religious Education

In the latter part of this essay, I describe the Catholic Church's internal language of religious education. But that language needs the context of a full meaning of religious education. There are two very distinct parts, or what I will call "faces," to religious education. The two faces are related, but one must first distinguish before uniting. A clear and consistent unity forbids a premature synthesis.

The first face of religious education is the fairly familiar one of a religious group trying to form new members who will carry on the practices and mission of the group. The experienced and devoted members show the learners how to perform the rituals and practices of the group. This work of education can be called formation, initiation, or induction. If a group is to function as a community that provides affection, support, and identity to the individual, then the group needs a boundary which distinguishes inside and outside. This boundary, however, need not create an epistemological dichotomy between uncritical conformist on the inside and objective observer on the outside. One can be a devout and loyal Roman Catholic and still take the view of outsider on occasion. In fact, that ability is the basis for the other face of religious education.

The second face of religious education is the providing of an understanding of religion. Whereas the first face is to shape the way people behave, this second is mostly a matter of the mind. Can we step back from our immediate involvement and try to understand? The object to be understood is religion, which includes one's own religion.

An openness to understand is the alternative to the tendency to attack, belittle, condemn, or dismiss. If what other people practice as religion seems bizarre or absurd, it is likely that we have not yet understood. Understanding presupposes a sympathetic readiness to listen attentively, reflect calmly, and judge fairly. An understanding of religion will find an outlet in social, political, and religious activity. But the person has to discover the link between understanding and external activity for himself or herself. The connection may take a long time to emerge and may never be obvious to other people.

A complete contrast between these two faces of religious education would include describing who, what, how, where, and why. I will concentrate on who are the recipients of religious education.

In the first kind of religious education, the recipients are inquirers or initiands of a religious body. The focus is very particular: this group of people wish to learn the practices of this religious community. With reference to age, most religions have traditionally concentrated on children. That statement hides an ambiguity because the term "children" is not as clear-cut as is often assumed. Some religious groups, adopting the premises of modern education, speak of education as if it began at age five or six. While supposedly concentrating on the children, they neglect the most formative time in children's lives. In a religious community, five or six years of age is rather late for learning the important attitudes and rituals of a religious life.

Those who believe that a person's religious formation has to continue throughout life are sometimes accused of neglecting children or even opposing the education of children. But children are not the enemy of lifelong education. An education that deserves the name "lifelong" would necessarily start at birth—at the latest.

Christian, Jewish, and Muslim emphasis upon the education of children was not misplaced. However, what has become increasingly clear in the twentieth century is the need for a shift of emphasis. Some of the shift is from later to earlier childhood; that would involve, of course, special concern for the parents of young children. In addition, a religious group has to recognize that the attitude of inquirer or initiand can continue throughout life. The patterns of church life continue to educate or miseducate every day. How the liturgy is performed, how men and women interact in the Church, how the old are respected, constitute a continuing education.

I said that the learners are already members of the community or seriously considering entrance. The individual is asking for immersion into and experience of the life of the community. A language is spoken within the group that expresses the intimate life of the community. A stranger wandering into a liturgical ceremony should find it alien. Some minimum preparation is necessary for appreciating the meaning of the community's prayer. The young child's absorption of the language is largely through parents and siblings.

In the second face of religious education, the ages of the audience can be from young child to older adult. But the capacity to understand religion takes many years to develop. Undoubtedly, three-year-olds can ask difficult questions about religion. Similar to children's questions about sex, questions of religion demand simple, honest answers without elaborate explanations. Young children have neither the ability nor the need to study religion. By age five or six children have begun to develop the thinking capacity presupposed in the understanding of religion. Many more years are needed before they can exercise critical judgments about their own religion in relation to the religion of others. Thus, the concentration of so much religious education in the years of elementary school lacks any clear logic. Those years are rather late for the first kind of religious education and rather early for the second kind.

As to the religious composition of the second audience for religious education, a manageable diversity is desirable. Some degree of otherness, some basis of comparison, is necessary for understanding anything. "Religion" as used in the modern world is plural in meaning; it was invented to describe the plurality found by explorers, anthropologists, and archeologists. Many Catholic leaders wish to have Catholics understand their own religion first before encountering others. One can sympathize with that desire but understanding still involves comparison. Often in the past, the comparison was to a straw man, an unintelligible alternative to the one, true, and (almost) perfect Catholic Church. The Catholic high school graduate who went to a secular university sometimes had the feeling of stepping off a cliff upon discovering that the comparisons were not that simple.

That problem is not so common as it was forty years ago. Catholic schools do a better job of teaching religion. These days there are better comparisons between a somewhat messy Catholic Church and alternatives that one can understand to some degree. When Catholic students understand Judaism, they do not convert to Judaism; the usual effect is that they understand their Catholicism better. Unfortunately, well-taught religion lessons still reach only a minority of Catholics. We still need a better distribution of resources within the Catholic Church.

It should be noted that the Catholic Church need not be the only sponsor of well-taught religion lessons to Catholics. Many of the students who have attended Catholic schools are ready to study with a more diverse group in the university. We need other experiences beyond the university with some mixing of religion for the purpose of understanding religion. Such study can be sponsored by a single religious community, several different religious bodies, or a nonreligious organization. Having a mixed religion group to study religion is still thought to be the exotic exception, rather than a common occurrence. A group of Catholics can understand Judaism, to a degree, and Judaism's relation to the Church. It is nonetheless a surer road to understanding if Jews are articulating the Jewish position.

The distinction I have drawn between the two faces of religious education does not locate people in separate compartments. Each individual at some time in life needs access to each kind of religious education. Both kinds may operate simultaneously, although at some moments of life one of them is likely to dominate. I suggested that in the first few years of life the formation into the religious group necessarily takes precedence. I suspect that in late adolescence or young adulthood, there is often a severe tension. As one's academic ability to understand reaches maturity, one may have resistance to the other kind of education, that is, formation within the community. If that stage can be negotiated without too much storminess, the older adult can hold in a calm and fruitful tension the two kinds of religious education.

A legitimate question that might be asked is why these two distinct realities need to have the same name. Could not "religious education" serve for one or the other of the two? The answer is that "religious education" already serves for both realities in different parts of the world. Instead of introducing ambiguity, I am calling attention to it. I am also suggesting that there is a good reason for it.

In the late twentieth century the world needs both faces of religious education. The comprehensive use of the term advocated here would open a fruitful dialogue between the two of them. Not every religious educator has to do both kinds of education. But while concentrating on one kind, the educator has to be aware of another aspect to the work. If there is a linguistic bridge, then the individual's passage from one side to the other would not be a jarring reversal.

Religious education is an idea born in the twentieth century. The widespread assumption in the nineteenth century that religion and education are opposites, that education would slowly eliminate religion, was countered at the turn of the century by the premise of the religious education movement. This premise was that religion and education are not only compatible but are beneficial to one another.

On one side of the relation, religious people were encouraged to become educated: to be intelligently and freely formed in the practices of their religious life and to understand that way of life in relation to a set of practices called "religion." Devout involvement in religious practice does not preclude understanding religion; it can be a helpful basis for a realistic assessment of religion.

In the other direction, scholars who would explain religion need a feel for religious practice. Someone is not cut off from all understanding of religion by reason of not belonging to a clearly defined religious community. But such a person needs sympathy not antipathy for the actual practice of a religious life. In the past a lot of the explaining of religion in secular universities turned out to be an explaining away of religion. Presuming that something should not exist is not an effective way of understanding it.

If the term "religious education" covers both the formation of life within a community and an intellectual understanding, which in principle goes beyond the community, the need for a respectful and sympathetic dialogue is highlighted. Academic instructors in religion ought not to be subject to tests of orthodoxy. But such teachers regularly have to examine what motivates their teaching and what is their relation to the religious practices they are trying to illuminate.

A religious education that does embrace these contrasting activities—formation into one religious community and an understanding of religion(s)—is threatened by opposite dangers. On one side an academic examination of religion can take over the term, leaving church, synagogue, and mosque without a link between their internal activities and the rest of the world's educational efforts in religion. This problem does not exist in the United States, but it is found in countries influenced by a British way of speaking about education. In these places, religious education usually means the name of a subject taught in state schools. This usage not only limits religious education to the school but encapsulates it as one course in the curriculum of the state school.

The way people speak is often not entirely logical, and outsiders should not be quick to criticize. But the strange evolution of "religious education" in British English has the effect of excluding church, synagogue, and mosque. The British borrowed the term from the United States before giving it a legal meaning in the 1940s. At that time, the term encompassed academic study and worship. When strong doubts arose about a common worship service in government schools, "religious education" tended to become equivalent only to an academic subject. This way of speaking has been in place for only about thirty years and, as educational debates in the late 1980s showed, it is not an entirely clear way of speaking.[1]

The United States presents not the preferable alternative but the opposite danger. Whatever religious education means in the United States, it does *not* mean a subject taught in state schools. Its common use in the United States is for an activity proper to church or synagogue but illegitimate in the public school.[2] "Religious education" was invented as a term to bridge the educational work of religious bodies and the public school. But hardly had the Religious Education Association been founded when the more conservative parts of Catholicism, Judaism, and Protestantism shied away from the term.

The recent effort to start or re-start a Catholic-Protestant-Jewish dialogue on education is admirable. However, it may obscure the fact that their original partner in dialogue was to be public education. When a group of people in the 1970s decided to address the question of religion in the public school, they felt it necessary to withdraw from the Religious Education Association and start an organization that came to be known as the National Council of Religion and Public Education. The split was an unfortunate one, and neither organization has flourished. Both groups may run interesting conferences and publish journals, but they have not been able to initiate on any national scale the badly needed discussion of religion and education: Christian, Jewish, Muslim, and other religious groups on one side of that relation; religiously affiliated schools, private schools, state schools, and other educational agencies on the other side. This relation, so central to the United States, does not have a framework for discussion.

The renewal of the term "religious education" since the 1960s was largely fueled by Catholic enthusiasm. From being slightly suspect and culturally alien until 1960, the Catholic Church found itself to be a major player in control of educational language. Today no individual institution has the power of the Catholic Church in determining the meaning of "religious education" in the United States. The drawback is that public schools (and even Protestant Christians) can be scared off by a term that Catholics wield as their own. It is incumbent on Catholics that in using the term "religious education" they are careful not to speak as if they were the owners of the term.

The Internal Language of Catholicism

This last point brings me into the second part of this essay: the Catholic Church's internal or intramural language of religious education. The direct reference is to the first face of religious education but with implications for the second face. The Catholic Church has the right and the duty to preserve its own internal language. What can be called religious education in that language are practices which, while formative of church membership, maintain a tension with a universal calling.

When the Catholic Church forgets that it shares in, rather than owns, religious education, a strange inversion of language can occur: Catholic religious education becomes a small and segregated part of the Church's work. To this day many people use "religious education" as interchangeable with "CCD." Even Andrew Greeley's writings after Vatican II have described a conflict of Catholic school versus religious education/CCD.[3] I do not argue with Greeley's data or his case for the Catholic school. I would think one good reason for supporting Catholic schools is that they provide religious education. I do not understand why Greeley accepts and affirms a language that cuts off the possibility of educational discussion within the Catholic Church and the Church's alliance with other educational bodies.

Catholic education since Vatican II has revolved around the term "catechetics" and its cognates "catechist," "catechize," "catechesis" and "catechism." All but the last of these words was unknown to most Catholics before 1960. After the council catechetical language quickly swept the field, but there were and are ambiguities. We are still early in the game of developing a language that will lead to cooperation rather than fragmentation in the Catholic Church's educational efforts.

After Vatican II the way to describe church activity has been with the idea of ministry. The council did not emphasize this term but the experience of Vatican II clearly inspired its reentry. Before the council Catholics either did not use the term "ministry" or used it to refer to the clergy. Some people still use the term to mean nothing but the clergy; an unhelpful reaction by other people is to use ministry for everyone's work in the Church except the clergy's. Overall, there has been progress in the Catholic reappropriation of the term to refer to the five, six, eight, or some small number of areas that define the essential work of the Church. It is no small progress that the Catholic Church now has names for certain people doing certain tasks that are crucial to church life.

Within the Catholic Church there would be general agreement that catechizing can be called a ministry. Unfortunately, most Protestant Churches resist catechetical language, even though it can be found in early Protestant history. This fact does not invalidate its usage as a language of intimacy within Catholicism. Although it is largely a postconciliar phenomenon, catechetical language has roots in the New Testament and the early Church.

It is important while preserving this language that it be kept in tension with language that transcends the Catholic Church. For example, I have often heard it said that "a catechist is not a mere teacher." This denial is an unwise acceptance of a dichotomy. "Catechist" needs some of the connotations of "teacher," and the modern secular meaning of "teacher" needs challenge by the activity of such people as catechists. Jaroslav Pelikan begins his book on the images of Jesus with the image of teacher, which, according to Pelikan, was the most universal and least controversial title of Jesus in the first century. Losing hold of that title is a devastating loss for Christians.[4]

When people say a catechist is not a teacher, I think they mean to distance themselves from the image and connotations of *school teacher*. There could be a helpful distinction here if made without disparagement to either side. The contrast is not between catechist and teacher but instead between different kinds of teaching.

The Catholic Church needs a kind of teaching that is not burdened with the assumptions of the classroom. Likewise, academic instruction should not be burdened with the role of catechizing. Teaching that is appropriate from the pulpit or in preparing a person for sacramental initiation may be inappropriate in the classroom. I find it frustrating that many statements from chanceries and the Vatican seem to have no suspicion of this distinction. Most people who work in classrooms every day discover the difference very quickly.

Catechizing is a form of teaching in which words predominate (in contrast to most teaching where words are secondary). In this respect, it is similar to school teaching. However, school teachers work in the context of classrooms and an academic curriculum; catechists work in the context of sacramental life. School teachers teach religion; catechists teach the Gospel and Christian doctrine. The catechetical venture is firmly within the framework of forming people to lead a Christian life. Catechesis is one of the ministries of the Catholic Church wherein the Gospel is announced, to be followed by an explanation of Christian doctrine.   ·

This description of the catechetical as a small but important aspect of Catholic religious education runs counter to a strong tendency of recent decades. People who take to any important task have a natural tendency to expand the conception of what they do beyond the boundaries that history, logic, and other people have determined. The catechetical aspect of the Catholic Church tends to overreach its place within the ministries of the Church. Some clear distinctions would avoid bruised feelings and stimulate cooperation. What, for example, is the relation between liturgy and catechetics? People whose main interest is liturgy tend to speak as if liturgy includes catechetics. People who promote catechetics sometimes speak as if liturgy were part of catechetics. Both positions are intelligible depending on where one's interests lie; neither assumption is helpful to cooperation. For the present context, catechetics needs the help of liturgy, but liturgy is not a part of catechetics. Liturgy is crucial in the formation of Christian life. By being itself, liturgy is formative and educational; it is not an instrument of anything else.

The *National Catechetical Directory* says that the tasks of the catechist are "to proclaim Christ's message, to participate in efforts to de-

velop community, to lead people to worship and prayer, and to motivate them to serve others."[5] Only the first of these four tasks—proclaiming Christ's message—is clearly the work of the catechist. Of
course, a case can be made that the first supports the other three or that
it is implied by the other three. Certainly catechists hope that both the
context of their work and the result of the work involve community,
worship, and service. However, the likely reading of this sentence in
the *National Catechetical Directory* is that catechetics is composed of
four elements: message, community, worship, and service. A survey of
written materials and annual conferences would, I think, indicate that
to be the widespread assumption.

From an historical and etymological point of view, such a meaning is not well supported. Message, community, worship, and service
are what church ministry is for. All four are part of the Catholic
Church's internal language of religious education. From a practical
point of view, the expansion of catechetical work places an excessive
burden on some church ministers and obstructs cooperation between
ministries.

Catechesis, understood to be one of the Church's educational
ministries, provides a realistic context for situating a catechism. The
new "universal catechism" can be no more than a compendium of
Christian doctrine. Like similar projects, the process of writing the
document may be more important than the finished product. I would
have liked a much simpler book that could have been a useful manual.
At best, the book will be a guide for one aspect of church life; at worst,
it will be one more book that does not sell or, if bought for appearance's sake, sits on the shelf.

The writers of the catechism wisely avoided trying to describe
other religions. To restrict a catechism's considerations to Catholic doctrine can be a way of respecting the autonomy of other religions and of
leaving the door open to other times, other places, and other books.

No book today can supply the answers of religious education—
within the Catholic Church as well as beyond. But there are questions
within catechetical ministry that do have answers, or least a range of
possible answers. Those who exercise this ministry need some preparation. They cannot be expected to be expert in every ministry. They
need to study the Bible, church history, and evolution of Christian
doctrine. That is where a catechism could be useful if it summarized
biblical, theological, and historical scholarship.

The catechist also needs a cooperative setting in which to catechize. With the help of other church ministers, many Catholics can
participate in catechetical work. Lest catechetics become encapsulated
in its own linguistic world, it needs the context of other languages

within the Church as well as language of encounter between church and non-church world. In 1970 I wrote an essay which a journal misleadingly titled "Catechetics R.I.P."[6] What the essay actually says is that in the 1960s the catechetical movement was amazingly successful. Now we needed other educational language that would complement the catechetical. A quarter century later I would assert the same statement even more strongly. Liturgists, theologians, parents, school teachers, parish administrators all have a part in the Church's educational mission and provide a context for catechizing.

The educational formation of a Catholic rests first not on catechetics but on worship and service. No educational reform within the Church can be successful if it is concentrated on catechisms, CCD, and textbooks. One learns to be a Catholic by participating in the liturgical life of the community. Perhaps the most successful educational model that has been developed since the council is the Rite of Christian Initiation of Adults. Here the role of the catechist is clearly situated in relation to sacramental life. The best renewals of parish life have carried that spirit into other formats. Educational programs based on the liturgy do not have to be elaborate and complex, suitable only for experts. All parishioners ought to be invited to take some part.

A service element can never be absent from programs of Catholic formation. Unlike liturgy and catechetics, service knows no church boundary. The language of feeding the hungry and bandaging the wounded is intelligible without any theological preparation. When liturgy is genuinely drawing people toward a center, it also impels them outward to serve those in need within the Church community and beyond.

The chief religious education that the Catholic Church provides to the rest of the world is in struggles against injustice, in the willingness of individuals and communities to protest against all forms of violence. When such witness is evident, then church explanations of what it stands for are intelligible to all and persuasive to some. If the witness is missing, then almost anything said by church spokespersons is suspect. The Church's books and pronouncements cannot educate if the words are not heard.

Two Testing Points

I would finally like to mention two litmus tests of how religious education is faring *within* the Catholic Church three decades after the council. Also important for my purposes is the question: How is religious education faring in relation *to* the Catholic Church? The first litmus test is graduate programs of religious education at Catholic universities; the second is the Director of Religious Education movement.

Immediately after the council a number of M.A. programs in religious education sprang up across the United States. Many of them were small and had little backing; they tended to wither quickly. Other programs were well planned and the universities invested resources to allow development; some of these programs prospered and turned out hundreds of graduates, to the benefit of parishes and Catholic schools.

For more than a decade there has been a drift away from the term "religious education " to describe these programs. A common alternative is "pastoral ministry" which may start out as a parallel program and then gradually absorb the religious education degree. Although this shift of names may be realistic and helpful for individuals concerned with jobs, I suspect that something is lost in this transition.

Universities have a responsibility to consider this issue carefully. I understand why a seminary would call its degree program "pastoral ministry"; the seminary is an ecclesiastical institution whose purpose is to train ecclesiastical ministers. The same is not true of a university, even one with a religious affiliation. The Catholic university's mission is to maintain a healthy tension between church and non-church worlds. A major part of its mission is to pose a challenge to the secular assumption that education excludes religion. The existence of a religious education program in a Catholic university ought to be a prod to every school of education in the country: Why is religion neglected when every school teacher in the country has to deal with it?

I am not suggesting that the Catholic university simply try to hold on to the population and program it had for a decade or two after the council. The programs were nearly always weak on the educational side: family education, counseling, administrative skills, as well as academic curriculum. The language of ministry as part of the context of religious education is appropriate in a university that is Catholic. But in a Catholic institution that is a university, religious education ought to be an integral part of a school of arts and sciences and/or a professional school for the preparation of educators.

Within the Church, the university ought to be challenging the diocesan and parochial structures to come up with jobs that have intellectual substance and professional standing. The university ought not to accept whatever ecclesiastical language seems fashionable. A master's degree should do more than prepare a person to be a general assistant to the pastor. Specific educational jobs should be available within parishes, in religiously affiliated schools, and in other schools for which a religious education degree would be preparation. Such jobs will not be there unless the university stands behind religious education as a legitimate and important venture for the future. The Catholic university should not have to carry the project alone, but the project will not be sustained without leadership from Catholic universities.

The second litmus test is one of the jobs to which the M.A. in religious education has led. Immediately after the council an educational reform movement was launched in the Twin Cities diocese of Minnesota. The movement took a decade to acquire a fairly standard name: Director of Religious Education.[7] The name has never reached universal acceptance, but the title of Director of Religious Education is found throughout the United States and encompasses many thousands of people. Although the title was consciously chosen to link it to an earlier Protestant movement, the Catholic movement far surpasses all other churches. And while there may be similar movements in other countries, the U.S. case is clearly the most dramatic one.

As in most reform movements, there is a moment when creativity is demanded by the exigencies of the time. As Catholic schools disappeared and teaching staffs shrunk in size, the Church was faced with either simply shrinking its educational work or trying new forms. In some places, the D.R.E. movement may have been interpreted as the cutting of the teaching staff from eight to one. In other places, it meant the parish would examine itself and start using its resources differently. I wrote in a book in 1970 that if you are being hired as D.R.E. it is probably for the best of reasons or for the worst of reasons; and it would be advisable to know which it is before being hired.[8] I believed at the time that the movement could not have the luxury of being a modest success. I still believe that to survive at all it has to be the forerunner of a rethinking of the Church's education.

Directors of Religious Education are among the most intelligent, loyal, and hard-working people in the Catholic Church. But they remain too isolated to accomplish the great claim of their title: the directing of religious education in the Catholic Church. The isolation is mostly not of their own making. However, they have not helped their own cause by talking about Directors of Religious Education as constituting "a profession." Although any group can claim to be a profession, the claim gets you nowhere unless there is a sufficient base of knowledge and an institutional support to make the claim credible. Otherwise, creating your own profession simply has the effect of isolating the group.[9]

The choice for most people who wish to have the respect professionals claim is to get help from one or more existing professions. Directors of Religious Education need help from church ministers and professional educators; they need support from within their own

Church and from outside the Church. Directing religious education in the Catholic Church means marshalling resources internal to the Church. It also means being aware of the fact that the Catholic Church turns a face toward the rest of the world.

Internal to the Church, there is a need to link the formative work of many ministries. The pastor does that in one way but there is room for another person doing it with explicit educational intent. The D.R.E. has to link message, worship, community, and service by inviting every parishioner to be involved in education. The tricky part is to end up the director of the program rather than the program itself.

The Director of Religious Education also stands at the intersection of the Church and non-church world of education. On one side, the D.R.E. is usually closer to ordinary parish life than are Catholic school teachers. On the other side, the D.R.E. usually has more contact with secular education than does the pastor and other church ministers. Thus, the D.R.E. embodies the two faces of religious education, sometimes acting against church policy for the sake of a better educated Church. The position is precarious, especially if your livelihood depends on a local pastor or parish council.

The U.S. Catholic Church's need to direct its religious education cannot be solved by a single, parochial position. Even the number of parishes that can hire a person (or persons) at a living wage and provide professional resources is likely to remain a minority. The D.R.E. movement has raised up the promise of the Catholic Church evolving into a truly educational Church, transformative of its own members and a force for justice in the world at large. But the Church still has a long way to go in developing institutional support not only for parish directors of religious education but for the hundreds of thousands of catechists, the millions of Catholic parents, and the tens of millions of actual or potential learners.

NOTES

1. For a summary of British history on the point, see Gabriel Moran, *Religious Education as a Second Language* (Birmingham: Religious Education Press, 1989) chapter 4; John Hull, *New Directions in Religious Education* (London: Falmer, 1982).

2. *Religion in the Curriculum* (Washington, D.C.: Association for Supervision and Curriculum Development, 1987).

3. Andrew Greeley and Peter Rossi, *The Education of Catholic Americans* (Chicago: Aldine, 1966); Andrew Greeley and William McCready, *Catholic Schools in a Declining Church* (Mission, Kans.: Sheed, Andrews and McMeel,

1976); Andrew Greeley, "Letter to the Editor, " *National Catholic Reporter* (June 30, 1989).

4. Jaroslav Pelikan, *Jesus through the Centuries* (New Haven: Yale University, 1985) chapter 1.

5. *Sharing the Light of Faith* (Washington, D.C.: United States Catholic Conference, 1978) #213

6. "Catechetics R.I.P., " *Commonweal* (December 18, 1970) 299–302 .

7. See Maria Harris, *The DRE Book* (New York: Paulist, 1976); Thomas Walters, *National Profile of Professional Directors of Religious Education* (Washington, D.C.: United States Catholic Conference, 1983); Thomas Walters, "The DRE: A Progressive Study, " *PACE* (December 1990) 92–5.

8. Gabriel Moran, *Design for Religion* (New York: Herder & Herder, 1970).

9. The classic study on this point is Harold Wilensky, "The Professionalization of Everyone," *American Journal of Sociology* 70 (1964) 137–58.

TEN

On Being Bi-Religious: Colonialism, Catholicism, and Conversion

June O'Connor

The ways in which religious communities conceive of themselves in relation to other communities, as open and receptive or as closed and separatist, is an issue that has taken on new urgency in our time. The pluralism of religions, cultures, and ethnicities that constitutes our society and the world at large is pressing for attention by religious persons and scholars of religion alike. The once common description of Catholic-Protestant-Jewish traditions as constituting religion in the United States, for example, has rightly surrendered to a more pluralistic and realistic description that accounts for Native American, Muslim, Buddhist, Hindu, Sikh, Humanist, Neo-pagan, and multiple other groups as well as those Christian and Jewish. Dialogues and trialogues have been established in many regions as people seek to understand and live with the religious "other" who is often the neighbor, the co-worker, the newly-acquired family member.

Current discussions about how to conceive of and relate to the "religious other" have yielded a variety of theories and typologies. In the debate to date, inclusivism, exclusivism, and pluralism are commonly accepted and commonly contested categories for grouping and assessing specific interpretations.[1] One of the assumptions of the debate is that because religious pluralism is a fact of contemporary social life, believers in given religious traditions must account for their truth-claims in relationship to the competing truth-claims of other traditions. Commonly expressed in the forms of convictions, beliefs, and

167

doctrines, truth-claims thereby stimulate and focus much of the current discussion on religious pluralism.

Another perspective on religious pluralism, however, compels my attention and in my view merits sustained attention far beyond this article. This perspective informs or reminds us that religious pluralism is not solely a problem regarding truth-claims between discrete and disparate parties. Religious pluralism is also *a way of being religious.* Just as "bi-lingual" and "bi-cultural" describe ways of being with respect to skills for understanding and communicating across diverse communities, so too "bi-religious" serves as an apt adjective for some religious peoples who identify with and participate in more than one religious tradition, community, or symbol system.[2] The stories of Rigoberta Menchu of Guatemala and Nicholas Black Elk of the United States illuminate the possibilities and complexities of bi-religious identity. First, however, to clarify these contrasting perspectives on religious pluralism as truth-claim adjudication, on the one hand, and ways of being religious, on the other, I wish to provide a glimpse into the debate to date.

The Debate to Date: Claims in Conflict

Focusing on competing truth-claims, the debate on religious pluralism thus far has generated a variety of positions. "Inclusivism" reflects a standpoint of openness and receptivity to the truthfulness of other religions. Inclusivism affirms other religions as avenues of truth and value, yet does so with qualification. Christian inclusivism states, for example, that although other religions may offer truth and goodness, they do so less fully than Christianity.[3] Sources of Christian inclusivism include Catholics Karl Rahner and Hans Küng and a variety of Vatican II documents, but also Anglican, Eastern Orthodox, Third World Protestant, and Process thinkers. Each nuances an inclusivist position in distinctive ways; details and emphases among these sources vary.[4] As the inclusivist rubric suggests, the "other" (religious group) is accepted in terms of and affirmed according to selected fundamental features or standards of a particular religion, such as searching for the truth, belief in one God, monistic realization of the Absolute, or love.

"Exclusivism" holds that a given, particular religion is the only true religion. The classical Christian formula for Christian exclusivism is the dictum from the Latin Church's Father Cyprian: outside the Church there is no salvation. From late antiquity to the nineteenth century, this was a widespread Christian view among Catholics and, later, Protestants alike.[5] Karl Barth's emphasis on the uniqueness of the Christian revelation as expressed in the New Testament illustrates the position. Barth pits "religion" against "revelation." In his view, religions (and this may well include some forms of Christianity, he admits) represent the human effort to anticipate or fabricate God's will rather than to receive God's initiating, revelatory, and saving word.[6]

Missionary outreach and Christian expansion in the modern era have been powerful cross-cultural expressions of this exclusivist viewpoint. Yet several forces have generated a Christian critique of exclusivism. Familiarity with non-Christian religions, due in part to the breakup of European colonial powers and the discovery of the destructive impact the exclusivist position has had on the non-Christian majority of the world's population, has rendered this position suspect. Nonetheless, exclusivism remains particularly visible in fundamentalist and evangelical Christianity, which holds that only a biblically-focused Christianity is true, and that the other religions, particularly non-Christian religions, provide erroneous and dangerous renderings of reality.

"Pluralism" maintains that a plurality of religions is not only a fact but is a good, that more religions than one are, or may be,[7] true in some sense. A variation on this is that all religions can be construed as symbol systems whose images may (or do) express or reflect something real or valid, some important truth or aspect of the truth. What differentiates a Christian pluralist position from Christian inclusivism is, in the words of Paul Knitter, its "move away from insistence on the superiority or finality of Christ and Christianity toward a recognition of the independent validity of other ways."[8] Pluralism does bring its own criteria to bear in assessing other religions, however, and in this sense bears some resemblance to inclusivism. To the extent that other religions participate in some reigning truth or value (for example, monotheism or charity or recognition of an Absolute or Reality-centeredness), they are regarded as true.

A fourth type proposed by Schubert Ogden is "pluralistic inclusivism," which claims that because one religion is true (Christianity, in Ogden's analysis) others might be or can be true "because or insofar as they give expression to substantially the same religious truth."[9] Ogden's christology does not require that Christ be constitutive of salvation but only that Christ be viewed as representative of salvation. And since there may be other representations of God's saving love expressed in other religions, Ogden argues, it is possible that other religions are true, as Christianity is true.[10]

The standpoints noted here vary from one another, yet a common assumption binds them. Inclusivism, exclusivism, pluralism, and Ogden's inclusive pluralism address the multiplicity of religions in society and culture in terms of competing truth-claims between the self and the other, one's own religion and the other's religion. This pertains, for example, to Catholic claims and Muslim claims; Evangelical Christian claims and Jewish claims; Buddhist claims and liberal Protestant claims; and so on.

Testimonial writings of indigenous peoples of the Americas, however, alert us to another perspective on religious pluralism. This perspective redirects the focus of discussions on religious pluralism from a primary concern with the theological and philosophical adjudication of truth-claims between discrete and disparate parties to a consideration of religious pluralism *as a way of being religious*. This second reading of religious pluralism acknowledges that religions blend, combine, and recombine in ever-changing ways within particular, individual, singular religious persons and communities. The confluence of Native American and Roman Catholic religious myths, symbols, and ritual practices provides one intriguing mixture which is exemplified in the stories of Rigoberta Menchu, Guatemalan Quiche Mayan Indian and Catholic catechist, and Nicholas Black Elk, Oglala Sioux holy man who also became a Catholic catechist. Their stories yield a glimpse into ways in which people draw upon two religious identities, they display some of the ways in which colonialism affects people's religious lives, and they point to important and fascinating questions about how the combinations of religions might best be construed and understood.

On Being Bi-Religious

Rigoberta Menchu: Quiche and Catholic

Rigoberta Menchu (c. 1959–) presents herself to her editor and readers as an Indian woman who prizes the ancestral customs and practices the religious ceremonies of her Quiche Mayan religious heritage, while simultaneously participating as a Catholic catechist in the life of her Church.[11] She is both Quiche practitioner and Catholic catechist. Describing her father as "a dedicated Christian" (80) and herself as a Catholic catechist from age twelve, Menchu explains that "by accepting the Catholic religion, we didn't accept a condition, or abandon our culture. It was more like another way of expressing ourselves" (80).

"Another way of expressing ourselves" (80, 81) and "another channel of expression" (9) serve as Menchu's chief categories of explanation of herself as both Quiche and Catholic. She writes,

> When the Catholic Action arrived, for instance, everyone started going to mass, and praying, but it's not their only religion, not the

only way they have of expressing themselves. Anyway, when a baby is born, he's always baptized within the community before he's taken to church. Our people have taken Catholicism as just another channel of expression, not our one and only belief. Our people do the same with other religions (9).

This blending of ways is reflected in ceremonies. With respect to baptism, for example, before the child is taken to church, the community performs its own ceremonies during which the child is regarded as "a child of God, our one father" (13). "We don't actually have the word God but that is what it is, because the one father is the only one we have," (13) Menchu continues, and "to reach this one father, the child must love beans, maize, and earth" (13). The community also prays to "Mother Earth":

> Mother Earth, you who gives us food, whose children we are and on whom we depend, please make this produce you give us flourish and make our children and our animals grow . . . (57).

Water and maize are the most important objects in this agriculturally-based community's life. Respect and reverence are seen as the most appropriate human responses (56). Water is considered sacred because the people have always depended on water to survive. "The idea that water is sacred is in us children, and we never stop thinking of it as something pure" (56). In Quiche ceremonies, maize and water represent man and woman; candles represent the earth. "Then we offer up a sheep or chickens," Menchu narrates, "because we believe sheep to be sacred animals, quiet animals, saintly animals, animals which don't harm other animals" (58).

Catholic and Quiche symbols employ common objects (water, candles, sheep, and ancestors). Menchu highlights the importance of ancestors in both traditions:

> For example, we believe we have ancestors, and that these ancestors are important because they're good people who obeyed the laws of our people. The Bible talks about forefathers too. So it is not something unfamiliar to us. We accept these Biblical forefathers as if they were our own ancestors, while still keeping within our own culture and our own customs (80).

Indeed, ancestors are seen as saints in Catholicism.

> We express ourselves through our designs, through our dress—our *huipul*, for instance, is like an image of our ancestors. They are like the

> saints of Catholic Action. This is where you see the mixture of
> Catholicism and our own culture. We feel very Catholic because we
> believe in the Catholic religion but, at the same time, we feel very
> Indian, proud of our ancestors (81).

Similarly, the biblical accounts of kings remind the Quiche of their
own kings and leaders of the past.

> For instance the Bible tells us that there were kings who beat Christ.
> We drew a parallel with our king, Tecún Umán, who was defeated
> and persecuted by the Spaniards, and we take that as our own real-
> ity. In this way we adjusted to the Catholic religion and our duties as
> Christians, and made it part of our culture. As I said, it's just another
> way of expressing ourselves (81).

"Just another way of expressing ourselves . . ." becomes a refrain in
Menchu's discussions of religion.

As with baptism, so, too, with marriage. Ceremonies are celebrated among the Quiche first in the community and later in the
Church (74). These twofold loyalties require that time be set aside for
both expressions.

> All this means we have to put aside time and attend to all the com-
> munity's affairs. We must have time for our ceremonies, our Indian
> festivities. We must have time for the Catholic religion. This is an-
> other means of expression and complicates our situation. But the
> whole village is ready to give the time. No-one disagrees, because
> most of our people are not atheists. We don't live like the ladinos
> [non-Indians] (86).

As the recipient of the 1992 Nobel Peace Prize, Rigoberta Menchu
has been internationally recognized for her work in resisting oppres-
sive Guatemalan and international social and economic structures.[12] In
the face of racism against the indigenous peoples and their exclusion
from social and economic opportunities, Menchu and her people developed various self-help efforts. Their community-organizing work
evoked repressive actions from the government and, as a result, she
and her fellow villagers were pressed to develop strategies for self-
defense and nonviolent resistance. "Our main weapon, however,"
Menchu comments, "is the Bible. We began to study the Bible as a text
through which to educate our village. There are many wonderful stories in the Bible" (130).

Focusing on texts in which they could see themselves, they identified with Moses and his effort to free his people from domination and
oppression, and with Judith, whose fight against her king "gave us a

vision, a stronger idea of how we Christians must defend ourselves" (132). The Bible, Menchu writes, assisted the people to discover that "it is not God's will that we should live in suffering . . . God did not give us that destiny, but . . . men on earth have imposed this suffering, poverty, misery and discrimination on us" (132). The liberating function of the Bible and the Church fed Menchu's work and commitment to her people. "I am a Christian," Menchu writes, "and I participate in this struggle as a Christian" (132). "As I was saying, for us the Bible is our main weapon. It has shown us the way" (134).

Menchu is critical as well as appreciative of her Church, noting the ways in which the early Catholic Action movement that was instrumental in her youth functioned also to keep the people where they were, failing to encourage resistance and change.[13] The Catholic Church focused too much on sin in those days, she felt later on, and not enough on change and hope. The institutional and bureaucratic features of the Church also complicated Quiche lives in unhelpful ways, such as requiring people to sign papers when they married— practices unknown and unnecessary to the ancient ways (76).

Menchu herein displays a discriminating sensibility about the multiple and sometimes conflicting ways in which religion functions in people's lives: as repressive and as liberating, as other-worldly and as this-worldly, as alert to the reality of evil even as it bespeaks the power of goodness and offers grounds for hope.

Menchu testifies to the compatibility, rather than the competition, between Quiche and Catholic. The emphasis on ritual and ceremony, on the tangible presence of the sacred, on active and approachable intermediaries, and on special, blessed objects are analogous features that make visible some areas of compatibility. The symbolic use of water, candles, prayer, and sheep, the strong sense of community past and present, and the prescribed, ritualized remembrance of ancestors that are characteristic of both religions enable Menchu to move easily from Quiche to Catholic and Catholic to Quiche. Each is "another channel of expression," another way of expressing themselves (9, 81, 86).

Another way of conceiving of these religions-in-relation is that they make differing, important contributions to a people with varied needs. Just as they do not compete, we might say, so they do not really combine. They simply function on different planes, as they speak to different needs and dimensions of life. For example, the Quiche religion focuses on nature as source of insight and symbolism while Catholicism draws on historical person and event. While both speak to the experience of a people struggling to survive, Quiche emphasizes survival on the land while the Catholic highlights survival through historical event and social change. The Quiche myths and rituals speak to the agricultural rootedness of the peoples' lives, expressing the hope of sustenance and fecundity. The Catholic myths and rituals bespeak a sense of historical rootedness and provide stories that yield models of and hope for change. The two heritages are thus seen as speaking to different dimensions of life and as offering distinctive resources for survival. Strategy and survival thus help to explain how these two religions can be accepted as two "channels of expression." The philosophical and theological adjudication of truth-claims is not the focus here.[14]

Quiche and Catholic operate as symbol systems that aid the people, as translations of one another, and as forms of communication and petition in relation to the source of life. As symbol systems, Quiche rituals celebrate the power of life in seasonal events as Catholic rituals inform and remind participants of the saving power of historical events. The confluence of ancestors and saints (ancestors as saints) is suggestive of ways in which religions can serve as translations of one another. And prayer to Mother Earth and Father God in ritual context illustrates the communicative and petitionary features of both religions.

The adaptability that Menchu displays in moving from Quiche to Catholic and Catholic to Quiche points also to an adaptability that many indigenous populations have demonstrated in the course of their encounters with and subsequent responses to colonialism. In precolonial times, the religio-cultural systems of diverse indigenous populations developed in ways expressive of their adaptations to the natural environment and natural phenomena. Ecological conditions gave rise to symbol systems. Thus, maize-cultivating peoples associated the life-sustaining sources of maize and water with sacrality; for some, mountains became a locus for contact with the transcendent; eagle feathers and tobacco become ritual objects for others. The natural and the supernatural worlds are experienced as interdependent, and this interdependence is expressed mythically and ritually with rich use of symbolism.[15]

European colonial expansion irrevocably altered the world experienced by indigenous peoples in pre-colonial times and forced people to adapt in order to survive. The familiar, traditional ways of conceptualizing the world and expressing oneself in the world were sometimes destroyed, at times hidden, neglected, or rendered inapplicable, at other times adapted and assimilated in new ways. To assert some sense of control, to find meaning, and to take action has required native people to utilize the resources at hand. Whatever their origin and intent, the colonialists' impositions, including their religions, eventually became part of the material through which or against which indigenous peoples emerged with an altered self-understanding and altered strategies for survival.[16]

Menchu's insistence that these two resources are simply different channels of expression suggests an acceptance that obviates a need to reconcile. Where those concerned with adjudicating truth-claims are likely to see contradiction, she experiences no antagonism, no competition. Rather, both of these religions serve as resources which help people to live and to hope and to produce in varying circumstances. They are, thus, different channels of expression, and time is set aside for each.

Various images and concepts have been proposed to explain the phenomenon of people tapping the resources of more than one religion and of combining and blending diverse religions. Syncretism is a commonly contested category in these discussions.[17] Additional concepts, such as translation, correspondence, fusion, symbiosis, mosaic, and mixture have been proposed to provide names for this phenomenon.[18] Notions of substitution, exchange,[19] dual citizenship,[20] and configurations of religious belief[21] have also been suggested on the basis of both theoretical inquiries and field studies.

Indigenous peoples who have long been considered on the "other side" or "underside"[22] of history are now providing information and interpretation about religion that are important to hear, for what we are learning from these voices often requires us to recast and reconfigure some of our most-favored conceptions.[23] Religious pluralism is one of these. The testimony of Rigoberta Menchu, a Quiche Indian Catholic catechist and community activist from Latin America, illustrates religious pluralism as a way of being religious. The story of Black Elk, an Oglala Sioux holy man from North America, provides another, quite different example.

Nicholas Black Elk: Oglala Holy Man-Become-Catholic Catechist

Although Black Elk is particularly well-known from John Neihardt's 1932 publication *Black Elk Speaks: Being the Life Story of a Holy Man of the Oglala Sioux*,[24] Neihardt's story covers only twenty-four years of Black Elk's approximately eighty-seven years of life. Yet the memorable Lakota mystic spent forty-six of those years as a member of the Catholic Church, and many of these as an active catechist. Critical studies by Raymond J. DeMallie, Paul B. Steinmetz, Michael F. Steltenkamp, Julian Rice, and Clyde Holler historicize and contextualize Neihardt's representation of Black Elk, filling in many details that are ignored in *Black Elk Speaks*. Citing a wide range of archival materials, oral histories, and contemporary Lakota religious practices, these studies address and seek to assess Black Elk's fuller religious identity.[25]

Unlike Rigoberta Menchu, who relates her two religious loyalties in the metaphor of a channel of expression, Black Elk does not articulate any metaphors or conceptual frameworks for relating his loyalties to the traditional (Oglala/Lakota) religion and to Catholicism. A chronological framework serves as a useful starting point for understanding Black Elk's relationship to these two religions. First, he was a traditional religious Oglala practitioner; later, following a conversion of some sort, he became a Catholic and a catechist. This sequential, chronological approach is not sufficient for understanding Black Elk's religious ways, however, for Black Elk's conversations and correspondence display some zigzagging between the two: first the old (Sioux ways), then the new (Catholic); later, the Catholic and then again, the Sioux.

DeMallie provides illuminating detail about Black Elk's religious sensibilities and expressions. Born in 1863,[26] Black Elk reported a powerful and dramatic religious vision at age nine. He felt himself visited by the "thunder beings" of the Lakota cosmology, who, with the Great Spirit, commissioned Black Elk to serve and heal his people. Burdened by the sense of responsibility that came with this vision, the young boy Black Elk suffered fear and timidity about his abilities to do what he felt the thunder beings expected of him. At about age seventeen or eighteen he shared his vision with Lakota elders and, at their encouragement, danced out his vision in a ceremonial form known as the horse dance. This relieved Black Elk of the pressures he felt from his vision by making public his sense of a spiritual calling. He enacted other rituals, including the fasting and purification disciplines that preceded his official "crying for a vision," a rite through which Oglalas seek wisdom and power. He also performed buffalo and elk ceremonies, sponsored a heyoka ceremony, and performed another horse dance. His spiritual authority thereby well-tested and well-proclaimed within the Lakota tradition, Black Elk served his people for several years as a medicine man known for his curative powers (DeMallie, 7–8).

In 1886, at age twenty-three, he joined the Buffalo Bill Wild West show, traveling for three years to New York and later to England, Germany, and France, before returning to the Northern Plains. He wrote to the Lakota people that he used this time to learn the ways of the white man. His desire to travel seems in part to have sprung from an effort to understand the social forces that were undermining the strength and power of his people as the old Lakota ways disappeared in the face of the incursion of the white population.

But his religious sensitivities were also at work, and Black Elk focused his attention on the religion of the whites. In a letter from

Europe to his people in Dakota, Black Elk wrote, "of the white man's many customs, only his faith, the white man's beliefs about God's will, and how they act according to it, I wanted to understand" (DeMallie, 9–10). Although Black Elk was baptized (most likely in the Anglican tradition) during his time with Buffalo Bill, DeMallie does not interpret this as an event of great importance nor even as a religious action by Black Elk, because Buffalo Bill made this a condition of his business contract (DeMallie, 10). The baptism positioned Black Elk to participate in and thereby learn a great deal about the white man's religion during his travels to New York and Europe.

Black Elk told Neihardt that in Europe he had lost his Lakota spiritual powers, but that these powers had returned to him when he himself returned to Pine Ridge (DeMallie, 11). Resuming his life in the Dakota plains, Black Elk became fascinated by the Ghost Dance movement. He saw in it something of a parallel to his own Lakota vision as a boy, and he approached the Ghost Dance festivities with a renewed sense of vision and hope. This renewed sense of Lakota spiritual power was short-lived, however, for the Wounded Knee massacre of 1890, in which two hundred Indians were killed by federal troops, disillusioned Black Elk as it did many Lakotas. One missionary observed that many Indians were distanced entirely from religion as a result of that event (DeMallie, 12).

In 1892, Black Elk married Katie War Bonnet, who is presumed to have been a Catholic since their three sons were baptized in the Catholic tradition. In 1904, Black Elk became a Catholic himself. Historical materials offer several explanations for this event. More than twenty years later, Black Elk explained to Neihardt that he had felt unwilling to follow a mandate of his Lakota vision that had instructed him at age thirty-seven [1900] to use "soldier weed, a destructive power that would wipe out his enemies—men, women, and children" (DeMallie, 14). In his refusal to take responsibility for this destruction, we are told, he turned to the Catholic Church.

His daughter Lucy offers a second explanation, citing an incident in which Black Elk used his powers to heal a seriously ill boy when a Jesuit priest arrived to administer the last rites. The priest condemned Black Elk's rites and urged Black Elk to come with him to the mission church. According to Lucy, Black Elk felt the priest's powers were greater than his own; thus, he accepted the priest's invitation, took religious instruction, and two weeks later—on December 6, 1904, the Catholic feast of St. Nicholas—he was baptized Nicholas Black Elk (DeMallie, 14).[27]

A third explanation takes very seriously Black Elk's interest in Christianity. Partly rooted in curiosity, partly rooted in a desire to better understand the white man through his religion, and partly rooted in his own heightened and enduring religious sensibilities and affinities, particularly with respect to notions about God and God's will (DeMallie, 9–10), Black Elk took initiative to understand white religion both as a form of knowledge and as a form of spiritual power. Black Elk's writings to his people highlight the centrality of love in Paul's Letter to the Corinthians and Jesus' attention to the poor. In a letter written in Lakota in 1909, for example, Black Elk exhorts his people to help one another "because our Savior came on this earth and helped all poor people" (DeMallie, 19).

A fourth explanation for Black Elk's conversion spotlights shifting patterns of social and economic power. As one form of white intervention, Christian presence affected Dakota life socially, politically, economically, educationally, and religiously. The old Lakota ways became inapplicable to the new circumstances of occupation and unworkable under new forms of governance. When Neihardt asked Black Elk on one occasion why he had put aside the old religion, Black Elk said, "My children had to live in this world" (DeMallie, 47). He was not alone. Given the movement of the white world into the life and land of the Indian, and given subsequent diminution of the old Indian ways, almost all the Lakotas joined one or another Christian denomination in at least a nominal way (DeMallie, 15). "Because my children had to live in this world" (DeMallie, 47) suggests that Black Elk's conversion was a resourceful response and strategic concession to vast cultural and social change.

Knowing all this, DeMallie judges that "Black Elk's conversion was unquestionably genuine" (DeMallie, 14), while reminding us that "conversion to Christianity must not be misunderstood as indicating loss of faith in traditional religion" (DeMallie, 92). Steinmetz puts it this way:

> Conversion to Christianity does not mean giving up a religious tradition but rather giving it a Christian meaning. To equate conversion with the substitution of one religion for another is an inaccurate notion which does no justice to the deep psychological relationship a person has with his or her past.[28]

Basing much of his research on the accounts provided by Black Elk's daughter, Lucy Looks Twice, Michael Steltenkamp offers interpretive detail:

> Black Elk understood his role as a Catholic catechist to be the desire of Wakan Tanka, "who had chosen him for this work," and he adopted this new form of religious expression with great zeal. The

old medicine man-turned-catechist appreciated his earlier tradition but adapted to a historical ethos that made his religious quest a response to Wakan Tanka in the changing circumstances of the here and now.[29]

Black Elk's involvements as a Catholic catechist enabled him to continue work he had earlier undertaken as a Lakota mystic and medicine man, for it provided him numerous outlets to aid and heal his people in practical and spiritual ways. For example, catechists conducted Sunday services in the Lakota language, led the people in prayers and hymns, read the gospel and instructed people in the faith, visited the sick, and in emergency settings, conducted baptisms and burials (DeMallie, 17). Many of the older religious, social, and political processes and forms of Oglala organization thereby persisted in new guise.[30] Religious activities became a primary means by which Lakota leadership, community, and sense of solidarity were continued in a world occupied by whites.

Clyde Holler's excellent study, *Black Elk's Religion*, concurs with this point, suggesting that Black Elk discerned significant overlap between the traditional Lakota ways and the Catholic Church (Holler, 202). Since conversion accounts often assume conversion to be a movement from one commitment (worldview, value, belief) to another, and since conversion commonly means "turning around," the notion of conversion, too, presses for renewed attention in the face of these stories.

Recent studies expand conventional views of conversion as movement from one referent to another by casting discussion of conversion in the language of transformation. Conversion as transformation is seen as a process that stimulates a powerful and profound, indeed, a transforming change in a person's ways of seeing, feeling, valuing, understanding, and relating. Probing the complexity of conversion and its impact on the total person, this perspective highlights the fact that the conversion process is constituted by an affective, cognitive, moral, and religious restructuring of one's outlook and orientation.[31] When conversion occurs within the contexts of colonialism and neo-colonialism, radical cultural and social (often violent) changes in the use and distribution of power also powerfully affect the restructuring process.

Black Elk himself describes his relationship to traditional Oglala religion and to Catholicism in different ways at different times. Sometimes his words suggest that he regarded his conversion as the displacement of the old Oglala religion by the new Catholic one. Yet other passages make clear that the traditional religion continued to claim his loyalty even as a Catholic. In support of the displacement model, a letter Black Elk published in the *Catholic Herald* in 1911 is noteworthy, for there he exhorts his fellow Sioux: "I am engaged in difficult work which is good unto death; let us not talk of our ways of the past, but think about the new ways our Savior has given to us" (DeMallie, 21). His daughter, Lucy Looks Twice, and others remember Black Elk primarily in terms of his active involvement with priests establishing Catholicism among his people. The seriousness with which he took his Catholic faith and the vigor he displayed in catechizing others is widely recognized by Black Elk's friends and family members; they are offended by those who refuse to take seriously Black Elk's Catholic commitments.[32]

However, when John Neihardt drove up to Black Elk's house in Manderson in 1930, hoping to interview him about the old Lakota ways, Black Elk welcomed the opportunity to release and reveal the Oglala vision that had remained vivid throughout his life. The words and the images of his vision were so clear and so bright that Black Elk reportedly said to his inquiring guest, "I did not have to remember these things; they have remembered themselves all these years."[33] With John Neihardt and Neihardt's daughters, and with his son, Benjamin, present, Black Elk prayed to the "Grandfather, Great Spirit" in the old Lakota way, and "everyone was deeply moved by the earnestness of the old man's prayer" (DeMallie, 46). Black Elk adopted John Neihardt and his daughters Hilda and Enid into the Oglala tribe by bestowing Indian names upon them (Flaming Rainbow, Daybreak Star Woman, and She Walks With Her Sacred Stick). The Neihardts felt that this event made them participants in the vision Black Elk revealed, and they felt a responsibility to communicate it to others (DeMallie, 36–37).

When published, *Black Elk Speaks* became a source of some embarrassment to Black Elk because of the furor it raised in Catholic circles (DeMallie, 61–62). The question that bothered some pertained to truth-claims. Did Black Elk believe in the Christian God who alone was seen as the source of salvation or did he believe in the thunder beings and grandfathers of *Black Elk Speaks*? An historical document signed by Black Elk after the book's publication demonstrates that he publicly announced being a Christian and reaffirmed his devotion to the Catholic faith as the "true Faith of God the Father, the Son, and the Holy Spirit" (DeMallie, 59).[34] Yet again, in a 1948 communication between Black Elk, his son Ben, and Charles Hanson, Jr., according to DeMallie, Black Elk said he had made a mistake in rejecting the old ways for Christianity. As late as two years before his death, he wondered whether the Lakota religion might have been better for his people (DeMallie, 72). Thus, Black Elk's religious story, given these and other like examples, exhibits a pattern of shifting, somewhat zigzagging loyalties: the old (Sioux ways) and then the new (Catholic ways); then the Catholic again, and then again the Sioux.

Catholic beliefs and Lakota beliefs were largely perceived in Catholic circles of the time in terms of contrast, opposition, and competition in contrast to the ecumenism of recent decades.[35] "Today such ecumenical sharing between native and Christian religious traditions is taken as a given by Catholic Lakotas," DeMallie comments, "but in Black Elk's day it was an idea yet unborn" (66).[36] The Jesuits who staffed the Pine Ridge Mission feared that Black Elk would "backslide" (62) into his old ways. Holding both religions "alongside" each other appears to be the more realistic probability. Historian Henry Warner Bowden comments generally on Plains Indian appropriation of Christianity as a process of absorbing "new values and behavioral standards but . . . without totally rejecting their precontact identity."[37]

This suggests that conversion in a context of occupation is more adequately construed as the including of new religious perspectives, or, perhaps better, in the case of Black Elk, as the movement back and forth from one religious perspective to another along a continuum. At one end of the continuum is the old Sioux way of life representing the time before contact with the white population; at the other end of the continuum is the post-contact world of the white ways. Indians used the continuum as a resource to be tapped situationally, as circumstances allowed or required.[38] Black Elk's apparently shifting loyalties are better understood, in this line of thought, less as a zigzagging movement that suggests ambivalence and far more as a capacity to tap the resources of two traditions.

Black Elk remained a member of the Catholic Church until the end of his life, and he received the sacraments of Holy Communion and Extreme Unction prior to his death (DeMallie, 71, 74). Buried in the chapel graveyard at St. Agnes Mission (where he had served as the first native catechist), a tombstone bears the brief inscription "Chief Black Elk." His Christian name (Nicholas) is absent. The Christian graveyard and the Oglala inscription thus become an intriguing symbol of Black Elk's twofold religious identity.

The white governmental and ecclesial social setting in which Black Elk lived did not allow an easy acceptance of both religions. Black Elk was pressured to choose between the Lakota or the Catholic way, and choose he did. Rigoberta Menchu, by contrast, apparently has comfortably combined Quiche and Catholic—or so goes the story she tells. Living in a time when religious interactions are seen as interesting and acceptable, her additive approach to religion is as acceptable to her Catholic community as it is to the Quiche. This was not so for Black Elk. Not unlike Rigoberta Menchu, Black Elk, too, was bi-religious. But because he lived in an occupied setting where being bi-religious was not allowed, his twofold loyalties had to be expressed one at a time, at discrete moments and distinctive places in his life.

Holler usefully details the plausibility of Black Elk's bi-religious identity. He alerts us to the fact that, whereas the concepts of true belief and salvation are central to Christianity, in the Lakota way it is power (cosmic power, spiritual power) and the continuity of the people that are the chief religious concerns. Whereas Catholicism commonly stresses the authority of church officers and teachings, Native American wisdom stresses the individual visions of holy men, which vary from one to another (Holler, 215). Thus, true belief is not the preoccupation of indigenous peoples such as Rigoberta Menchu and Nicholas Black Elk, as it tends to be for many Christians.

> In other words, it is simply ethnocentric to assume without further ado that Black Elk must have experienced Christianity and traditional religion primarily as conflicting belief systems. It seems much more likely that Black Elk was predisposed to see religious statements as symbolic expressions of truths that could not be fully captured outside the context of religious ecstacy. If two holy men could have different visions without threatening the Lakota concept of religion, why could not two cultures have different visions of the sacred? (Holler, 215).

In this view, spiritual *power,* far more important to Black Elk than truth-claims, renders Black Elk receptive to a Catholic Christian path that demonstrated its power in ritual, but also in cultural influence and social standing. The Catholic Church thus became a resource and a path in relation to which, perhaps within which, traditional religion could continue. Does this mean that Black Elk's conversion was ungenuine? Does it suggest that Black Elk used Catholicism for his own Lakota ends without really believing in it? To these implied accusations, Raymond DeMallie and Clyde Holler answer, "no." On the basis of Black Elk's own words and the testimony of his contemporaries, they see Black Elk's conversion and commitment to Christianity as sincere, honest, and real.

Clyde Holler suggests that the key to understanding the possibility of Black Elk's being bi-religious rests in an understanding of religions as symbolic discourse rather than as competing systems of propositional truth-claims. The question is often raised that Black Elk must be either a sincere Christian or a sincere traditionalist, for it is not possible to be both. To this, Holler responds:

> If Black Elk did not share our culture-bound concept of religion as propositional truth, what reason is there to believe that he even felt the conflict? If they were to him two alternate ways of envisioning the sacred—or two stories about the sacred—not two mutually exclusive and absolute truth claims, it becomes easier to see how he could accept Christianity as a further unfolding of his vision, weaving Christian elements back into his account of his original power vision (Holler, 217).

This interactive reading presents Black Elk as far more than "a pitiful old man" who concludes *Black Elk Speaks* (Neihardt, 230). Rather, Black Elk's bi-religious loyalties and commitments highlight a creative religious agent, who, within a context of subjugation, developed his religious life by way of adding, combining, and reconfiguring mediating symbols that communicated meaning, efficacy, and direction.[39] Holler admires Black Elk's intellectual creativity and resourcefulness in tapping two religions as alternate ways of envisioning, representing, and relating to the sacred.

Although in keeping with the times Black Elk was pressed to choose between two religions, two spiritualities, and two loyalties, it is more plausible that Black Elk found meaning and efficacy in both religions and spiritualities, but that he lacked a vocabulary to express this and a social context that would accept it. Where the missionaries saw opposition and competition, Black Elk, the evidence suggests, found two sources of meaning, direction, and power. Conversion in this setting is aptly understood, then, as a form of adaptability, an expression of flexibility and creativity through which more is embraced rather than something displaced.

Holler's findings and interpretations, together with those of DeMallie, Steinmetz, and Steltenkamp, thus press us to notice the multiple motivations and creative combinations that characterize religious conversion and commitment within the context of cultural conflict and colonialism.

Questions for Future Research

Categorization as a fundamental concern of inquiry and interpretation presses us to find adequate categories to name the combining of religions. Rigoberta Menchu casts her experience in terms of distinctive forms or channels of expression. Black Elk's place and time prevented him from such an easy and explicitly acknowledged combination. Yet Black Elk did draw upon his two traditions, entering and tapping two worlds that he found meaningful and powerful.

Many stories are needed more fully to illuminate the ways in which religions blend and are blended, and a variety of metaphors are to be expected to describe those relationships. As noted above, the proposals are many. Religions-in-relation within individuals are seen by some as translations of one to the other; as alternative or parallel paths to a goal; as two worlds accessible to each other by way of a bridge; as forms of exchange or of dual citizenship or of symbiosis; as a mosaic; as alternative channels of expression; or as differing configurations of religious belief and practice that serve as resourceful strategies useful to the needs and circumstances of a given time. It is likely that other metaphors that display the concept of religious conversion as appropriation and addition rather than displacement and replacement will be garnered from additional research.

Testimonials, autobiographies, interviews, and oral histories that give sustained attention to this question carry the potential for generating an important data base. A sampling of questions that researchers might pursue include the following. As religions blend and combine in distinctive ways affected by socio-political-cultural-specific settings, what images most accurately describe the interactions, exchanges, and combinations? How do the combinations take form and in what ways do they take expression conceptually, ritually, ethically, and institutionally? Given the fact that analogies are always similar and dissimilar simultaneously, in what ways does a given metaphor or analogy (for example, another channel of expression, translation, continuum, separate planes, or dual citizenship) illuminate the experience of religious pluralism as bi-religiosity and in what ways does it fail to do so? How do the differences between propositional and symbolic modes of interpretation shape or prevent the possibility of bi-religiosity? What examples of irresolvable tensions and contradictions emerge and how are these dealt with?

A broader base of information and interpretation on this issue carries the potential for contributing to a number of issues widely debated today: (a) the impact of colonialism, neocolonialism, and other forms of occupation on people's religious lives; (b) the ways in which contemporary missionization efforts support or subvert the flow and distribution of social, political, and economic power; (c) the place of truth-claims in the lives of religious persons (for example, is the concern with religious truth-claims and an insistence on their adjudication a mark of privileged social status? Do the stories of Rigoberta Menchu and Black Elk press us to recognize religions as resourceful strategies in the face of the most basic struggles for food, space, and meaning?); (d) the concern with power, ritual participation, aesthetic engagement, and commitment to the continuity of a community as attractive features of religions that for some are far more important than beliefs and truth claims; (e) the tensions and the attractions of being drawn to multiple religions and the ways in which people actually do participate in more than one religion; (f) the dynamics by which "the religious other" becomes, in fact, "the self" when the other (religion) has been appropriated by the self and the newly bi-religious self becomes other than one was.

NOTES

1. See, for example, John Hick and Brian Hebblethwaite, eds., *Christianity and Other Religions: Selected Readings* (Philadelphia: Fortress, 1981); John Hick and Paul Knitter, eds., *The Myth of Christian Uniqueness: Toward a Pluralistic Theology of Religions* (Maryknoll, N.Y.: Orbis Books, 1987); Gavin D'Costa, ed., *Christian Uniqueness Reconsidered: The Myth of a Pluralistic Theology of Religions* (Maryknoll, N.Y.: Orbis Books, 1990); Paul F. Knitter, *No Other Name? A Critical Survey of Christian Attitudes Toward the World Religions* (Maryknoll, NY..: Orbis Books, 1985, 1992); Schubert Ogden, *Is There Only One True Religion or Are There Many?* (Dallas: Southern Methodist University Press, 1992); John Hick, *An Interpretation of Religion: Human Responses to the Transcendent* (New Haven, Conn.: Yale University Press, 1989); and Dan Cohn-Sherbok, ed., *Many Mansions: Interfaith and Religious Intolerance* (London: Bellew Publishing, 1992). Diana Eck's account of her religio-intellectual journey is cast within the context of religious pluralism in *Encountering God: A Spiritual Journey from Bozeman to Banares* (Boston: Beacon Press, 1993).

2. Joseph Murphy's illuminating and provocative study, *Santeria: An African Religion in America* (Boston: Beacon Press, 1988), alerted me to this rich and suggestive image of being "bi-religious." He credits Mary Ann Borello of New York whose work with Puerto Rican spiritualists led her "to model ideas of religious syncretism on bilingualism." See Murphy, 171, n. 23. I wish to acknowledge Professor Murphy's helpful comments on an earlier version of this article.

3. Inclusivism is not unique to Christian thinkers. Hindu inclusivism, for example, maintains that religions other than Hinduism are true insofar as they express some centrally-named feature of Hinduism. Indian philosopher Sarvepalli Radhakrishnan illustrates this point. For him, other religions can be affirmed in terms of the extent to which they identify the saving or liberating experience to consist in a monistic realization of the Absolute which is seen as the true law, the perennial, transcendent truth of philosophical (Advaita) Hinduism. See S. Radhakrishnan, "Conflict of Religions: The Hindu Attitude," in *The Hindu View of Life* (New York: Macmillan, 1968), and Julius J. Lipner, "Religion and Religions," in G. Parthasarathi and D. P. Chattopadhyaya, eds., *Radhakrishnan: Centenary Volume* (Delhi: Oxford University Press, 1989) 146. The essentialist viewpoint that Radhakrishnan represents has many critics. Raimundo Panikkar is one: ". . . Hinduism can hardly be called a religion. It

is rather a bundle of religious traditions. We should readily understand the in-
stinctive reaction of the people of India against being levelled down to a single
'Hinduism.' Strictly speaking, Hinduism does not exist." See *The Unknown
Christ of Hinduism*, rev. ed. (London: Darton, Longman & Todd, 1977) 38.

4. For a well-detailed discussion of various authors, see Knitter's *No
Other Name?*, chapter 7, 120–44.

5. Ogden, *Is There Only One True Religion or Are There Many?*, 28–9.

6. See Karl Barth, "The Revelation of God as the Abolition of Religion,"
in Hick and Hebblethwaite, eds., *Christianity and Other Religions*, 32–51; and
Knitter's discussion of Barth's position in *No Other Name?*, 80–7.

7. Ogden discusses inconsistencies in the language of pluralists on this
issue of *is* or *may be*. See *Is There Only One True Religion or Are There Many?*,
23–6.

8. Knitter, "Preface," in John Hick and Paul F. Knitter, eds., *The Myth of
Christian Uniqueness*, viii. See also Gavin D'Costa's response to this which challenges Knitter's claim and gives rise to his book: "Preface," in Gavin D'Costa,
ed., *Christian Uniqueness Reconsidered*, ix.

9. Ogden, *Is There Only One True Religion or Are There Many?*, 103.

10. Additional positions, beyond the four discussed, require recognition.
Fifth, if one holds that there is simply no way to know, one faces frontally the
epistemological limits of the human situation and admits agnosticism.
Religious truth-claims become unverifiable and thus undebatable. Sixth, if one
holds that no religion is true, the question of choosing or negotiating competing truth-claims becomes meaningless. A seventh position is that, given the
track record of human community over time, and given the role of human beings in the practice and perpetuation of religions, all religions are very likely
both true in some respects and false in other respects; the challenge is to discern the difference. Such discernment requires interpretive theory and skills,
critical and self-critical reflection, and the positing of criteria for judgment. An
eighth possibility is conceptual relativism which makes comparison impossible since it offers no norm by which to critique or affirm traditions. Each is
contained in its own language system.

11. *I, Rigoberta Menchu: An Indian Woman in Guatemala*, ed. and introd.
Elisabeth Burgos-Debray, trans. Ann Wright (London: Verso, 1984). Page references in the text refer to this edition.

12. For a series of analyses of the conditions in Guatemala written by anthropologists and other social scientists, see Robert M. Carmack, ed., *Harvest of
Violence: The Maya Indians and the Guatemalan Crisis* (Norman, Okla: University
of Oklahoma Press, 1988).

13. Catholic Action was a large-scale catechist movement that came to
Guatemala in the mid-1940s. Anthropologist Robert Carmack notes that although it had conservative roots, seeking to evangelize in competition with
Protestant groups, Catholic Action became active in establishing cooperatives
among the people and in fostering educational efforts to assist the Indians that
they might improve their social conditions. "Classes on social welfare and political consciousness were part of the program that became known as Catholic

Action." See "The Story of Santa Cruz Quiche," in Robert M. Carmack, ed., *Harvest of Violence*, 49.

14. My colleague George Ramos provided the image of these two religions operating on separate planes. Insofar as these religions address distinctive needs, the people do not require connection, reconciliation, or integration. He also regularly reminds me that native people's religions are, in his view, generated and embraced far more as pragmatic strategies than as truth-claims. As creative responses to the pressures and struggles of life, these expressions are indeed authentic, "true" for the people who live them. But they are not "truth-claims" to be asserted or defended as "ultimate truths."

15. Ake Hultkrantz has developed these themes in his ecology of religions perspective. See "An Ecological Approach to Religion," *Ethnos* 31/1–4 (1966) 131–50.

16. George Ramos, unpublished communication.

17. Andre Droogers outlines the many meanings of syncretism in "Syncretism: The Problem of Definition, the Definition of the Problem," in Jerald Gort, Hendrik Vroom, et al., *Dialogue and Syncretism: An Interdisciplinary Approach* (Amsterdam: Editions Rodopi, 1989) 7–25; W. A. Visser 't Hooft argues for a Christian condemnation of syncretism in *No Other Name: The Choice between Syncretism and Christian Universalism* (Philadelphia: Westminster Press, 1963); Robert D. Baird considers syncretism as a category in the history of religions in *Category Formation and the History of Religions* (Mouton, The Netherlands: Mouton, 1971) 142–51; B. C. Hedrick illustrates syncretism in Spanish America in a short piece entitled *Religious Syncretism in Spanish America* (Greeley: Colorado State College, Museum of Anthropology Miscellaneous Series, no. 2, 1967); Antonio Gualtieri contrasts syncretism with indigenization in *Christianity and Native Traditions: Indigenization and Syncretism Among the Inuit and Dene of the Western Arctic* (Notre Dame, Ind.: Cross Roads Books, 1984). Charles Stewart and Rosalind Shaw (editors) highlight the politics of religious syncretism in a collection of essays entitled *Syncretism/Anti-syncretism: The Politics of Religious Synthesis* (New York: Routledge, 1994).

18. Murphy, *Santeria*, 116, 120–4. See also Roger Bastide, *African Civilizations in the New World*, trans. Peter Green (London: C. Hurst and Company, 1971) 152–68, and Melville J. Herskovits, *The New World Negro* (Bloomington, Ind.: Indiana University Press, 1966) 321–53.

In an interview on Latino religion in the U.S., Otto Maduro comments that syncretism is a feature of all religions: "Whatever term we use, all religions . . . are living traditions that have adopted and adapted an infinite number of elements from the seeking where they took root and developed, starting with the language but ending with the rituals, the vestments, the prayers, the modes of organization, the conceptions of power and authority, the concepts of God, the sacred, the holy, sanctity, etc. So in a way, without the expression being at all derogatory, all religions result from a process of syncretization, including the Italian-Vatican Catholicism or Iberian 16th-century Catholicism, or 19th-century Irish Roman Catholicism." In "U.S. Latinos and Religion: An Interview with Otto Maduro," *America* (August 14–21, 1993) 18.

19. Carl Gustav Diehl, "Replacement or Substitution in the Meeting of Religions," in Sven S. Hartman, ed., *Syncretism: Based on Papers Read at the Symposium on Cultural Contact*, Meeting on Religious Syncretism Held at Abo on September 8–10, 1966 (Stockholm: Almqvist & Wiksell, 1969) 137–61.

20. Antonio Gualtieri, *Christianity and Native Traditions*, 8.

21. Ake Hultkrantz, "Configurations of Religious Belief among the Wind River Shoshoni," in Christopher Vecsey, ed., *Belief and Worship in Native North America* (Syracuse, N.Y.: Syracuse University Press, 1981) 28–47.

22. Gustavo Gutierrez speaks of the "other side" in "Towards the Fifth Centenary," in Leonardo Boff and Virgil Elizondo, eds., *1492–1992: The Voice of the Victims*, Concilium 1990/6 (London: SCM, 1990) 1. Elise Boulding employs "underside" imagery; see *The Underside of History: A View of Women Through Time* (Boulder, Colo.: Westview Press, 1976).

23. June O'Connor, "Stories from the South: The Voices of Latin American Women [As a Resource for Comparative Religious Ethics]," in Harlan Beckley, ed., *The Annual: Society of Christian Ethics 1993* (Boston: SCE, 1993) 283–90, and "Comforting the Sorrowful: From Charity to Solidarity," in Francis Eigo, ed., *Rethinking the Spiritual Works of Mercy* (Villanova, Pa.: Villanova University Press, 1993) 67–96.

24. New York: Pocket Books, 1972.

25. Raymond J. DeMallie, ed., *The Sixth Grandfather: Black Elk's Teachings Given to John G. Neihardt* (Lincoln and London: University of Nebraska Press, 1984); Paul B. Steinmetz , S.J., *Pipe, Bible, and Peyote among the Oglala Lakota: A Study in Religious Identity*, rev. ed. (Knoxville: University of Tennessee Press, 1990); Julian Rice, *Black Elk's Story: Distinguishing Its Lakota Purpose* (Albuquerque: University of New Mexico Press, 1991); Michael F. Steltenkamp, *Black Elk: Holy Man of the Oglala* (Norman, Okla.: University of Oklahoma Press, 1993); Clyde Holler, *Black Elk's Religion: The Sun Dance and Lakota Catholicism* (Syracuse, N.Y.: Syracuse University Press, 1995) .

26. Neihardt and DeMallie cite 1863; Joseph Epes Brown writes, "According to his [Black Elk's] own account, he was born in 1862" (Preface to *The Sacred Pipe: Black Elk's Account of the Seven Rites of the Oglala Sioux* (New York: Penguin, 1971) xiv; Black Elk's tombstone lists 1858 as the time of birth; Black Elk's daughter, Lucy Looks Twice, judged it to be 1866 (Michael Steltenkamp, *Black Elk: Holy Man of the Oglala*, 131 and 189, n. 2).

27. Steltenkamp, *Black Elk: Holy Man of the Oglala*, 33–5 .

28. Steinmetz, *Pipe, Bible, and Peyote among the Oglala Lakota*, 188–9.

29. Steltenkamp, *Black Elk: Holy Man of the Oglala*, 136.

30. William K. Powers, *Oglala Religion* (Lincoln, Neb.: University of Nebraska Press, 1977) 129. See also Steltenkamp, *Black Elk: Holy Man of the Oglala*, 48–51.

31. See Bernard Lonergan, *Method in Theology* (London: Darton, Longman & Todd, 1971); "Theology in Its New Context, " in W.F.J. Ryan and B. J. Tyrrell, eds., *A Second Collection* (London: Darton, Longman & Todd, 1974) 55–67. Also Walter Conn, "Bernard Lonergan' s Analysis of Conversion, " *Angelicum* 53/3, 362–404, and *Christian Conversion: A Developmental Interpretation of Autonomy and Surrender* (New York: Paulist Press, 1986).

32. Michael Steltenkamp, *Black Elk: Holy Man of the Oglala*, xvii, 140–1, 155; also Paul Steinmetz, *Pipe, Bible, and Peyote among the Oglala Lakota*, 179–85.

33. *Black Elk Speaks*, 41.

34. See also Michael Steltenkamp, *Black Elk: Holy Man of the Oglala*, 82–4.

35. Harvey Markowitz writes that Catholic mission thinking at the time of Black Elk "rejected the notion that a Lakota could participate in traditional Indian ceremonies and simultaneously be a Catholic." See "The Catholic Mission and the Sioux: A Crisis in the Early Paradigm," 124, in Raymond J. DeMallie and Douglas R. Parks, eds., *Sioux Indian Religion: Tradition and Innovation* (Norman, Okla.: University of Oklahoma Press, 1987) 113–37. The paradigm of "cultural replacement" characterized white policy; both the missionary effort and government educational policy sought to replace Sioux traditions (122, 136). See also Robert Hilbert, S.J., "Contemporary Catholic Mission Work Among the Sioux," ibid., 142–3.

36. In "The Catholic Mission and the Sioux," Markowitz attributes the shift in Catholic Indian mission paradigms to the 1963–1965 Vatican Council II, ibid., 113–37. See also Hilbert, ibid., 139–47.

37. *American Indians and Christian Missions: Studies in Cultural Conflict* (Chicago: University of Chicago Press, 1981) 191. Also DeMallie and Parks, eds., "Introduction," *Sioux Indian Religion*, 13.

38. William K. Powers uses the continuum image with respect to the two cultures generally in *Oglala Religion*, 205; it is an image that seems applicable to and useful in resolving these questions of religious identity and participation as well. See also Paul Steinmetz's use of the continuum image: ". . . when a Lakota does go back to his end of the continuum, he does not always go back to a pure Lakota identity but to one that has been modified by Christianity. And when he selectively returns to the white man's end, he returns to a Christianity that has been modified by Lakota tradition, so that in fact the distance between the two ends becomes shorter" (*Pipe, Bible, and Peyote among the Oglala Lakota*, 169–70).

39. On the notion of "mediating symbols," see Paul B. Steinmetz, S.J., "Three Types of Religious Acculturation Among the Oglala Lakota," in Peter Slater and Donald Wiebe, eds., *Traditions in Contact and Change* [Selected Proceedings of the XIVth Congress of the International Association for the History of Religions] (Waterloo: Wilfrid Laurier University Press, 1983) 527–41. On the themes of innovation and change in Sioux religions in particular, see DeMallie and Parks, eds., *Sioux Indian Religion*. Steinmetz's *Pipe, Bible, and Peyote among the Oglala Lakota* examines the contemporary religious dynamics of cultural interaction and religious acculturation on the Sioux Pine Ridge reservation. He challenges and extends acculturation studies by examining acculturation not only in terms of Indian-white relations but also in terms of Indian-Indian relations, thereby taking seriously the diversity that exists among Indian groups as well.

ELEVEN

Pope John Paul II on Islam

Mahmoud Ayoub

I. Historical Overview

Muslim-Christian relations are as old as the Islamic tradition itself. Before his prophetic mission, while still a youth, Muḥammad's prophethood is believed to have been recognized and foretold by the Christian monk Baḥirah.[1] The truth of Muḥammad's mission and authenticity of the scripture revealed to him were confirmed by the aged Christian savant Waraqah b. Nawfal. Waraqah's testimony to the truth of Muḥammad's apostolic mission confirmed him in his resolve to preach his new message of faith in the One God to an idolatrous and stubborn people.[2] When some of the Prophet's followers could no longer endure the persecution of the hostile men of Makkah, he advised them to seek protection with the Christian king of Abyssinia.[3]

Christians are described in the Qur'ān as "the nearest in amity" to the Muslims (Q. 5:82). Twice they are numbered among the religious communities whose faith and good works will be richly rewarded by God, "and no fear shall come upon them nor will they grieve."[4] Yet the Christians are sternly reproached for their extremist claims concerning Jesus and even accused of rejection of faith.[5]

Thus the Islamic position towards Christians has from the beginning been an ambivalent one. This ambivalence is characteristic not only of the Islamic view of Christians but of Christian-Muslim relations generally and on both sides. One fundamental reason for this ambivalence is that both faiths are intensely missionary oriented. Each claims to have exclusively a universal message of truth and salvation for all of humankind. Each community, moreover, considers the other to be in grave error in its basic understanding of God, his nature, and relationship to humanity and its history.

While it may be argued that Muslim-Christian relations are now better than they have ever been, in fact little has changed in the basic attitudes of the Church and the *Ummah* towards one another. There has been on both sides a grudging recognition of their common faith in the One God but also a deep mistrust of the aims and intentions of each community towards the other. This mistrust stems from long-held distortions and misrepresentations of the faith and culture by both communities of one another. These distorted images have often been used to justify long and bloody conflicts between Western Christendom and the world of Islam.

On the basis of this common faith in God and commitment to do his will, in 1077 Pope Gregory VII wrote to the *sulṭān* al-Nāṣir, ruler of Bejaya in present day Algeria, reminding him of this common faith and commitment. The Pope admonished the Muslim ruler, "God approves nothing in us so much as that after loving Him, one should love his fellow." He continued: "You and we owe this charity to ourselves, specially because we believe and confess one God. . . ."[6] Less than two decades later, in 1095, Pope Urban II sounded an entirely different note at the Council of Clairmont, which he used to launch the first Crusade against the Muslims. In his famous address the Pontiff contrasted the Franks, "the beloved of God," with the Muslims, whom he called, "an accursed race, a race utterly alienated from God. . . ."[7]

II. New Hopes and Old Prejudices

The millennium following these harsh words has seen many positive changes in Muslim-Christian relations. A new era of meaningful and constructive dialogue began with Vatican II, 1962–1965. In this essay we are concerned with the position of the Catholic Church towards Islam and Muslims, and more specifically with the pronouncements of Pope John Paul II on Islam. It must be noted at the outset that the following analysis of his holiness's pronouncements will mirror the same ambivalence that has characterized the relations between the two communities throughout their long history.

In many ways the pronouncements of Pope John Paul II on Islam echo the spirit and letter of the Vatican II. In particular, *Nostra aetate,* one of the Council's major documents expressing the Church's new spirit of openness to dialogue with "non-Christians" has been the primary inspiration for the Pope's approach to Islam. Nevertheless, his holiness often returns to old and conservative attitudes of the Church towards Islam and Muslims. This is particularly the case, as we shall see, when he addresses Catholic clerics living in Muslim lands. The issue that will concern us in this study is, therefore, the apparent inconsistencies in the Holy Father's pronouncements on Islam and what this means to the commitment of both the Church and the *Ummah* to interfaith dialogue.

Pope John Paul II has been more prolific on Islam than any pontiff before him. This is undoubtedly due in large part to his numerous pastoral visits to Christian minorities living in Muslim lands.[8] No less important in this regard is the participation of the Pontifical Council for Interreligious Dialogue in international interfaith activities. On such occasions the Pope addressed Muslim participants on behalf of the Catholic Church. Other reasons for the Pope's concern with Muslims and Islam have been international conflicts such as the Lebanese civil strife, the Gulf War, and the tragic interreligious conflict in the former Yugoslavia. Still another reason is the diplomatic relations of the Vatican with many Muslim nations.

We shall selectively examine the statements of Pope John Paul II on Islam chronologically over a fifteen-year period, 1979–1994. These statements will be considered under three categories, those addressed to Muslims directly and those addressed to Christians about Islam. The third and equally important category is the Pope's writings, especially his encyclical *Mission of the Redeemer* (1991) and the book *Crossing the Threshold of Hope* (1994). These two recent documents provide the theological framework for the Pope's personal position towards other religions in general and Islam in particular.

The first journey of the Pope to a predominantly Muslim country was to Turkey in November 1979, slightly over a year after his accession to the pontifical office. In a homily delivered at the chapel of the Italian Embassy in Ankara, the Pope exhorted the Catholic community to live in peace and amity with fellow Muslim citizens. He praised Turkey's secular system which allows all citizens to practice their own religion without any discrimination. "Although they do not acknowledge Jesus as God," the Pope observed, Muslims "revere him as a prophet, honor the virgin Mary and await the day of Resurrection." He extolled Islamic moral, spiritual, and social values which Christians also hold. The Pope finally called on both Muslims and Christians to collaborate on the basis of their common faith in God in promoting peace and brotherhood "in the free profession of faith proper to each."[9]

It is important to note here that honoring Jesus and his mother is not an Islamic gesture of good will towards Christians. It is rather an essential part of their faith. But to "acknowledge Jesus as God" is for Muslims to associate other gods with God, which is the only unforgivable sin.[10] While we believe such theological issues should not be ignored by Christians and Muslims in their efforts to promote better understanding through honest dialogue, they should be recognized and dealt with patiently and with great sensitivity.

In May 1980, first in Kenya and then in Ghana, the Pope echoed the same sentiments in his addresses to Muslim leaders of the two African countries. He found in the worship of the One God, the creator of heaven and earth, a uniting bond of Christians and Muslims. He affirmed the Church's commitment to dialogue with Islam, but also asked that ". . . her own heritage be fully known specially to those who are spiritually attached to Abraham and who profess monotheism."[11] This somewhat veiled reference to missionary work among the Muslims of Africa is more openly expressed in later speeches, particularly to African bishops and missionaries engaged in medical, educational, and other humanitarian services.

The dual mission of the Church as a "good Samaritan" to the poor and suffering peoples of the world, and also as the maker of disciples for Christ "of all nations,"[12] was emphasized by the Pope during a two-day stop in Pakistan on his way to the Far East. His holiness exchanged expressions of good will with the late Pakistani President Zia ul Haqq. He observed that, while the primary mission of the Church is a spiritual one, she nonetheless always seeks to promote the dignity of all human beings through schools and other educational, charitable, and social institutions. Then reflecting the spirit of Vatican II, the Holy Father concluded his address with the prayer that mutual understanding between Christians and Muslims grow deeper and that ways of greater cooperation be found "for the good of all."[13]

The attitude of mutual mistrust and hostility which have on the whole characterized relations between the Christian West and the Muslim world had its roots not only in fundamental theological differences, but also in political, economic, and military rivalries. Within less than a century of the Prophet's death, Christendom lost to Muslim domination some of its most central provinces. Asia Minor, Egypt, and North Africa were very early irrevocably lost, and for centuries the Iberian Peninsula and other important parts of Christian Europe were centers of Islamic learning and power.

While, moreover, significant Christian minorities survived in Egypt and other Middle Eastern lands, in North Africa, or the lands of the Arab West (al-Maghrib), the home of Cyprian, Ambrose, and Augustine, Christianity disappeared forever. Yet North Africa's pre-Islamic religious heritage left an indelible mark on its popular Sufi piety. This piety in turn provided the basis of spiritual fellowship with mystically inclined Christians such as the well-known Christian marabout Charles de Foucauld. De Foucauld tried and succeeded in sharing his Christ-like life with Muslims in Algeria, who saw in him a Sufi saint as well as a saintly Christian hermit. He thus broke the religious barriers that had long separated Muslims and Christians without compromising his own religious convictions.[14]

Another equally significant point of contact with the West has been the deep penetration of French education and culture of most North African societies. Therefore, in spite of the disappearance of indigenous Christianity in North Africa, the Church has enjoyed long and spiritually fruitful relations with the region.

In his address to North African bishops on November 23, 1981, the Pope spoke of the need to strengthen the small Catholic communities in that region in order that they may "bear a genuinely Christian witness among those who receive them." He also observed that this witness may be enriched by Muslim culture and piety. The Pope, however, cautioned that empathy for Islamic spirituality should not obscure the primary responsibility of the Christian, which is to "witness to the faith in Christ and to Christian values." He finally counselled that Catholic women married to Muslim men should always be an object of solicitude by the Church. For, he asserted, their presence in Muslim families allows them to witness directly to their faith.[15]

The approach of Pope John Paul II to Muslims centers on two essential concepts, interfaith dialogue and Christian witness. These appear to be in the Holy Father's mind two closely interrelated terms. Thus the purpose of dialogue is to facilitate Christian witness. But the aim of both is ultimately the conversion of Muslims to Christianity.

This goal was enjoined upon the bishops of Mali during their *ad limina* visit to Rome on November 26, 1981. The Holy Father encouraged the bishops to engage in dialogue with Muslims as well as people of other faiths. "But dialogue itself," he asserted, "would lack an important dimension if it did not foresee the possibility of one freely asking for baptism."[16]

Were this goal to be directed at the followers of African and other non-monotheistic traditions, an argument could be made that the aim is to lead them to faith in God. But with Muslims, dialogue ought to be a dialogue of faith among the worshipers of the God of Abraham and all the prophets including Muḥammad. Otherwise dialogue, whatever form it may take, would be simply a cover for some form of postcolonial proselytization. This is particularly the case when dialogue is conducted in the context of Western Church-related medical, social, and educational missions.

The Pope is, according to Catholic tradition, not only the successor of St. Peter as the head of the universal Church, he is also an international political figure. Understandably, therefore, the Pope would have many and at times conflicting agendas, depending on the time, place, and audience that he addresses. This may account, at least in part, for the apparent inconsistencies in his statements.

Speaking to Muslims in Nigeria on February 14, 1982, the Pope called for better understanding and cooperation between Christians and Muslims on the basis of common spiritual and moral values: faith in God and submission to God's holy will, and the commitment to defend human life and dignity. The context of this address was the family and its sanctity as "a precious nucleus of society." On the basis of a common spiritual and moral patrimony, he insisted, we can "in a true sense call one another brothers and sisters in the faith of the one God."[17]

The Holy Father called for safeguarding religious freedom, particularly in the education of children, which is usually taken to mean the freedom to teach the Christian faith. Yet there was no allusion to missionary activities of any kind. Rather, he counselled that religious education be used as a means to "counter the efforts of those who wish to destroy the spiritual aspects of man."[18]

In a highly significant speech addressed to the leaders of the Muslim and Jewish communities in Lisbon on May 14, 1982, the Pope presented a genuinely pluralistic theology of dialogue among the peoples of the Abrahamic traditions. Behind this religious pluralism, he averred, there must exist a unity of faith confirmed by personal conduct. The spiritual life of the faithful of all three communities would, the Pope further argued, help those who are searching for the Transcendent. It may help such sensitive souls to enjoy an inner glimmer of the reality of God in their lives. He continued: "Since, convinced as we are of the good which belief in God constitutes for us, the desire to share this good with others is spontaneous."[19]

The Pope went on to assert that for many people in today's world, God is either unknown or erroneously symbolized by ephemeral human powers. Therefore, interfaith dialogue could foster greater appreciation of the spirituality of every religious tradition. In this way interreligious dialogue could expose the myth of building a new and harmonious world-order without God, one that is solely based on anthropocentric humanism. In doing this, the Pope concluded, we would contribute to the common good of humanity.[20]

This theology of reconciliation and the freedom of faith, spiritual reform, mutual tolerance, and dialogue among peoples of different faith-traditions constituted an essential component of the Pope's message to the world, at least in the early years of his papacy. Concrete expression of this theology of universal faith in the One God was given in the apostolic letter of John Paul II, in celebration of the jubilee year of redemption.[21] One of the themes of this letter is the role of Jerusalem as a symbol of peace and harmony for the followers of the three Abrahamic faiths.

After speaking of the place of the Holy City in the devotional life of the three faith-communities, the Pope declared:

> I think of and long for the day on which we shall be so taught by God, that we shall listen to His message of peace and reconciliation. I think of the day on which Jews, Christians and Muslims will greet each other in the city of Jerusalem with the same greeting of peace with which Christ greeted the disciples after the resurrection, "peace be with you" (John 20:19).

The diversity of expressions of faith and culture in the Holy City should, his holiness counselled, be "an effective aid to concord and peace."[22]

The theology of the unity of faith among all the believers in God, which the Pope so eloquently presented to the leaders of the three monotheistic religions in Lisbon in May 1982, was again expounded at the Vatican three years later. The occasion was a colloquium on the theme of holiness in the two traditions.[23] The Holy Father began his address to that interfaith-international gathering with the Qur'ānic affirmation, "Your God and ours is one and the same, and we are brothers and sisters in the faith of Abraham."[24] He then compared and contrasted the concept of holiness in the three monotheistic traditions and its manifestation as a quality of life in the Christian and Muslim communities. He contrasted the holy life of such virtues as uprightness, righteous living and goodness, which the two religions enjoin, with such "self-centered tendencies as greed, the lust for power and prestige, competition, revenge, lack of forgiveness and the quest for earthly pleasures." These and similar vices, the Pope observed, turn humankind away from the path to goodness, "which God has intended for all of us." He concluded by observing that there are countless men and women—Muslims, Christians, and others around the world—who "quietly live authentic lives of obedience to God and selfless service to others." Such holy lives "offer humanity a genuine alternative—God's way to a world which otherwise would be destroyed in self-seeking hatred and struggle.[25]

To Muslims and Jews, as we saw, the Pope's message of good will and cooperation in promoting peace and social justice is usually based on a common faith and religious kinship. But when he spoke to

Muslim and Hindu representatives in Nairobi, Kenya, on August 18, 1985, he emphasized social action based on general moral and spiritual values common to all the major religions. He thus argued that the communities of these world religions should not remain passive in the face of spiritual and social needs, violations of human rights, wars, and other disasters.

In that gathering the Pope acknowledged religious diversity but also unity in the worship of God. He asserted, "God's will is that those who worship him, even if not united in the same worship, would nevertheless be united in brotherhood and in common service for the good of all." This common quest for spiritual and moral fulfillment, the Pope asserted, should motivate us all to work together in facing the challenge of helping the world to "live in peace and harmony with respect for the human dignity of all."[26]

In a notable address to Moroccan youths delivered on the following day in Casablanca, the Pope added a humanistic dimension to this universal message of good will. Since the Pope referred often to this address in later encounters with Muslims, it must be regarded as an especially significant statement of his position towards Islam and Muslims. The irenic tone of this speech was perhaps determined by its audience. Among other world issues, the Pope addressed the need for more justice in world affairs, the lack of North-South solidarity, and the plight of refugees. The earth, the Pope asserted, is God's gift to all of humankind. All are equally entitled to its resources, and all have the right to live on it in peace and security. Furthermore, since every human being is in a certain sense the image and representative of God, we must love and respect every human being. He added, "Man is the road that leads to God. . . ."[27]

For the purpose of this study, however, it must be noted that in this address the Pope spoke unequivocally of the common religious heritage of Muslims and Christians. He said: "I believe that we Christians and Muslims must recognize with joy the religious values that we have in common and give thanks to God for them."

In keeping with his role as a pastor, the Pope presented to Moroccan youths a long list of common beliefs and practices which bind Muslims and Christians. These include prayers, fasting, and almsgiving, as well as hope in God's mercy both in this world and the next. He concluded: "We hope that after the resurrection God will be satisfied with us, and we know that we will be satisfied with him."[28]

His Holiness repeated many of the same ideas in a homily which he preached in the same city and on the same day. But since he was speaking then to Christians, he repeated his call for witness to Christ to Muslims. Again, he couched this call to witness in the pastoral language of Christian love and charity. In their dialogue with Muslims—which the Pope admitted was not always easy—Christians should be ever conscious of the mystery of salvation, which they must communicate to others with love. As the theme of the homily was love, the Holy Father concluded, "If we have no love, our presence here will do nothing. Our witness will remain empty."[29]

On February 26, 1986, in Vatican City, the Pope received in audience Jewish, Christian, and Muslim participants in a colloquium organized under the auspices of the Jerusalem Hope Center for Interfaith Understanding and Reconciliation. The theme of the colloquium was "One God and three Religions." The Pope appropriately highlighted the two divine attributes of mercy and justice, which both the Bible and the Qur'ān teach. He also expressed the oft-repeated hope of peace and reconciliation among the three faith-communities through the city of peace, Jerusalem, which is a living symbol of God's will for all to live in peace and mutual respect. He continued: "In today's world it is more important than ever that people of faith place at the service of humanity their religious convictions, founded on daily practice of listening to God's message and encountering Him in prayerful worship."[30]

It is noteworthy that when the Holy Father speaks to representatives of the three religions, he places the three faiths on an equal footing as legitimate paths to God. Furthermore, his call for placing religious convictions at the service of humanity gives dialogue its true meaning and purpose. Still another noteworthy point is the absence in such addresses of any missionary motives.

This conciliatory attitude, however, raises an important question. Why does the Holy Father insist on missionary work among Muslims when he talks to Christians, and even to Muslims, but avoids any reference to it when he addresses Jews? One reason, we believe, is that Jewish-Christian dialogue has made far better progress towards achieving a common language among equal participants than has Muslim-Christian dialogue. Another reason is that for most of world Jewry has for centuries shared with the West a common history and culture. Islam, on the other hand, has for long been "the mysterious other" and the Muslim world an arch rival to Western Christendom. Be that as it may, at a time when Christians and Muslims live as neighbors in every Western metropolis, the old ambivalence which remains characteristic of some of the Pope's pronouncements on Islam is hardly conducive to constructive dialogue.

Despite the fact that the Holy Father has enthusiastically participated in interfaith gatherings, he nonetheless appears to be uncomfortable with such undertakings. This may be because interfaith activities mean *de facto* recognition of the equal validity of all religions as paths to the divine or ultimate reality. This admission would of course question the Pope's view of the Church's missionary mandate. The Pope's cautionary attitude may conversely be due to the recognition of the uniqueness and integrity of every religion, which must not be compromised through interfaith activities, particularly those involving interfaith common prayers.

Both the enthusiasm and ambivalence of the Pope towards inter-religious common devotions were clearly evinced in his opening address to the World Day of Prayer for Peace, held in Assisi on October 27, 1986. His Holiness began by observing the great value of so many religious leaders coming together for such a noble cause. This shows, he said, "that there exists another dimension of peace and another way of promoting it, which is not the result of negations, political compromise or economic bargaining."[31] Through religious diversity, the Pope further asserted, prayers for peace express a common spiritual bond and a relationship with the Power that surpasses all our human capabilities.

As for His Holiness's ambivalence, it may be discerned in the following qualifications that he placed on the aims of the meeting under discussion. He argued that the purpose of the gathering was not to seek religious consensus among the participants or negotiate their faith convictions. Nor does it mean, the Pope said, that "religions could be reconciled at the level of common commitment in an earthly project which would surpass them all." Nor should such a gathering be regarded as a concession to relativism in religious beliefs, "because every human being must sincerely follow his or her upright conscience with the intention of seeking and obeying the truth."[32] But is not the ultimate goal of dialogue to achieve a fellowship of faith, a sort of "religious consensus" that would see in the diversity of expressions of this common faith a divine blessing?

III. Dialogue or Evangelization?

It was observed above that Vatican II ushered in a new era of Muslim-Catholic relations. However, the council did not declare acceptance of Islam as a theological belief-system but only an end to hostility towards Muslims and an appreciation of Muslim piety. All that the council did, therefore, was open the door for Muslim-Catholic dialogue in an atmosphere of mutual respect and tolerance. This new approach, however, still calls for the evangelization of Muslims, as the Pope's attitude towards Islam indicates. But the question remains, is this openness true dialogue, or could it be simply condescending tolerance aimed at facilitating evangelization?

Since the beginning of his pontificate, Pope John Paul II has been consciously urging African and Asian bishops to engage in friendly dialogue with Muslims, but at the same time to intensify their efforts in "spreading the Good News."[33] Yet in an address to a Christian-Muslim colloquium on religious education in modern society, he went a long way towards espousing a completely free and open approach in dialogue with Muslims and others on the basis of their common humanity. The Pope first admitted that there are basic differences between the two faiths, but he continued: "Christians and Muslims both hold that the true path towards human fulfillment lies in carrying out the divine will in our personal and social lives."[34] A pre-condition for dialogue is sound religious education, which should inculcate respect for others and openness to them as children of God, regardless of race, religion, economic status, gender, or ethnic identity.[35]

From our limited survey of his pronouncements, it appears that the Holy Father's attitude toward Islam and religious pluralism in general grew more conservative through the years of his papacy. This may perhaps be a reaction to the epochal world-events of the last two decades, as well as the increasing secular and liberal challenges within the Church itself. The Pope's attitude towards religious pluralism is expressed in a growing emphasis on evangelization.

In a papal letter addressed to the fifth plenary assembly of the Federation of Asian Bishops, held in Bandung, Indonesia, in July 1990, His Holiness advocated an ever greater commitment to evangelization for the Asian local churches. The praise which he lavished on these churches for their dynamic "witness to the Gospel" is significant in view of the fact that among the most "dynamic local churches" is the Indonesian church. Thus Muslims around the world believe that Indonesia's large Muslim population is a prime target of this evangelization. Whether true or not, this belief helps perpetuate old Muslim suspicions of Christian motives.

The Pope grounded his strong call to evangelization in the document of Vatican II, *Nostra aetate*, which declares:

> Although the Church gladly acknowledges whatever is true and holy in the religious traditions of Buddhism, Hinduism and Islam as a reflection of the truth which enlightens all men, this does not lessen her duty and resolve to proclaim without fail Jesus Christ who is "the way, the truth and the life" (John 14:6).[36]

Moreover, he acknowledged the validity of the theological idea—based on the classical notion of the seminal divine word *(logos spermatikos)*—that the righteous followers of other religions may be saved by Christ without the ordinary means which God had established for salvation. Yet he still insisted that this "does not cancel the call to faith and baptism which God wills for all people."[37]

Carrying the logic of this argument to its ultimate conclusion, His Holiness repudiated the principle of religious pluralism which is crucial to any meaningful dialogue. He argued that the idea that the Church is only one of many ways to salvation is contrary to the Gospel and to the Church's very nature. He rejected as well the principle of sharing one's faith with another person in the hope of deepening the other's faith within his or her own religious tradition.[38]

Pope John Paul II's position towards other religions is clearly and emphatically argued in an encyclical which he issued shortly after the Gulf War.[39] Although this important document says nothing about Islam in particular, the Pope may have had Muslims, and particularly the Arabs, in mind when he called on people in the latter category everywhere to "open the doors to Christ."[40] In traditional fashion, the Pope divides humanity into two camps, Christians and those who do not know Christ. Since the number of such people in the latter category has doubled since Vatican II, he urged the entire Christian Church to become a missionary Church.

The thrust of the main argument of this encyclical is stated in the opening declaration of the first chapter: "Jesus Christ the only savior." The Pope elaborated this point thus: ". . . God has established Christ as the one mediator. . . ." God also established the Church as the "universal sacrament of salvation." He then concluded, "To this catholic unity of the people of God, therefore, all are called."[41]

To the important question "why mission?" the Pope replied that the Church's faith is that true liberation can be attained only through Christ. Only in Christ can humanity be saved from slavery to sin and death. While no one can question the centrality of this doctrine to the Church's faith, it is not one that Islam and Judaism accept, either as part of their own faith or as a common basis for dialogue with Christians. Nor can it serve in today's pluralistic world as a basis for dialogue with any other faith-community. This is because this doctrine leaves no room for a genuine fellowship of faith, which must be the ultimate goal of interreligious dialogue.

On the eve of the twenty-first century, after the development and dissemination of the scientific study of religion and the steady advance of global communication, meaningful dialogue is only possible on the basis of religious and cultural pluralism. This means that Christians and Muslims must accept the fact that God did not only speak Hebrew, Greek, or Arabic, but rather he speaks to every people in their own tongue and to their own cultural and spiritual situation. Furthermore, the universality of divine revelation is attested in both the New Testament and the Qur'ān.[42]

While the Pope admits that God mysteriously guides all nations to know him, he insists that true knowledge of God can only be attained through Christ and the Church "which is the instrument of salvation." He further asserts, ". . . the Holy Spirit offers everyone the possibility of sharing in the Paschal mystery in a manner known to God."[43] But this only means the possibility for everyone to be a Christian, and that should be the Church's universal mission. On this principle of the inner *preparatio evangelica* of every human being, the papal encyclical calls for "mission to the Nations." The objective of this mission is to found Christian communities everywhere and to develop mature and fully functioning churches in areas where Christianity has not taken roots.[44]

On the basis of this encyclical and other papal statements of the 1990s, it may be concluded that Pope John Paul II is clearly committed to the old doctrine, *"extra Ecclesiam nulla salus."* But inasmuch as he advocates interreligious dialogue, he may be considered a neo-exclusivist. He is more aware of the diversity and richness of religious traditions than the ancient Church Fathers who first advocated this ex-clusivist doctrine. But like them, he cannot accept genuine religious pluralism, because it compromises the Church's mission to the na-tions. He therefore views dialogue as simply an instrument of mission. "Interreligious dialogue," the Pope wrote, "is a part of the Church's evangelizing mission." Dialogue, he further argued, should be based on the conviction that the Church "alone possesses the fullness of the means of salvation."[45]

IV. Conclusion

The theme of the universality of divine guidance to all human beings to the knowledge of God is taken up by His Holiness at some length in his book *Crossing the Threshold of Hope.*[46] Here, however, he does not take seriously such phenomena as animism and ancestor worship as legitimate religious practices, but wishes to use them as openings for introducing the Christian faith to the followers of these traditions. In the veneration of ancestors the Pope sees some sort of preparation for the Christian concept of the Church as the communion of saints, "in which all believers, whether living or dead, form a single community, a single body."[47] Therefore, missionaries, the Pope observes, find it easier to speak a common language with these people than with the followers of the higher religions.

The Pope's position toward Islam in this book is especially sig-nificant, because here he speaks not as the Pope but as a private person. We must therefore conclude that what he says about Islam in this book represents his own convictions. He calls Muslims "believers in Allāh,"[48] forgetting that Allah is only the Arabic name for God which was used by Arab Jews and Christians long before Islam. Anyone who knows the Old and New Testaments, the Pope avers, can clearly see how the Qur'ān "completely reduces divine revelation." The Qur'ān therefore moves away from what God said about himself in the two Testaments, "first through the prophets and finally . . . through his son." He concludes: "In Islam all the richness of God's revelation which continues the heritage of the Old and New Testaments has definitely been set aside."[49]

We noted earlier the Pope's Qur'anic affirmation in his address to the colloquium on holiness, "Your God and ours is the same, and we are brothers and sisters in the faith of Abraham."[50] In this book he says: "Although beautiful names are given to the god of the Qur'ān, he remains a god outside the world, a god who is only majesty, never Immanuel, 'God with us.'"[51] Thus we see that the "all-merciful God" of whom His Holiness so often reminded Muslims as the God of us all is absent in his book. The major fault of Islam for His Holiness is ultimately that Islam is not Catholic Christianity.

It was argued above that the ultimate goal of true dialogue is a fellowship of faith. This existential fellowship will not be achieved between institutions, or perhaps even their official representatives. It remains the quest of sincere seekers after the truth, pious men and women of whom Christ said, "You shall know the truth and the truth shall set you free" (John 8:32).

NOTES

1. Alfred Guillaume, *Life of Muhammad: A Translation of Ibn Ishāq's Sīrat Rasūl Allah* (Oxford: Oxford University Press, 1955) 79–82.

2. Waraqah was the cousin of Muḥammad's wife Khadījah and may have been a priest. See ibid., 107.

3. According to Islamic hagiographical tradition, the Nagus *(najāshī)* of Abyssinia not only received the Muslims hospitably, but he is reported to have agreed with the Qur'anic view of Jesus and finally died a Muslim. The personality of al-Najāshī represents an interesting example of Muslim-Christian encounter. See ibid., 146–55; see also Montgomery Watt, *Muhammad at Mecca* (Oxford: Clarendon Press, 1953) 109–17.

4. This ecumenical assertion occurs nearly verbatim near the beginning and end of the Prophet's Madinan career, 2:62 and 5:69.

5. See for example Q. 4:171, 5:17, 72-73 and 77.

6. Quoted by His Holiness Pope John Paul II in his *'īd al-fiṭr* (end of the fasting month of Ramaḍān) April 3, 1991. For the correspondence between the *sulṭān* and Pope Gregory VII, see Rev. Thomas Mishel, S.J., and Mons. Michael Fitzgerald, M. Afr., *Recognize the Spiritual Bonds Which Unite Us. 16 Years of Muslim-Christian Dialogue* (Vatican City: Pontifical Institute for Interreligious Dialogue, 1994) 3–4.

7. Edward Peters, ed., *The First Crusade: The Chronicle of Fulcher and Chartres and Other Source Materials* (Philadelphia: University of Pennsylvania Press, 1971) 2; see also 2–5.

8. Between 1978, when he took office, and 1994, Pope John Paul II made 60 trips to 109 countries. See Michel and Fitzgerald, *Spiritual Bonds,* 14.

9. *Origins* 9:26 (December 13, 1979) 420.

10. The Qur'ān states: "God will not forgive that associates be ascribed to Him, but other than this, he forgives whomsoever he will" 4:48.

11. *Origins* 10:2 (May 29, 1980) 20.

12. See Luke 10:25-37 and Matt 28:19.

13. *Origins* 10:37 (February 26, 1981) 592.

14. For a Muslim appreciation of the life and work of this remarkable man, see Zoe Hersov, "A Muslim's View of Charles de Foucauld. Some Lessons for the Christian-Muslim Dialogue," *Muslim World* 85, 3–4 (July–October 1995) 295–316.

15. *Bulletin Secretariatus pro non Christianis* 48 (1981) 182–3.

16. Ibid., 187.

17. *Origins* 11:37 (February 25, 1982) 588.

18. Ibid., 588.

19. *Bulletin* 55 (1984) 25–6.

20. Ibid., 26.

21. *Redemptionis Anno, Origins* 14:20 (May 24, 1980) 31–2.

22. Ibid., 32.

23. I had the honor of being one of the participants in that colloquium, which included visits to Assisi and other holy sites in Italy. It was a memorable experience.

24. The Pope here paraphrased part of Q. 29:46 and alluded to Q. 3:64, which invites all the people of the Book to unity of faith in the One God.

25. For the Pope's address and all the proceedings of that colloquium, see *Islamo-Christiana* 11 (1985) 201–8.

26. Cf. *Bulletin* 60 (1985) 233–7. A few days earlier, on August 12, the Pope delivered the same message to the multi-religious society of Cameroon. See Michel and Fitzgerald, *Spiritual Bonds,* 42, 44.

27. Michel and Fitzgerald, *Spiritual Bonds,* Ibid., 65.

28. Ibid., 65.

29. Ibid., 66.

30. *Bulletin* 62 (1986) 147.

31. *Bulletin* 64 (1987) 29.

32. Ibid., 30.

33. This was his message to the bishops of Mali in March 1988, the bicentenary year of mission. See *Bulletin* 70 (1988) 14–5.

34. The colloquium was organized in Rome jointly by the Pontifical Council for Interreligious Dialogue and the Royal Jordanian Ahl al-Bayt Foundation, December 6–8, 1989. *Bulletin* 73 (1990) 14.

35. Ibid., 14–5.

36. Quoted by the Pope in *Bulletin* 75 (1990) 229.

37. Ibid., 230.

38. Ibid., 231.

39. Papal Encyclical #8, *Redemptoris Missio,* January 1991 (hereafter, RM).

40. RM 3.

41. RM 4 .

42. Cf. Acts 14:17; Heb 1:1; and Q. 35:27.

43. RM 21.

44. RM 48.

45. RM 55.

46. John Paul II, *Crossing the Threshold of Hope,* Vitorio Missori (New York: Alfred A. Knopf, 1994) 77ff.

47. Ibid., 82.

48. Ibid., 91.

49. Ibid., 92.

50. See n. 24 above.

51. John Paul II, *Threshold,* 92.

TWELVE

The Writings of Gerard S. Sloyan: 1950–1995

Compiled by Regina A. Boisclair

The writings of Gerard S. Sloyan are listed under one of the following subject headings: Biblical Studies, Catholic Thought and Practice, Christianity and Judaism, Jesus Christ, Lectionaries and Homiletics, Liturgy, Morality, Religious Education and Spirituality, and Miscellaneous Other Topics. However, researchers should be aware that some titles pertain to more than one of these subjects. Under each subject, his books and pamphlets are listed before his essays, homilies, or articles and appear in the chronological sequence of publication. Book reviews by Sloyan are provided in a separate chronological list.[1]

Biblical Studies

Books and Pamphlets

The Gospel of St. Mark. Introduction and Commentary. Collegeville: The Liturgical Press, 1960 (also in Spanish and Malayalam).
The Books of Ruth and Tobit. Collegeville: The Liturgical Press, 1968.

1. This partial bibliography is based on listings in the *National Union Catalog,* the Online Computer Library Catalog (OCLC), the ATLA *Index* on CD ROM and the *Catholic Periodical and Literature Index* available in December 1995. Additional data was provided by the catalogs of the Jesuit-Krauss-McCormick Library in Chicago and Illinois Library Network (LLINET). I thank Dr. Stephen W. Holloway of ATLA for attempting to update the information of the CD ROM that is at present available in libraries. A few entries that are not in the resources listed above were either known to the compiler or graciously supplied by Gerard S. Sloyan.

New American Bible. Washington, D.C.: National Center for Religious Education, 1971 (English editor, New Testament).

Jesus on Trial: The Development of the Passion Narratives and Their Historical and Ecumenical Implications. Philadelphia: Fortress, 1973.

Commentary on the New Lectionary. New York: Paulist, 1975.

Is Christ the End of the Law? Philadelphia: Westminster, 1978.

John. A Biblical Commentary for Teaching and Preaching. Atlanta: John Knox, 1988 (also in Japanese).

What Are They Saying About John? New York: Paulist, 1991.

So You Mean to Read the Bible! Some Tips for Absolute Beginners. Collegeville: The Liturgical Press, 1992.

Walking in the Truth. Perseverers and Deserters: The First, Second and Third Letters of John. Valley Forge, Pa.: Trinity Press International, 1995.

Essays and Articles

"Read the Bible and . . . ," *Worship* 26 (February 1952) 144–51.

"Reading the Bible: Some Suggestions," *Worship* 26 (May 1952) 310–5.

"From Christ in the Gospel to Christ in the Church," *Catholic College Teachers of Sacred Doctrine. Proceedings* 1 (Villanova, Pa.: Catholic College Teachers of Sacred Doctrine, 1955) 10–24.

"The Gospel According to St. Matthew. The Semitic Character of the Gospel," *Worship* 32 (June 1958) 342–51.

"The Gospel According to St. Mark," *Worship* 32 (October 1958) 547–57.

"The Gospel According to St. Luke," *Worship* 33 (November 1959) 633–41.

"'Primitive' and Pauline Concepts of the Eucharist," *Catholic Biblical Quarterly* 23 (June 1961) 1–13.

"The Holy Eucharist as an Eschatological Meal," *Worship* 36 (July 1962) 444–51.

"The New American Bible," *Living Light* 7 (Fall 1970) 87–104.

"Last Days of Jesus," *Judaism* 20 (Winter 1971) 56–68.

"Recent Literature on the Trial Narratives of the Four Gospels," in Thomas J. Ryan, ed., *Critical History and Biblical Faith.* Proceedings of the College Theology Society, 1977 (Villanova, Pa.: College Theology Society, 1977) 136–76.

"Letter of James," in Reginald Fuller, et al., *Hebrews, James, 1 and 2 Peter* (Philadelphia: Fortress, 1977) 28–49.

"Biblio File," *Liturgy* 24 (May–June 1979) 9–10.

"Biblio File," *Liturgy* 24 (July–August 1979) 7–8.

"Biblio File," *Liturgy* 24 (September–October 1979) 39–40.

"Biblio File," *Liturgy* 24 (November–December 1979) 44.

"Biblio File," *Liturgy* 25 (January–February 1980) 45.

"Biblio File," *Liturgy* 25 (March–April 1980) 41.

"The Bible and Christian Prayer," *Liturgy* 1 (1980) 3–8.

"Come Lord Jesus: The View of the Post-Resurrection Community," in Francis A. Eigo, ed., *Who Do People Say I Am?* (Villanova, Pa.: Villanova University Press, 1980) 91–122.

"Response to Samuel Terrien's *The Elusive Presence*," in Lawrence Frizzell, ed., *God and His Temple. Reflections on Professor Samuel Terrien's* The Elusive Presence: Toward a New Biblical Theology (South Orange, N.J.: Institute of Judaeo-Christian Studies, Seton Hall University, 1980) 66–71.

"Discipleship of Christ in the Book of Revelation," *New Catholic World* 225 (January–February 1982) 38–40.

"The Samaritans in the New Testament," *Horizons* 10 (Spring 1983) 7–21.

"Jewish Ritual of the First Century C.E. and Christian Sacramental Behavior," *Biblical Theology Bulletin* 15 (July 1985) 98–103.

"Outreach to Gentiles and Jews: New Testament Reflections," *Journal of Ecumenical Studies* 22 (Fall 1985) 764–9.

"The Bible as the Book of the Church," *Worship* 60 (January 1986) 9–21.

"Biblical Theology," in Joseph A. Komonchak, Mary Collins, Dermot A. Lane, eds., *The New Dictionary of Theology* (Wilmington, Del.: Glazier, 1987) 118–29.

"Colossians" and "Ephesians," in Bernhard W. Anderson, ed., *The Books of the Bible*, II (New York: Scribner's Sons, 1989) 282–92, 301–10.

"What Is John 17 Saying to the Churches?" *Liturgy* 10 (Spring 1992) 53–5.

"Not Even Solomon in All His Splendor. The New Testament and Creation," *Pastoral Musician* 18 (December 1993–January 1994) 25–6, 33–5.

"The Role of the Bible in Catechesis according to the Catechism," in Berard L. Marthaler, *Introducing* Catechism of the Catholic Church (New York: Paulist, 1994) 32–42.

"Demons and Exorcisms," *Bible Today* 32 (January 1994) 21–6.

"The Use of the Bible in A New Resource Book," *Biblical Theology Bulletin* 25 (Spring 1995) 3–13.

"Preaching," "Teach/Teaching," in Carroll Stuhlmueller, ed., *The Collegeville Pastoral Dictionary of Biblical Theology* (Collegeville: The Liturgical Press, 1966) 765–9, 974–7.

Catholic Thought and Practice

Books and Pamphlets

The Sacrament Idea. Washington D.C.: National Council of Catholic Men, 1954 (Catholic Hour radio addresses, NBC).

Essays and Articles

"The Problem of Prohibited Books and the American Catholic Intellectual," *Society of Catholic College Teachers of Sacred Doctrine Proceedings* 6 (Villanova, Pa.: Catholic College Teachers of Sacred Doctrine, 1960) 83–9.

"Marian Prayers," in Juniper B. Carol, ed., *Mariology* vol. 3 (Milwaukee: Bruce, 1961) 64–87.

"Faith and Modern Subjective Thought," *Catholic Theological Society of America Proceedings* 18 (1963) 77–87.

"Changes Coming in Penance," *Catholic Layman* 80 (March 1966) 46–9.
"Spirituality for the Secular Priesthood," in Gerard S. Sloyan, ed., *The Secular Priest in the New Church* (New York: Herder & Herder, 1967) 55–76.
"The Age of First Confession," *Catholic Theological Society of America Proceedings* 22 (1967) 201–13.
"What About the Dutch Catechism?" *U.S. Catholic* 33 (December 1967) 6–10.
"Orthodoxy and Heterodoxy: The Situation in the Church Today," *Catholic Theological Society of America Proceedings* 25 (1970) 137–54.
"Biblical and Patristic Motives for Celibacy of Church Ministers," in William Bassett and Peter Huizing, eds., *Celibacy in the Church, Concilium,* vol. 78 (New York: Herder and Herder, 1972) 13–29.
"Postbiblical Development of the Petrine Ministry," in James W. Flanagan, ed., *No Famine in the Land. Studies in Honor of John L. McKenzie* (Missoula, Mont.: Scholars Press, for the Institute for Antiquity and Christianity, 1975) 223–33.
"Roman Catholic Eucharistic Reforms. A Basis for Dialogue?" *Journal of Ecumenical Studies* 13 (Spring 1976) 286–91, and in Leonard Swidler, ed., *Eucharist in Ecumenical Dialogue* (New York: Paulist, 1976) 96–101.
"The Resurrection of the Body and Life Everlasting—Personal Fulfillment," *Furrow* 37 (December 1986) 747–55.
"The Catholic-Protestant Conflict in Northern Ireland," in Charles Fu and Gerhard Spiegler, eds., *Movements and Issues in World Religions. A Sourcebook and Analysis of Developments Since 1945* (Westport, Conn.: Greenwood, 1987) 39–55.
"A Theological and Pastoral Critique of *Catechism of the Catholic Church,*" *Horizons* 21 (Spring 1994) 159–71.
"Do Catholics Understand the Sacraments?" *Church* 11 (Autumn 1995) 12–17.

Christianity and Judaism

Books

[with Leonard Swidler]. *A Commentary on the Oberammergau* Passionsspiel *in Regard to Its Image of Jews and Judaism.* New York: Anti-Defamation League of B'nai B'rith, 1978.
[with Leonard Swidler]. *The Passion of the Jews. Recommended Changes in the Oberammergau Passion Play after 1984.* New York: Anti-Defamation League of B'nai B'rith, 1984.

Essays and Articles

"Buber and the Significance of Jesus," *The Bridge: Yearbook of Judaeo-Christian Studies* 3 (1958) 209–33.
"A Theology of Election: Review of Joachim Jócz's Book," *The Bridge: Yearbook of Judaeo-Christian Studies* 4 (1962) 361–70.

"The Meaning of Israel as Idea and Reality" in Philip J. Scharper, ed., *Torah and Gospel. Jewish and Catholic Theology in Dialogue* (New York: Sheed & Ward, 1966) 215–28.
"The Last Days of Jesus," *Judaism* (1971) 56–68.
"Jesus in Jewish-Christian-Muslim Dialogue," *Journal of Ecumenical Studies* 14 (Summer 1977) 448–65.
"Who Are the People of God?" in Asher Finkel and Lawrence Frizzell, eds., *Standing Before God. Studies on Prayer in Scripture and in Tradition. Essays in Honor of John M. Oesterreicher* (New York: Ktav, 1981) 103–14.
"Faith and Law: An Essay Toward Jewish-Christian Dialogue," *Journal of Ecumenical Studies* 18 (Winter 1981) 93–103.
"Some Theological Implications of the Holocaust," *Interpretation* 39 (October 1985) 402–13.
"Christianity's View of the Religious 'Other,'" *Drew Gateway* 58 (Spring 1989) 47–51.
[with Lester Dean, Lewis Eron, Leonard Swidler]. "A Jewish-Christian Dialogue about Paul," *Bursting the Bonds? A Jewish-Christian Dialogue on Jesus and Paul* (Maryknoll, N.Y.: Orbis, 1990) 125–216.
"Christian-Jewish Dialogue: An Annotated Book List," *Living Light* 30 (Autumn 1993) 93–9.

Jesus Christ

Books

Christ the Lord. New York: Herder & Herder, 1962; Doubleday Echo, 1965.
Jesus in Focus: A Life in Its Setting. Mystic, Conn.: Twenty-Third Publications, 1983; rev. ed., 1994.
The Jesus Tradition. Images of Jesus in the West. Mystic, Conn.: Twenty-Third Publications, 1986.
Jesus: Redeemer and Divine Word. Wilmington, Del.: Glazier, 1989.
The Crucifixion of Jesus: History, Myth, Faith. Minneapolis: Fortress, 1995.

Essays and Articles

"The Mystery of Christ," *North American Liturgical Week Proceedings* 24 (1963) 16–21.
"What Has Christianity to Do with Jesus?" *Monastic Studies* 8 (Spring 1972) 45–66.
"Some Problems in Modern Christology," in George Devine, ed., *A World More Human, a Church More Christian.* 1972 Proceedings of the College Theology Society (Villanova, Pa.: College Theology Society, 1972) 27–51.
"An Annotated Bibliography of Selected Titles in Christology," *Living Light* 10 (Winter 1973) 566–71.
"Jesus of Nazareth: Today's Way to God," *Journal of Ecumenical Studies* 17 (Winter 1980) 49–56.
"Jesus in Focus," *Today's Parish* 15 (October 1983) 8–10.

"Jesus and History," in Randolph Crump Miller, ed., *Empirical Theology: A Handbook* (Birmingham, Ala.: Religious Education Press, 1992) 142–54.
"The Jesus in Whom the Churches of the Apostolic Age Believed," Presidential Address, *The Catholic Theological Society of America Proceedings* 48 (1994) 65–79.

Lectionaries and Homiletics

Books

To Hear the Word of God. Homilies at Mass. New York: Herder & Herder, 1965.
Nothing of Yesterday Preaches. Homilies for Contemporaries. New York: Herder & Herder, 1966.
[with Howard Clark Kee]. *Pentecost 3.* Philadelphia: Fortress, 1974.
Rejoice and Take It Away: Sunday Preaching from the Scriptures. 2 vols. Wilmington, Del.: Michael Glazier, 1984.
Worshipful Preaching. Philadelphia: Fortress, 1984.
Advent, Christmas. Philadelphia: Fortress, 1985.
Holy Week. Philadelphia: Fortress, 1988.
Pentecost 1: Interpreting the Lessons of the Church Year. Minneapolis: Fortress, 1994.

Homilies, Essays, and Articles

"Preaching at Mass," *North American Liturgical Week Proceedings* 24 (1963) 191–4
"English Literature on the Homily," in P. Benoit, R. E. Murphy, and B. van Iersel, eds., *The Dynamism of Biblical Tradition, Concilium,* vol. 20 (New York: Paulist, 1967) 124–30.
"The Jews and the New Roman Lectionary," *Face to Face* 2 (1976) 5–8.
"The Lectionary as a Context for Interpretation," *Interpretation* 31 (April 1977) 131–8.
"An Instructional Cycle to Prop Up the Lectionary?" *Living Light* 17 (Summer 1980) 182–6.
"The Lectionary as a Context for Interpretation," *Liturgy* 2 (1982) 43–9.
"Preparation for Preaching," *Christian Ministry* 15 (July 1984) 5–7.
"A Light of Revelation to the Gentiles [Homily for Epiphany]," in John T. Pawlikowski and James A. Wilde, eds., *When Catholics Speak About Jews* (Chicago: Liturgy Training Publications, 1987) 35–7.
"Is Church Teaching Neglected When the Lectionary Is Preached?" *Worship* 61 (March 1987) 126–40.
"Forming Catechumens Through the Lectionary," in James Wilde, ed., *Before and After Baptism: The Word of Teachers and Catechists* (Chicago: Liturgy Training Publications, 1988) 27–37.
"Some Suggestions for a Biblical Three-Year Lectionary," *Worship* 63 (November 1989) 521–35.

"The Lectionary. Richer Fare for God's People," *Liturgy 90* 21 (July 1990) 8–10.
"The Lectionary. A Treasure-House of Images," *Liturgy 90* 21 (August–September 1990) 7–9, 15.
"The Lectionary. The Hebrew Scriptures Apart from Their Fulfillment in Christ," *Liturgy 90* 21 (October 1990) 9–11.
"The Lectionary. The Four Gospels: Four Interpretations of Jesus," *Liturgy 90* 21 (November–December 1990) 9–11.
"The Lectionary. The Independent Second Readings and the Psalter," *Liturgy 90* 22 (January 1991) 8–10, 13.
"Studying the Lectionary," *Liturgy 90* (May–June 1991) 8–11.
"Book Roundup: Preaching Matthew," *Church* 8 (Winter 1992) 51–4.
"Homily, Brooklyn, New York. [Liturgy of Christian Burial of R. W. Hovda]," *Worship* 66 (May 1992) 267–70.
"The Scriptures of the Season: Eastertime," *Liturgy* 11 (1993) 43–53.
"The Homily and Catechesis. The Catechism and/or the Lectionary?" in Berard L. Marthaler, ed., *Introducing* Catechism of the Catholic Church (New York: Paulist, 1994) 133–41.
"Liturgical Preaching," in William H. Willimon and Richard Lischer, eds. *Concise Encyclopedia of Preaching* (Louisville: Westminster/John Knox, 1995) 311–3.
"A People Delights in the Triune NAME: Preaching the Readings," *Liturgy* 13 (1996) 4–9.

Liturgy

Books and Pamphlets

Commentary on The Constitution of the Sacred Liturgy of the Second Vatican Council and the Motu Proprio of Pope Paul VI. Glen Rock, N.J.: Paulist, 1964.
Liturgy in Focus. Glen Rock, N.J.: Paulist, 1964.
Worship in a New Key: What the Council Teaches on the Liturgy. Washington, D.C.: Liturgical Conference, 1965; New York: Doubleday Echo, 1968.

Essays and Articles

"Mary in the Temporal Cycle—Easter Season," *National Liturgical Week Proceedings* 15 (1954) 115–35.
"Liturgical Week," *Worship* 31 (October 1957) 544–9.
"Liturgy in the Colleges," *North American Liturgical Week Proceedings* 18 (1957) 141–6.
"Pastoral Formation as an Aim of the Seminary Liturgy Course," *Yearbook of Liturgical Studies,* vol. 1 (Notre Dame, Ind.: Fides, 1960) 3–14.
"Liturgical Proclamation of the Word of God," *North American Liturgical Week Proceedings* 22 (1961) 7–15.
"The Liturgy and the Word of God," *Worship* 35 (January 1961) 105–7.
"Liturgy and Catechetics," in Frederick R. McManus, ed., *The Revival of the*

Liturgy: Gift to Father Godfrey Diekmann on His Jubilee as Editor of Worship (New York: Herder and Herder, 1963) 42–61.

"The Liturgy and the Average Priest," *Homiletic and Pastoral Review* 64 (Summer 1964) 105–17.

"Progress Report on the Liturgy," *America* 111 (August 22, 1964) 179–83.

"The Constitution on the Sacred Liturgy and Prayer Life in the College." Society of Catholic College Teachers of Sacred Doctrine. *Proceedings of the 10th Annual Convention* (1964) 107.

"Debate on the Eucharist, The Real Presences" *Commonweal* 84 (June 17, 1966) 357–61.

"Is There Any Hope for Liturgy?" *Commonweal* 93 (March 27, 1970) 56–60.

"The New Rite for Celebrating Marriage," *Worship* 44 (May 1970) 258–67.

"Visions of Unity in Bible and Liturgy," *Liturgy* 23 (November 1978) 9–14.

"We're Not Ready For It," *Pastoral Music* 4 (March 1980) 64–5.

"The Bible on Sacred Space," *Liturgy* 2 (1983) 21–7.

"Liturgical Basis for Social Policy: A Catholic Viewpoint," in Daniel F. Polish and Eugene J. Fisher, eds., *Liturgical Foundations of Social Policy in the Catholic and Jewish Traditions* (Notre Dame, Ind.: University of Notre Dame Press, 1983) 169–79.

"Word and Sacrament in the Life of the Spirit," *Liturgy* 5 (1986) 59–69.

"Response to the Berakah Award," *Worship* 60 (July 1986) 305–11.

"The Paschal Triduum: An Enduring Drama," *Pastoral Musician* (August–September 1989) 15–8.

"A Response to the Study [of post-Vatican II liturgy in 15 U.S. parishes] from the Standpoint of Christology," in Lawrence J. Madden, ed., *The Awakening Church: 25 Years of Liturgical Renewal* (Collegeville: The Liturgical Press, 1992) 46–54.

"Easter's Fifty Days," *Liturgy* 11 (1993) 64–5.

"The Fiftieth Day," *Liturgy* 11 (1993) 66.

"Thirty Years after the Constitution on the Sacred Liturgy," *Liturgical Ministry* 3 (Summer 1994) 111.

"Presence and Absence in the Eucharist," *Worship* 69 (May 1995) 263–9.

Morality

Books and Pamphlets

How Do I Know I'm Doing Right? Toward the Formation of a Christian Conscience. New York: Pflaum, 1967; rev. ed., 1976.

Catholic Morality Revisited. Origins and Contemporary Challenges. Mystic, Conn.: Twenty-Third Publications, 1990.

Essays and Articles

"Springs of Morality in Current Catholic Ethics," *Worship* 31 (March 1957) 188–9.

"Blessed Are Certain of the Peacemakers," *Spiritual Life* 13 (Winter 1967) 231–43 and in Thomas Quigley, ed., *American Catholics and Vietnam* (Grand Rapids: Eerdmans, 1968) 27–38.

"Doing Right Revisited," *Religion Teacher's Journal* 9 (November—December 1975) 37–9.

"Moral Education and Development: Forming a Right Conscience," *Today's Catholic Teacher* 11 (May 1978) 24–5.

"Conscience," in Richard A. Boulet, ed., *Moral Education and Development* (Dayton: Pflaum, 1979).

Religious Education and Spirituality

Books

Christian Concepts in Social Studies in Catholic Elementary Education. Washington, D.C.: The Catholic University of America, 1948, 1950.

Speaking of Religious Education. New York: Herder & Herder, 1968.

Essays and Articles

"On Educating Leaders," *Catholic Educational Review* 49 (November 1951) 577–85.

"That I May Never Be Thirsty," *Catholic Educational Review* 50 (April 1952) 223–34.

"School: Religion's Too Secret Weapon," *Columbia* (September 1952) 4–5.

"Catholic High School: Idea and Reality," *Catholic Educational Review* 51 (April 1953) 217–33.

"Curriculum in Transition," *National Catholic Educational Association Bulletin* 50 (August 1953) 341–7.

"They're All Ours and It's No Picnic," *Columbia* 33 (October 1953) 11–21ff.

"Working with Men of Good Will: 50th Anniversary Convention of the R.E.A., *National Catholic Educational Association Bulletin* 50 (February 1954) 7–17.

"Chalk Dust on a Black Suit. William H. Russell," *Columbia* 33 (June 1954) 15ff.

"Some Factors in the Teaching of Sacred Doctrine," *Catholic Educational Review* 53 (January 1955) 1–17.

"Shaping the Christian Message," *Commonweal* 64 (June 27, 1956) 413–7.

"Religious Education Today (Antwerp Congress)," *Catholic Educational Review* 54 (December 1956) 577–88.

"Catechism and the Word," *Commonweal* 65 (March 8, 1957) 586–9.

"Eucharist and the Aims of Christian Education," *Worship* 31 (May 1957) 312–9.

"Experience of Mystery. Requisite for Theology," *Catholic Educational Review* 55 (May 1957) 289–99.

"Shaping the Christian Message," in Gerard S. Sloyan, ed., *Shaping the Christian Message. Essays in Religious Education* (New York: Macmillan, 1958) 11–45.

"Catholic Catechism," *Worship* 32 (April 1958) 305–8.
"Some Problems of Religious Formation in Our Day," *Catholic Educational Review* 57 (April 1959) 217–26.
"Religion in the State University," *Commonweal* 71 (October 2, 1959) 7–10.
"Roman Catholic Religious Education," in Marvin J. Taylor, ed., *Religious Education* (New York: Abingdon, 1960) 396–409.
"Undergraduate Studies in Sacred Doctrine at One U.S. University," *Lumen Vitae* 15 (1960) 712–22.
"The International Study Week on Mission Catechetics (Eichstaett, Germany)," *Worship* 35 (December 1960) 48–57.
"Amerika, Die Vereinigte Staaten von," in Leopold Lentner, ed., *Katechetisches Lexikon* (Freiburg: Herder, 1961) cols. 11–26.
"Fifty Years of Telling the Good News," *Worship* 35 (March 1961) 210–3.
"Catechetical Progress," *Worship* 35 (November 1961) 661–9.
"The Good News and the Catechetical Scene in the United States," in Josef A. Jungmann, *The Good News Yesterday and Today,* ed. and trans. William A. Huesman (New York: Sadlier, 1962) 211–28.
"Bibliography of Landmarks in the History of Catechizing," *Worship* 36 (May 1962) 371–3.
"Catechetical Roundup," *Worship* 36 (May 1962) 366–71.
"Use of Sacred Scripture in Catechetics," *Religious Education* 57 (October 1962) 329–34.
"Roman Catholic Education in the U.S.A.," in Kendig Brubaker Cully, ed., *Westminster Dictionary of Religious Education* (Philadelphia: Westminster, 1963) 576–81.
"Catechetical Renewal (A Midstream Evaluation)," *Worship* 37 (January 1963) 96–102.
"Religious Education," *Commonweal* 77 (January 25, 1963) 459–60.
"Catechetics Today," *Perspectives* 8 (October 1963) 132–7.
"God's Secret Design Summed Up in Christ. The Heart of Catechizing," *Bible Today* 7 (October 1963) 412–7.
"Relation of the Catechism to the Work of Religious Formation," in Gerard S. Sloyan, ed., *Modern Catechetics: Message and Method in Religious Formations* (New York: Macmillan, 1963) 63–101.
"Seminary Training and Religious Education," in Gerard S. Sloyan, ed., *Modern Catechetics: Message and Method in Religious Formations* (New York: Macmillan, 1963) 291–303.
"Religious Education Analyzed," *North American Liturgical Week Proceedings* 27 (1966) 49–56.
"The Parish as Educator," *Commonweal* 84 (March 25, 1966) 20–3.
"Books on Religious Education 1955–65," *Worship* 40 (April 1966) 209–17.
"Religious Education as a Correlate of 'Religious Knowledge': Some Problem Areas," *Religious Education* 61 (July–August 1966) 286–91, 298.
"The Parish as Educator," in James O'Gara, ed., *The Postconciliar Parish* (New York: Kenedy, 1967) 127–36.
"On Christian Education," *North American Liturgical Week Proceedings* 28 (1967) 23–30.

"Catechetics" and "Catechisms," *New Catholic Encyclopedia,* vol. 3 (New York: McGraw-Hill, 1967) 220–5, 225–31.

"A Statement on Teaching Religion," *America* 116 (January 7, 1967) 16–20.

"Religious Studies in Roman Catholic Colleges and Universities," *Theological Education* 3 (Spring 1967) 376–83.

"A New Catechism: Catholic Faith for Adults, 1967," *Religious Education* 63 (July–August 1968) 328–30.

"The New Role of the Study of Religion in Higher Education. What Does It Mean?" *Journal of Ecumenical Studies* 6 (Winter 1969) 1–17.

"Seminaries in America," *Commonweal* 73 (October 7, 1970) 37–40.

"Why Is Christianity Resisted Today?" *Spirituality Today* 31 (June 1979) 149–56.

"Obeying for Conscience' sake," in Kevin Nichols, ed., *Voice of the Hidden Waterfall. Essays on Religious Education in Honour of Francis Drinkwater* (Middlegreen, Slough, England: St. Paul Publications, 1980) 61–75.

"Transmitting the Heritage of Faith through Libraries," *Catholic Library World* 53 (July–August 1984) 15–20.

"To Be the Best We Can Be," *Religion Teacher's Journal* 25 (February 1991) 24–5.

"Make Us to Be One Body, One Spirit in Christ," *Sisters Today* 64 (1992) 377–85.

Miscellaneous Other Topics

Books and Pamphlets

The Trinity. Glen Rock, N.J.: Paulist, 1963.

Three Persons in One God. Englewood Cliffs: Prentice Hall, 1964 (in the eleven-textbook "Foundations of Catholic Theology Series," ed. Gerard S. Sloyan).

Essays and Articles

"Thomas Wolfe: A Legend of a Man's Youth in His Hunger," in Harold C. Gardiner, ed., *Fifty Years of the American Novel, 1900–1950* (New York: Charles Scribner's Sons, 1951) 197–215.

"In Quest of God," *Commonweal* 67 (February 21, 1958) 531–3.

"Good News?" *The Priest* (July 1960) 615–19.

"The Joy of Christ," *Furrow* 11 (February 1960) 91–8.

"The Youth of the Church," in Donal Flanagan, ed., *The City. Essays on the Church* (Dublin, Ireland: Gill, 1960) 5–12.

"Is It Good News or Isn't It?" *Catholic Book Reporter* 1 (May 1961) 10–1.

"Faith Comes Through Healing," *North American Liturgical Week Proceedings* 26 (1965) 125–31.

"How Worldly Must the Church Be?" *North American Liturgical Week Proceedings* 27 (1966) 49–56.

"Meaning and Qualities of Ministry: The Office of the Permanent Deacon," *Living Worship* 5/7 (September 1969) 1–6.

"The Permanent Diaconate: A New Servant Class?" *Commonweal* 94 (March 26, 1971) 56–60.

"Christianity" (plotting of maps and text), in Isma'il al Faruqi, ed., *A Historical Atlas of the Religions of the World* (New York: Macmillan, 1974) 201–36.

Book Reviews by Gerard S. Sloyan[2]

Albert Descamps, *Les Justes et la justice dans Les évangiles et dans Le christianisme primitif hormis la doctrine proprement paulinienne* (Louvain, 1950), *American Ecclesiastical Review* 24 (1951) 476–8.

Alexander Jones, *Unless Some Man Show Me* (London: Sheed & Ward, 1951). *Catholic Biblical Quarterly* 14 (January 1952) 86.

John L. McKenzie, *The Two-edged Sword: An Interpretation of the Old Testament* (Milwaukee: Bruce, 1956). *Catholic Biblical Quarterly* 18 (October 1956) 429–31.

Alfred Durand, *Word of Salvation: Translation and Explanation of the Gospel According to St. Matthew and the Gospel According to St. Mark,* trans. J. J. Heenan (Milwaukee: Bruce, 1957). *Catholic Biblical Quarterly* 20 (January 1958) 123.

Andrés Fernandez Truyols, *The Life of Jesus Christ,* trans. Paul Barrett (Westminster: Newman, 1958). *Catholic Biblical Quarterly* 21 (April 1959) 230.

André Robert, ed., *Introduction à la Bible,* Vol. 2: *Nouveau Testament* (Tournai: Desclée, 1959) *Catholic Biblical Quarterly* 22 (January 1960) 97–100.

Paul Palmer, ed., *Sacraments and Forgiveness: History and Doctrinal Development of Penance, Extreme Unction and Indulgences* (Westminster, Md.: Newman, 1959). *Theological Studies* 22 (September 1961) 679–81.

Francis Clark, *Eucharistic Sacrifice and the Reformation* (Westminster, Md.: Newman, 1960). *Worship* 35 (October 1961) 590–2.

George Lindbeck, *The Future of Roman Catholic Theology: Vatican II, Catalyst for Change* (London: SPCK; Philadelphia: Fortress, 1970). *Worship* 44 (June–July 1970) 376–7.

Gèza Vermes, *Jesus the Jew* (London: Collins, 1973). *Judaism* 23 (Fall 1974) 497–9.

2. This list of reviews is based on listings in the ATLA *Index* on CD ROM and every volume of the *CPLI* available in January 1996. Until very recently, the *Catholic Periodical and Literature Index* did not index book reviews under the authors of each review. The *CPLI* has long listed reviewers with the journal in which each review appears under the authors of the titles that were reviewed. Thus, when *CPLI* is issued on CD ROM in 1996 it may then be possible to identify many more reviews that Gerard Sloyan supplied to journals indexed by the *CPLI* that are at present impossible to locate under his name.

John Meyendorff, *Byzantine Theology: Historical Trends and Doctrinal Themes*
(New York: Fordham University Press, 1975).
Horizons 3 (Fall 1976) 265–7.

Elisabeth Schüssler Fiorenza, ed., *Aspects of Religious Propaganda in Judaism and
Early Christianity* (Notre Dame, Ind.: University of Notre Dame Press,
1976).
Worship 51 (March 1977) 320–1.

Urban T. Holmes III, *Ministry and Imagination* (New York: Seabury, 1976).
Worship 51 (March 1997) 166–8.

Paul S. Minear, *To Heal and To Reveal: The Prophetic Vocation According to Luke.*
(New York: Seabury, 1976).
Religious Education 73 (January–February 1978) 97–8.

John A. T. Robinson, *Redating the New Testament* (Philadelphia: Westminster,
1976).
Horizons 5 (Spring 1978) 96–9.

A. E. Harvey, *Jesus on Trial: A Study in the Fourth Gospel* (Atlanta: Knox, 1977).
Catholic Biblical Quarterly 40 (October 1978) 633–4.

Raymond E. Brown, *The Birth of the Messiah: A Commentary on the Infancy
Narratives in Matthew and Luke* (Garden City, N.Y.: Doubleday, 1977).
Interpretation 33 (January 1979) 81–4.

James D. G. Dunn, *Unity and Diversity in the New Testament* (Philadelphia:
Westminster, 1977).
Horizons 6 (Spring 1979) 124–6.

Samuel Sandmel, *Anti-Semitism in the New Testament* (Philadelphia: Fortress,
1978).
Catholic Biblical Quarterly 41 (July 1979) 497–8.

_____, *Judaism and Christian Beginnings* (London: Oxford University Press,
1978).
Horizons 6 (Fall 1979) 286.

Samuel Terrien, *The Elusive Presence: Toward a New Biblical Theology* (San
Francisco: Harper and Row, 1978).
Worship 53 (November 1979) 553–4.

R. Kevin Seasoltz, *New Liturgy, New Laws* (Collegeville: The Liturgical Press,
1980).
Worship 54 (September 1980) 465–6.

William Skudlarek, *The Word in Worship: Preaching in a Liturgical Context* (New
York: Abingdon, 1981).
Worship 55 (September 1981).

John Koenig, *Jews and Christians in Dialogue: New Testament Foundations*
(Philadelphia: Westminster, 1979).
Interpretation 35 (July 1981) 312–4.

Michael Cook, *Mark's Treatment of the Jewish Leaders* (Leiden: Brill, 1978).
Journal of Ecumenical Studies 19 (Summer 1982) 615–6.

Giuseppe Maffei, *Il Dialogo Ecumenico sulla Successione attorno all' Opera di Oscar
Cullmann (1952–1972)* (Rome: LES, 1980).
Journal of Ecumenical Studies 19 (Summer 1982) 604–5.

James D. G. Dunn, *Christology in the Making* (London: SCM; Philadelphia: Westminster, 1980).
Horizons 9 (Spring 1982) 134–6.
Edward C. Schillebeeckx, *Christ: The Experience of Jesus as Lord,* trans. John Bowden (New York: Seabury, 1980).
Journal of the American Academy of Religion 50 (June 1982) 314–5.
John Riches, *Jesus and the Transformation of Judaism* (London: Darton, Longman and Todd, 1980).
Journal of Ecumenical Studies 20 (Summer 1983) 497–8.
Joseph A. Fitzmyer, *The Gospel According to Luke, I–IX* (Garden City, N.Y.: Doubleday, 1981).
Horizons 10 (Fall 1983) 370–1.
Wayne A. Meeks, *The First Urban Christians: The Social World of the Apostle Paul* (New Haven: Yale University Press, 1983).
Horizons 10 (Fall 1983) 352–4.
W. D. Davies, *Jewish and Pauline Studies* (Philadelphia: Fortress, 1983).
Journal of Ecumenical Studies 21 (Summer 1984) 563–4.
Howard Clark Kee, *Miracle in the Early Christian World: A Study in Sociohistorical Method* (New Haven: Yale University Press, 1984); Harold Remus, *Pagan-Christian Conflict over Miracle in the Second Century* (Cambridge, Mass.: Philadelphia Patristic Foundation, 1983); Gerd Theissen, *The Miracle Stories of the Early Christian Tradition* (Philadelphia: Fortress, 1983).
Horizons 11 (Fall 1984) 431–3.
August Strobel, *Die Stunde der Wahrheit: Untersuchungen zum Strafverfahren gegen Jesus* (Tübingen: Mohr, 1980).
Catholic Biblical Quarterly 46 (April 1984) 375–6.
C. K. Barrett, *Essays on Paul* (London: SPCK; Philadelphia: Westminster, 1982).
Journal of Ecumenical Studies 21 (Summer 1984) 563.
Krister Stendahl, *Meanings: The Bible as Document and Guide* (Philadelphia: Fortress, 1984).
Theology Today 41 (January 1985) 478–82.
Koshi Usami, *Somatic Comprehension of Unity: The Church in Ephesus* (Rome: Pontifical Biblical Institute Press, 1983).
Catholic Biblical Quarterly 47 (January 1985) 176–8.
E. Earl Ellis, *The World of St. John: The Gospel and the Epistles* (Grand Rapids: Eerdmans, 1984), and Jacob Jervell, *Jesus in the Gospel of John* (Minneapolis: Augsburg, 1984).
Theology Today 42 (April 1985) 146–7.
Jack D. Kingsbury, *The Christology of Mark's Gospel* (Philadelphia: Fortress, 1983).
Dialog 24 (Spring 1985) 151–2.
Jean Carmignac, *La naissance des Evangiles synoptiques,* 2nd ed. (Paris: OEIL, 1984); Pierre Grelot, *Evangiles et tradition apostoliques: Réflexions sur un certain "Christ hébreu"* (Paris: Cerf, 1984); and Claude Tresmontant, *Le Christ hébreu: La langue et l'âge des Evangiles* (Paris: OEIL, 1983).
Catholic Biblical Quarterly 47 (October 1985) 745–7.

Ernst Haenchen, *A Commentary on the Gospel of John,* ed. Robert W. Funk and Ulrich Busse, 2 vols. (Philadelphia: Fortress, 1984).
Theology Today 42 (October 1985) 397–8.

Pheme Perkins, *Resurrection: New Testament Witness and Contemporary Reflection* (Garden City, N.Y.: Doubleday, 1984).
Horizons 12 (Fall 1985) 358–60.

Douglas J. Moo, *The Old Testament in the Gospel Passion Narratives* (Sheffield, England: Almond Press, 1983).
Interpretation 40 (January 1986) 94–5.

Jacob Neusner, *Messiah in Context* (Philadelphia: Fortress, 1984); *Midrash in Context: Exegesis in Formative Judaism* (Philadelphia: Fortress, 1983); and *Torah: From Scroll to Symbolism in Formative Judaism* (Philadelphia: Fortress, 1985).
Journal of Ecumenical Studies 23 (Winter 1986) 119–20.

John H. P. Reumann, *The Supper of the Lord* (Philadelphia: Fortress, 1985).
Journal of Ecumenical Studies 23 (Summer 1986) 549.
Catholic Biblical Quarterly 48 (October 1986) 757–8.

John Koenig, *New Testament Hospitality: Partnership with Strangers as Promise and Mission* (Philadelphia: Fortress, 1985).
Horizons 14 (Spring 1987) 142–3.

Hugh J. Schonfield, *The Original New Testament* (New York: Harper and Row, 1985).
Journal of Ecumenical Studies 24 (Spring 1987) 312–3.

Francis J. Moloney, *Woman: First among the Faithful* (London: Darton, Longman and Todd, 1985).
Worship 61 (March 1987) 188–9.

Paul D. Duke, *Irony in the Fourth Gospel* (Atlanta: John Knox, 1985).
Interpretation 41 (July 1987) 318–9.

Philip Sigal, *The Halakah of Jesus of Nazareth according to the Gospel of Matthew* (Lanham, Md.: University Press of America, 1986).
Judaism 37 (Winter 1988) 122–4.

Clemens Thoma and Michael Wyschogrod, eds., *Understanding Scripture: Explorations of Jewish and Christian Traditions of Interpretation* (New York: Paulist, 1987).
Journal of Ecumenical Studies 25 (Spring 1988) 294–5.

Arland J. Hultgren, *Christ and His Benefits: Christology and Redemption in the New Testament* (Philadelphia: Fortress, 1987).
Theology Today 45 (July 1988) 359–61.

John Painter, *Theology as Hermeneutics: Rudolf Bultmann's Interpretation of the History of Jesus* (Sheffield, England: Almond Press, 1987).
Catholic Biblical Quarterly 50 (July 1988) 541–2.

Judith Herrin, *The Formation of Christendom* (Oxford: Blackwell, 1987).
Horizons 15 (Fall 1988) 390.

Wofgang Roth, *Hebrew Gospel: Cracking the Code of Mark* (Yorktown Heights, N.Y.: Meyer Stone Books, 1988).
Journal of Ecumenical Studies 26 (Spring 1989) 396–7.

Marcus J. Borg, *Jesus, A New Vision: Spirit, Culture and the Life of Discipleship* (San Francisco: Harper and Row, 1987).
Worship 63 (May 1989) 270–2.

David Rensberger, *Johaninne Faith and Liberating Community* (Philadelphia: Westminster, 1988).
Theology Today 46 (July 1989) 241–2.

Richard A. Horsley, *Jesus and the Spiral of Violence: Popular Resistance in Roman Palestine* (San Francisco: Harper and Row, 1987).
Horizons 16 (Fall 1989) 380–2.

Harold W. Attridge, *Epistle to the Hebrews: A Commentary,* ed. Helmut Koester (Philadelphia: Fortress, 1989).
Journal of Ecumenical Studies 27 (Winter 1990) 127.

Earl Richard, *Jesus: One and Many—The Christological Concept of New Testament Authors* (Wilmington, Del.: Michael Glazier, 1988).
Horizons 17 (Fall 1990) 326–7.

Shlomo Simonsohn, *The Apostolic See and the Jews: Documents: 492–1404,* Studies and Texts 94; *Documents: 1394–1464,* 95; *Documents: 1464–1521,* 99 (Toronto: Pontifical Institute of Mediaeval Studies, 1988–90); *Documents: 1522–38,* 104; *Documents: 1539–45,* 105; *Documents: 1546–55,* 106; *History,* 110; *Addenda, Corrigenda, Bibliography and Indexes,* 110 (idem., 1990–91).
Journal of Ecumenical Studies 27 (Fall 1990) 783–4; 33 (Spring 1996).

Gerald P. Fogarty, *American Catholic Biblical Scholarship: A History from the Early Republic to Vatican II* (San Francisco: Harper and Row, 1989).
Catholic Biblical Quarterly 53 (January 1991) 133–4.

Raymond E. Brown, Joseph A. Fitzmyer, and Roland E. Murphy, eds., *The New Jerome Biblical Commentary* (Englewood Cliffs, N.J.: Prentice-Hall, 1992).
Horizons 18 (Spring 1991) 143–4.
Journal of Ecumenical Studies 29 (Spring 1992) 273–4.

Richard J. Coggins and James Leslie Houlden, eds., *A Dictionary of Biblical Interpretation* (London: SCM, 1990).
Catholic Biblical Quarterly (April 1992) 388–9.

Francis E. Peters, ed., *Judaism, Christianity, and Islam: The Classical Texts and Their Interpretation.* 3 vols. (Princeton, N.J.: Princeton University Press, 1990).
Journal of Ecumenical Studies 28 (Summer 1991) 507–8.

Richard A. Horsley, *Sociology and the Jesus Movement* (New York: Crossroad, 1989).
Horizons 18 (Fall 1991) 317–8.

Kenneth Grayston, *Dying We Live: A New Enquiry into the Death of Christ in the New Testament* (Oxford: Oxford University Press, 1991).
Journal of Ecumenical Studies 29 (Winter 1992) 117.

James W. Douglas, *The Non-Violent Coming of God* (Maryknoll, N.Y.: Orbis, 1991).
Sisters Today 64 (Spring 1992) 382–3.

Ben Witherington III, *The Christology of Jesus* (Minneapolis: Augsburg-Fortress, 1990) and *Women and the Genesis of Christianity* (Cambridge: Cambridge University Press, 1990).
Horizons 19 (Fall 1992) 312–3.

John Dominic Crossan, *The Historical Jesus: The Life of a Mediterranean Jewish Peasant* (San Francisco: Harper, 1991) and John P. Meier, *A Marginal Jew. Rethinking the Historical Jesus,* vol. 1: *The Roots of the Problem and the Person* (New York: Doubleday, 1991).
Horizons 20 (Spring 1993) 143–5.

James D. G. Dunn, *The Partings of the Ways: Between Christianity and Judaism and Their Significance for the Character of Christianity* (Philadelphia: Trinity Press International, 1991).
Interpretation 47 (April 1993) 209–10.

Jeffrey Siker, *Disinheriting the Jews: Abraham in Early Christian Controversy* (Louisville: Westminster/Knox, 1991).
Catholic Biblical Quarterly 55 (April 1993) 296–7.

Carmine Di Sante, *Jewish Prayer: The Origins of Christian Liturgy,* trans. Matthew J. O'Connell (New York: Paulist 1991).
Worship 67 (May 1993) 287–8.

James T. Burtchaell, *From Synagogue to Church: Public Services and Offices in the Earliest Christian Communities* (Cambridge: Cambridge University Press, 1992)
Worship 68 (January 1994) 80–1.

Raymond F. Collins, *Divorce in the New Testament* (Collegeville: The Liturgical Press, 1992).
Catholic Biblical Quarterly 56 (April 1994) 362–4.

Pierre Létourneau, *Jésus, fils de l'homme et fils de Dieu: Jean 2:23–3:36 et la double christologie johannique* (Paris: Cerf, 1993).
Catholic Biblical Quarterly 57 (January 1995) 183–4.

William L. Holladay, *The Psalms through Three Thousand Years: Prayerbook of a Cloud of Witnesses* (Minneapolis: Fortress, 1993).
Worship 69 (March 1995) 180–2.

Contributors

Mahmoud M. Ayoub is Professor of Islamic Studies at Temple University and Research Fellow at the Middle East Center of the University of Pennsylvania. He is the author of many books and articles, including *Redemptive Suffering in Islam* and *The Qur'an and Its Interpreters.*

James E. Biechler is Emeritus Professor of Religion at La Salle University, Philadelphia, Pennsylvania. His publications on Nicholas of Cusa include *The Religious Language of Nicholas of Cusa* and (with H. Lawrence Bond) *Nicholas of Cusa On Interreligious Harmony.*

Regina A. Boisclair's Ph.D. dissertation at Temple was directed by Gerard Sloyan. She has held both teaching and library positions at several institutions. She is preparing a book for The Liturgical Press to be titled *Proclaiming Teachings of Contempt: Anti-Judaism in the Sunday Lectionaries.*

Mary Collins, O.S.B., is a professor in the Department of Religion and Religious Education at the Catholic University of America in Washington, D.C., where she teaches Liturgical Studies and directs the M.A. Program in Liturgy.

Charles E. Curran is the Elizabeth Scurlock University Professor of Human Values at Southern Methodist University. He has served as President of the American Theological Society, The Catholic Theological Society of America, and the Society of Christian Ethics. His latest books are: *History and Contemporary Issues: Studies in Moral Theology* and *The Origins of Moral Theology in the United States: Three Different Approaches.*

David P. Efroymson is Professor Emeritus of Religion at La Salle University. He co-edited *Within Context: Essays on Jews and Judaism in the New Testament.*

Monika K. Hellwig spent one career teaching Theology at Georgetown University and is now Executive Director of the Association of Catholic Colleges and Universities. She has written several books and is co-editor of *The Modern Catholic Encyclopedia.*

Elizabeth A. Johnson, C.S.J., is Professor of Theology at Fordham University in New York City. She is the author of several books, including *She Who Is: The Mystery of God in Feminist Theological Discourse,* and has served as President of the Catholic Theological Society of America.

223

Gabriel Moran is Director of the Religious Education Program at New York University. He is the author of seventeen books, the most recent being *Showing How: The Act of Teaching*.

June O'Connor, Professor of Religious Studies at the University of California, Riverside, is the author of *The Moral Vision of Dorothy Day: A Feminist Perspective* and numerous scholarly articles. She is a member of the steering committee for the Religion and Human Rights consultation of the American Academy of Religion.

John C. Raines is Professor of Christian Social Ethics and Chair of the Department of Religion at Temple University. His most recent book is *Modern Work and Human Meaning*.

Leonard Swidler is Professor of Catholic Thought and Interrreligious Dialogue at Temple University. He is co-founder and editor of the *Journal of Ecumenical Studies,* and is author or editor of over 50 books including, most recently, *Toward a Catholic Constitution*.

The Rev. Dr. Paul M. van Buren, D. Theol., Professor Emeritus of Temple University, taught in its Department of Religion from 1964 until 1986 and since then has been reading and writing in Maine. Among his many books is the 3-volume *A Theology of the Jewish-Christian Reality*.

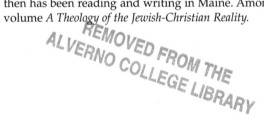